PHP 7 Data Structures and Algorithms

Leverage the power of PHP data structures and crucial algorithms to build high-performance applications

Mizanur Rahman

BIRMINGHAM - MUMBAI

PHP 7 Data Structures and Algorithms

Copyright © 2017 Packt Publishing

First published: May 2017

Production reference: 1240517

Published by Packt Publishing Ltd.
Livery Place
35 Livery Street
Birmingham
B3 2PB, UK.

ISBN 978-1-78646-389-0

www.packtpub.com

Credits

Author

Mizanur Rahman

Reviewer

Andrew Caya

Commissioning Editor

Kunal Parikh

Acquisition Editor

Nitin Dasan

Content Development Editor

Zeeyan Pinheiro

Technical Editor

 Kunal Mali

Copy Editor

Safis Editing

Project Coordinator

Vaidehi Sawant

Proofreader

Safis Editing

Indexer

Rekha Nair

Graphics

Jason Monteiro

Production Coordinator

Shraddha Falebhai

About the Author

Mizanur Rahman is a technology enthusiast and problem solver from Dhaka, Bangladesh, who loves web and mobile application development. Over the years, he has been working with PHP, Laravel, CodeIgniter, Symfony, JavaScript, C, C++, Java, Node.js, Socket.io, and React.js. He is a Zend Certified PHP 5 programmer with 14 years of experience. He is also a Certified Scrum Master (CSM) and the first Certified Scrum Professional (CSP) from ScrumAlliance in Bangladesh. He is also a Certified Scrum Product Owner (CSPO), Certified Scrum Developer (CSD), and SAFe Agilist (SA).

He got a degree in computer science from the North South University, Bangladesh, in 2003. He is currently working as the head of software development at Telenor Health AS. He has two start-ups of his own, Informatix Technologies and TechMasters. He previously worked for companies such as TrustPilot, Denmark, and Somewherein Inc along with Relisource technologies and TigerIT from Bangladesh.

He has been involved in different technology communities from Bangladesh for over 10 years. He is the administrator for PHPXperts, the largest PHP-based group in the south-east Asia with more than 25,000 members. He is also involved in Agile and Scrum movement in Bangladesh. He is the founder and the administrator of the Agile Bangladesh community. He is also a problem solver for Project Euler.

He has published two books: MediaWiki Administrators' Tutorial Guide and MediaWiki 1.1 Beginner's Guide, both by Packt Publishing. He is a regular speaker at various development conferences, technology seminars, and agile events in Bangladesh and Asia.

He lives in Dhaka with his lovely wife, Nisha, and two cute sons, Adiyan and Mikhael. When he is not working, he spends his time with his family and travel around the world. You can reach him at `mizan@informatixbd.com`, or follow his personal blog.

About the Reviewer

Andrew Caya discovered his passion for computers at the age of 11 and started programming in GW-BASIC and QBASIC in the early 90s. He earned a master's degree in Information Science and Master's Short Programme in Public Administration. After doing some software development in C, C++, and Perl, and some Linux system administration, he became a PHP developer more than 7 years ago. He is also a Zend Certified PHP Engineer and a Zend Certified Architect.

He is the creator of *Linux for PHP*, a lightweight, Docker-based, custom Linux project that allows PHP developers to easily compile and use recent versions of PHP in a variety of ways. He is also the lead developer of a popular Joomla extension and has the great pleasure of contributing code to many open source projects.

He is currently a professional contract programmer in Montreal, Canada, a technical reviewer for Packt Publishing, and a loving husband, and father.

www.PacktPub.com

For support files and downloads related to your book, please visit www.PacktPub.com.

Did you know that Packt offers eBook versions of every book published, with PDF and ePub files available? You can upgrade to the eBook version at www.PacktPub.com and as a print book customer, you are entitled to a discount on the eBook copy. Get in touch with us at service@packtpub.com for more details.

At www.PacktPub.com, you can also read a collection of free technical articles, sign up for a range of free newsletters and receive exclusive discounts and offers on Packt books and eBooks.

https://www.packtpub.com/mapt

Get the most in-demand software skills with Mapt. Mapt gives you full access to all Packt books and video courses, as well as industry-leading tools to help you plan your personal development and advance your career.

Why subscribe?

- Fully searchable across every book published by Packt
- Copy and paste, print, and bookmark content
- On demand and accessible via a web browser

Customer Feedback

Thanks for purchasing this Packt book. At Packt, quality is at the heart of our editorial process. To help us improve, please leave us an honest review on this book's Amazon page at `https://www.amazon.com/dp/178646389X`.

If you'd like to join our team of regular reviewers, you can e-mail us at `customerreviews@packtpub.com`. We award our regular reviewers with free eBooks and videos in exchange for their valuable feedback. Help us be relentless in improving our products!

I want to dedicate this book to my parents, Mr. M. A. Jalil and Mrs. Rokeya Jalil.

Table of Contents

Preface

Data structures and algorithms are an integral part of software application development. Whether we are building a web-based application, a CMS, or a standalone backend system using PHP, we need to apply algorithms and data structures all the time. Sometimes, we do that without noticing and sometimes without giving proper attention to it. Most developers think that these two topics are really difficult and there is no point in paying attention to details as PHP has lots of built-in support for data structures and algorithms. In this book, we will focus on the basics and practical examples of PHP data structures and algorithms so that we know what data structures are, why to choose them, and where to apply which algorithms. This book is designed for novice as well as experienced PHP programmers. The book starts from basic topics and moves on to more advanced topics. We have tried to accommodate lots of examples with images and explanations in this book so that you can understand the concepts properly in visual form and with practical examples.

What this book covers

Chapter 1, *Introduction to Data Structures and Algorithms*, focuses on different data structures, their definitions, properties, and examples. This chapter also includes the way in which we analyze algorithms and find their complexities, with special emphasis on Big Oh (O) notation.

Chapter 2, *Understanding PHP Arrays*, focuses on a very basic and built-in data structure in PHP -- PHP arrays. This also covers what we can achieve through PHP arrays and their advantages and disadvantages. We focus on how to use arrays to implement other data structures.

Chapter 3, *Using Linked Lists*, covers the different types of linked lists. It focuses on the classification of different variances of linked lists and their construction process, with examples.

Chapter 4, *Constructing Stacks and Queues*, focuses on two of the most important data structures in this chapter--stacks and queues. We see how to construct stacks and queues using different methods and discuss their operation and usage with examples.

Chapter 5, *Applying Recursive Algorithms - Recursion*, focuses on one important topic with algorithms--recursion. We cover the different ways in which we can solve a problem using recursive algorithms and the advantages and disadvantages of using this technique. We also cover some basic day-to-day programming problems that we can solve using recursion.

Chapter 6, *Understanding and Implementing Trees*, talks about a non-hierarchical data structure--the tree. We cover tree properties and how to construct them, and understand the cases in which the tree data structure will be important to us.

Chapter 7, *Using Sorting Algorithms*, demonstrates how to implement different sorting algorithms and their complexity, as sorting is a very important topic in the programming world and the search for an efficient sorting algorithm is always on. At the end of the chapter, we also cover the built-in PHP sorting algorithms.

Chapter 8, *Exploring Search Options*, states how searching is important in the programming world. In this chapter, we focus on different searching techniques and when to use which algorithms. We also discuss whether we should sort before searching. This chapter contains lots of examples and implementations of different algorithms.

Chapter 9, *Putting Graphs into Action*, explains how graph algorithms are one of the most widely used algorithms in the programming paradigm. In this chapter, we focus on different graph-related problems and solve them using different algorithms. We cover implementations of the shortest path algorithm and minimal spanning trees with examples and explanations.

Chapter 10, *Understanding and Using Heaps*, talks about the last data structure topic in the book--the heap. It is a very efficient data structure and is used in many implementations in the real world. We show how to build heaps and their uses, including the implementations of the heap sort algorithm.

Chapter 11, *Solving Problems with Advanced Techniques*, focuses on different techniques to solve problems. We focus our discussion on topics such as memoization, dynamic programming, greedy algorithms, and backtracking, along with examples and solutions for practical problems.

Chapter 12, *PHP's Built-In Support for Data Structures and Algorithms*, shows the built-in support we have for data structures and algorithms. We talk about PHP's functions, PECL libraries, and also some references for online resources.

Chapter 13, *Functional Data Structures with PHP*, sheds some light on functional programming and functional data structures using PHP, as functional programming is creating a lot of hype these days. We introduce a functional programming library called Tarsana and show different examples of using it.

What you need for this book

All you need to have is the latest PHP version (minimum requirement is PHP 7.x) installed on your machine. You can run the examples from a command line, which does not require a web server. However, if you want, you can install Apache or Nginx, or the following:

- PHP 7.x+
- Nginx/apache (optional)
- PHP IDE or code editor

Who this book is for

This book is for those who want to learn data structures and algorithms with PHP for better control over application-solution, efficiency, and optimization.
A basic understanding of PHP data types, control structures, and other basic features is required.

Conventions

In this book, you will find a number of text styles that distinguish between different kinds of information. Here are some examples of these styles and an explanation of their meaning.

Codes are written with a different font from the book text fonts to highlight the code block.

A block of code is set as follows:

```
[default]
class TreeNode {
    public $data = NULL;
    public $children = [];
    public function __construct(string $data = NULL) {
        $this->data = $data;
    }
    public function addChildren(TreeNode $node) {
        $this->children[] = $node;
    }
}
```

When we wish to draw your attention to a particular part of a code block during the explanation, the code is highlighted within the text like this: **addChildren**.

Any command-line input or output is written as follows:

```
Final
-Semi Final 1
--Quarter Final 1
--Quarter Final 2
-Semi Final 2
--Quarter Final 3
--Quarter Final 4
```

New terms and **important words** are shown in bold. Words that you see on the screen, for example, in menus or dialog boxes, appear in the text like this: "Clicking the **Next** button moves you to the next screen."

Warnings or important notes appear in a box like this.

Tips and tricks appear like this.

Reader feedback

Feedback from our readers is always welcome. Let us know what you think about this book-what you liked or disliked. Reader feedback is important for us as it helps us develop titles that you will really get the most out of.

To send us general feedback, simply e-mail `feedback@packtpub.com`, and mention the book's title in the subject of your message.

If there is a topic that you have expertise in and you are interested in either writing or contributing to a book, see our author guide at `www.packtpub.com/authors`.

Customer support

Now that you are the proud owner of a Packt book, we have a number of things to help you to get the most from your purchase.

Downloading the example code

You can download the example code files for this book from your account at `http://www.p acktpub.com`. If you purchased this book elsewhere, you can visit `http://www.packtpub.com/support` and register to have the files e-mailed directly to you.

You can download the code files by following these steps:

1. Log in or register to our website using your e-mail address and password.
2. Hover the mouse pointer on the **SUPPORT** tab at the top.
3. Click on **Code Downloads & Errata**.
4. Enter the name of the book in the **Search** box.
5. Select the book for which you're looking to download the code files.
6. Choose from the drop-down menu where you purchased this book from.
7. Click on **Code Download**.

Once the file is downloaded, please make sure that you unzip or extract the folder using the latest version of:

* WinRAR / 7-Zip for Windows
* Zipeg / iZip / UnRarX for Mac
* 7-Zip / PeaZip for Linux

The code bundle for the book is also hosted on GitHub at `https://github.com/PacktPublishing/PHP7-Data-Structures-and-Algorithms`. We also have other code bundles from our rich catalog of books and videos available at `https://github.com/PacktPublishing/`. Check them out!

Downloading the color images of this book

We also provide you with a PDF file that has color images of the screenshots/diagrams used in this book. The color images will help you better understand the changes in the output. You can download this file from `https://www.packtpub.com/sites/default/files/downloads/PHP7DataStructuresandAlgorithms_ColorImages.pdf`.

Errata

Although we have taken every care to ensure the accuracy of our content, mistakes do happen. If you find a mistake in one of our books-maybe a mistake in the text or the code-we would be grateful if you could report this to us. By doing so, you can save other readers from frustration and help us improve subsequent versions of this book. If you find any errata, please report them by visiting http://www.packtpub.com/submit-errata, selecting your book, clicking on the **Errata Submission Form** link, and entering the details of your errata. Once your errata are verified, your submission will be accepted and the errata will be uploaded to our website or added to any list of existing errata under the Errata section of that title.

To view the previously submitted errata, go to https://www.packtpub.com/books/content/support and enter the name of the book in the search field. The required information will appear under the **Errata** section.

Piracy

Piracy of copyrighted material on the Internet is an ongoing problem across all media. At Packt, we take the protection of our copyright and licenses very seriously. If you come across any illegal copies of our works in any form on the Internet, please provide us with the location address or website name immediately so that we can pursue a remedy.

Please contact us at copyright@packtpub.com with a link to the suspected pirated material.

We appreciate your help in protecting our authors and our ability to bring you valuable content.

Questions

If you have a problem with any aspect of this book, you can contact us at questions@packtpub.com, and we will do our best to address the problem.

1

Introduction to Data Structures and Algorithms

We are living in a digital era. In every segment of our life and daily needs, we have a significant use of technology. Without technology, the world will virtually stand still. Have you ever tried to find what it takes to prepare a simple weather forecast? Lots of data are analyzed to prepare simple information, which is delivered to us in real time. Computers are the most important find of the technology revolution and they have changed the world drastically in the last few decades. Computers process these large sets of data and helps us in every technology-dependent task and need. In order to make computer operation efficient, we represent data in different formats or we can call in different structures, which are known as data structures.

Data structures are very important components for computers and programming languages. Along with data structures, it is also very important to know how to solve a problem or find a solution using these data structures. From our simple mobile phone contact book to complex DNA profile matching systems, the use of data structures and algorithms is everywhere.

Have we ever thought that standing in a superstore queue to payout can be a representation of data structure? Or taking out a bill from a pile of papers can be another use of data structure? In fact, we are following data structure concepts almost everywhere in our lives. Whether we are managing the queue to pay the bill or to get to the transportation, or maintaining a stack for a pile of books or papers for daily works, data structures are everywhere and impacting our lives.

PHP is a very popular scripting language and billions of websites and applications are built using it. People use **Hypertext Preprocessor** (**PHP**) for simple applications to very complex ones and some are very data intensive. The big question is--should we use PHP for any data intensive application or algorithmic solutions? Of course we should. With the new release of PHP 7, PHP has entered into new possibilities of efficient and robust application development. Our mission will be to show and prepare ourselves to understand the power of data structures and algorithms using PHP 7, so that we can utilize it in our applications and programs.

Importance of data structures and algorithms

If we consider our real-life situation with computers, we also use different sorts of arrangements of our belongings and data so that we can use them efficiently or find them easily when needed. What if we enter our phone contact book in a random order? Will we be able to find a contact easily? We might end up searching each and every contact in the book as the contacts are not arranged in a particular order. Just consider the following two images:

One shows that the books are scattered and finding a particular book will take time as the books are not organized. The other one shows that the books are organized in a stack. Not only does the second image show that we are using the space smartly, but also the searching of books becomes easier.

Let us consider another example. We are going to buy tickets for an important football match. There are thousands of people waiting for the ticket booth to open. Tickets are going to be distributed on a first come first served basis. If we consider the following two images, which one is the best way of handling such a big crowd?:

The left image clearly shows that there is no proper order and there is no way to know who came first to get the tickets. But if we knew that people were waiting in a structured way, in a line, or queue, then it will be easier to handle the crowd and we will hand over the tickets to whoever came first. This is a common phenomenon known as a *queue* which is heavily used in the programming world. Programming terms are not generated from outside the world. In fact, the majority of the data structures are inspired from real life and they use the same terms most of the times. Whether we are preparing our task list, contact list, book piles, diet charting, preparing a family tree, or organization hierarchy, we are basically using different arrangement techniques which are known as data structures in the computing world.

We have talked a little about data structures so far but what about algorithms? Don't we use any algorithms in our daily lives? Definitely we do. Whenever we are searching for a contact from our old phone book, we are definitely not searching from the beginning. If we are searching for *Tom*, we will not search the page where it says *A, B,* or *C*. We are directly going to the page *T* and will find if *Tom* is listed there or not. Or, if we need to find a doctor from a telephone directory, we will definitely not search in the foods section. If we consider the phone book or telephone directory as data structures, then the way we search for particular information is known as algorithms. While data structures help us to use data efficiently, algorithms help us to perform different operations on those data efficiently.

For example, if we have 100,000 entries in our phone directory, searching a particular entry from the beginning might take a long time. But, if we know the doctors are listed from page 200 to 220, we can search only those pages to save our time by searching a small section rather than the full directory:

We can also consider a different way of searching for a doctor. While the previous paragraph takes the approach of searching a particular section of the directory, we can even search alphabetically within the directory, like the way we search a dictionary for a word. That might even reduce the time and entries for our searching. There can be many different approaches to find solutions of a problem, and each of the approaches can be named as algorithms. From the earlier discussion we can say that for a particular problem or task, there can be multiple ways or algorithms to perform.

Then which one should we consider to use? We are going to discuss that very soon. Before moving to that point, we are going to focus on **PHP data types** and **Abstract Data Types (ADT)**. In order to grasp the data structure concept, we must have a strong understanding of PHP data types and ADT.

Understanding Abstract Data Type (ADT)

PHP has eight primitive data types and those are booleans, integer, float, string, array, object, resource, and null. Also, we have to remember that PHP is a weakly typed language and that we are not bothered about the data type declaration while creating those. Though PHP has some static type features, PHP is predominantly a dynamically typed language which means variables are not required to be declared before using it. We can assign a value to a new variable and use it instantly.

For the examples of data structures we have discussed so far can we use any of the primitive data types to represent those structures? Maybe we can or maybe not. Our primitive data types have one particular objective: storing data. In order to achieve some flexibility in performing operations on those data, we will require using the data types in such a way so that we can use them as a particular model and perform some operations. This particular way of handling data through a conceptual model is known as Abstract Data Type, or ADT. ADT also defines a set of possible operations for the data.

We need to understand that ADTs are mainly theoretical concepts which are used in design and analysis of algorithms, data structures, and software design. In contrast, data structures are concrete representations. In order to implement an ADT, we might need to use data types or data structures or both. The most common example of ADTs is *stack* and *queue*:

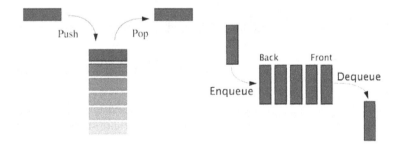

Considering the stack as ADT, it is not only a collection of data but also two important operations called push and pop. Usually, we put a new entry at the top of the stack which is known as *push* and when we want to take an item, we take from the top which is also known as *pop*. If we consider PHP array as a stack, we will require additional functionality to achieve these push and pop operations to consider it as stack ADT. Similarly, a queue is also an ADT with two required operations: to add an item at the end of the queue also known as *enqueue* and remove an item from the beginning of the queue, also known as *dequeue*. Both sound similar but if we give a close observation we will see that a stack works as a **Last-In, First-Out** (**LIFO**) model whereas a queue works as a **First-In, First-Out** (**FIFO**) model. These two different mathematical models make them two different ADTs.

Here are some common ADTs:

- List
- Map
- Set
- Stack
- Queue
- Priority queue
- Graph
- Tree

In coming chapters, we will explore more ADTs and implement them as data structures using PHP.

Different data structures

We can categorize data structures in to two different groups:

- Linear data structures
- Nonlinear data structures

In linear data structures, items are structured in a lincar or sequential manner. Array, list, stack, and queue are examples of linear structures. In nonlinear structures, data are not structured in a sequential way. Graph and tree are the most common examples of nonlinear data structures.

Let us now explore the world of data structures, with different types of data structures and their purposes in a summarized way. Later on, we will explore each of the data structures in details.

There are many different types of data structures that exist in the programming world. Out of them, following are the most used ones:

- Struct
- Array
- Linked list
- Doubly linked list
- Stack
- Queue
- Priority queue
- Set
- Map
- Tree
- Graph
- Heap

Struct

Usually, a variable can store a single data type and a single scalar data type can only store a single value. There are many situations where we might need to group some data types together as a single complex data type. For example, we want to store some student information together in a student data type. We need the student name, address, phone number, email, date of birth, current class, and so on. In order to store each student record to a unique student data type, we will need a special structure which will allow us to do that. This can be easily achieved by *struct*. In other words, a struct is a container of values which is typically accessed using names. Though structs are very popular in C programming language, we can use a similar concept in PHP as well. We are going to explore that in coming chapters.

Array

Though an array is considered to be a data type in PHP, an array is actually a data structure which is mostly used in all programming platforms. In PHP, the array is actually an ordered map (we are going to know about maps after a few more sections). We can store multiple values in a single array as a single variable. Matrix type data are easy to store in an array and hence it is used widely in all programming platforms. Usually arrays are a fixed size collection which is accessed by sequential numeric indexes. In PHP, arrays are implemented differently and you can define dynamic arrays without defining any fixed size of the array. We will explore more about PHP arrays in the next chapter. Arrays can have different dimensions. If an array has only one index to access an element, we call it a single dimension array. But if it requires two or more indexes to access an element, we call it two dimensional or multidimensional arrays respectively. Here are two diagrams of array data structures:

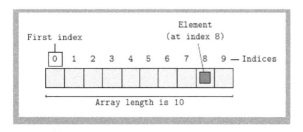
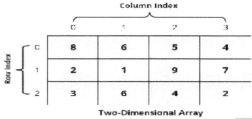

Linked list

A linked list is a linear data structure which is a collection of data elements also known as nodes and can have varying sizes. Usually, listed items are connected through a pointer which is known as a link and hence it is known as a **linked list**. In a linked list, one list element links to the next element through a pointer. From the following diagram, we can see that the linked list actually maintains an ordered collection. Linked lists are the most common and simplest form of data structures used by programming languages. In a single linked list, we can only go forward. In Chapter 3, *Using Linked Lists* we are going to dive deep inside the linked list concepts and implementations:

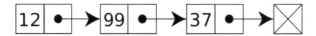

Doubly linked list

A doubly linked list is a special type of linked list where we not only store what is the next node, but we also store the previous node inside the node structure. As a result, it can move forward and backward within the list. It gives more flexibility than a single linked list or linked list by having both the previous and next pointers. We are going to explore more about these in Chapter 3, *Using Linked Lists*. The following diagram depicts a doubly linked list:

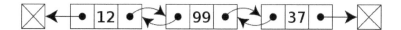

Stack

As we talked about the stack in previous pages, we already know that stack is a linear data structure with the LIFO principle. As a result, stacks have only one end to add a new item or remove an item. It is one of the oldest and most used data structures in computer technology. We always add or remove an item from a stack using the single point named *top*. The term push is used to indicate an item to be added on top of the stack and pop to remove an item from the top; this is shown in the following diagram. We will discuss more about stacks in Chapter 4, *Constructing Stacks and Queues*.

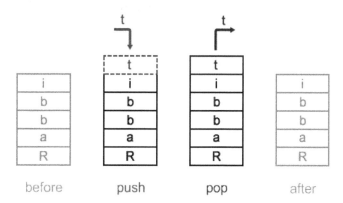

Queue

A queue is another linear data structure which follows the FIFO principle. A queue allows two basic operations on the collection. The first one is *enqueue* which allows us to add an item to the back of the queue. The second one is *dequeue* which allows us to remove an item from the front of the queue. A queue is another of the most used data structures in computer technology. We will learn details about queues in Chapter 4, *Consrtucting Stacks and Queues*.

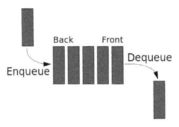

Set

A set is an abstract data type which is used to store certain values. These values are not stored in any particular order but there should not be any repeated values in the set. Set is not used like a collection where we retrieve a specific value from it; a set is used to check the existence of a value inside it. Sometimes a set data structure can be sorted and we call it an ordered set.

Map

A map is a collection of key and value pairs where all the keys are unique. We can consider a map as an associative array where all keys are unique. We can add and remove using key and value pairs along with update and look up from a map using a key. In fact, PHP arrays are ordered map implementations. We are going to explore that in the next chapter.

Tree

A tree is the most widely used nonlinear data structure in the computing world. It is highly used for hierarchical data structures. A tree consists of nodes and there is a special node which is known as the *root* of the tree which starts the tree structure. Other nodes descend from the root node. Tree data structure is recursive which means a tree can contain many subtrees. Nodes are connected with each other through edges. We are going to discuss different types of trees, their operations, and purposes in `Chapter 6`, *Understanding and Implementing Trees*.

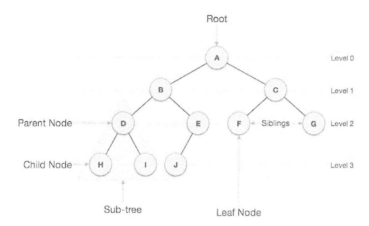

Graph

A graph data structure is a special type of nonlinear data structure which consists of a finite number of vertices or nodes, and edges or arcs. A graph can be both directed and undirected. A directed graph clearly indicates the direction of the edges, while an undirected graph mentions the edges, not the direction. As a result, in an undirected graph, both directions of edge are considered as a single edge. In other words, we can say a graph is a pair of sets (V, E), where V is the set of vertices and E is the set of edges:

$$V = \{A, B, C, D, E, F\}$$

$$E = \{AB, BC, CE, ED, EF, DB\}$$

In a directed graph, an edge *AB* is different from an edge *BA* while in an undirected graph, both *AB* and *BA* are the same. Graphs are handy to solve lots of complex problems in the programming world. We are going to continue our discussion of graph data structures in Chapter 9, *Putting Graphs into Action*. In the following diagram, we have:

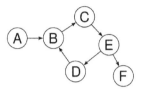

Heap

A heap is a special tree-based data structure which satisfies the heap properties. The largest key is the root and smaller keys are leaves, which is known as **max heap**. Or, the smallest key is the root and larger keys are leaves, which is known as **min heap**. Though the root of a heap structure is either the largest or smallest key of the tree, it is not necessarily a sorted structure. A heap is used for solving graph algorithms with efficiency and also in sorting. We are going to explore heap data structures in Chapter 10, *Understanding and Using Heaps*.

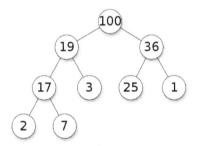

Solving a problem - algorithmic approach

So far we have discussed different types of data structures and their usage. But, one thing we have to remember is that just putting data in a proper structure might not solve our problems. We need to find solutions to our problems using the help of data structures or, in other words, we are going to solve problems using data structures. We need algorithms to solve our problem.

An algorithm is a step by step process which defines the set of instructions to be executed in a certain order to get a desired output. In general, algorithms are not limited to any programming language or platform. They are independent of programming languages. An algorithm must have the following characteristics:

- **Input**: An algorithm must have well-defined input. It can be 0 or more inputs.
- **Output**: An algorithm must have well-defined output. It must match the desired output.
- **Precision**: All steps are precisely defined.
- **Finiteness**: An algorithm must stop after a certain number of steps. It should not run indefinitely.
- **Unambiguous**: An algorithm should be clear and should not have any ambiguity in any of the steps.
- **Independent**: An algorithm should be independent of any programming language or platforms.

Let us now create an algorithm. But in order to do that, we need a problem statement. So let us assume that we have a new shipment of books for our library. There are 1000 books and they are not sorted in any particular order. We need to find books as per the list and store them in their designated shelves. How do we find them from the pile of books?

Now, we can solve the problem in different ways. Each way has a different approach to find out a solution for the problem. We call these approaches algorithms. To keep the discussion short and precise, we are going to only consider two approaches to solve the problem. We know there are several other ways as well but for simplicity let us keep our discussion only for one algorithm.

We are going to store the books in a simple row so that we can see the book names. Now, we will pick a book name from the list and search from one end of the row to the other end till we find the book. So basically, we are going to follow a sequential search for each of the books. We will repeat these steps until we place all books in their designated places.

Writing pseudocode

Computer programs are written for machine reading. We have to write them in a certain format which will be compiled for the machine to understand. But often those written codes are not easy to follow for people other than programmers. In order to show those codes in an informal way so that humans can also understand, we prepare **pseudocode**. Though it is not an actual programming language code, pseudocode has similar structural conventions of a programming language. Since pseudocode does not run as a real program, there is no standard way of writing a pseudocode. We can follow our own way of writing a pseudocode.

Here is the pseudocode for our algorithm to find a book:

```
Algorithm FindABook(L,book_name)
   Input: list of Books L & name of the search book_name
   Output: False if not found or position of the book we are looking for.

   if L.size = 0 return null
   found := false
   for each item in L, do
     if item = book_name, then
        found := position of the item
   return found
```

Now, let us examine the pseudocode we have written. We are supplying a list of books and a name that we are searching. We are running a `foreach` loop to iterate each of the books and matching with the book name we are searching. If it is found, we are returning the position of the book where we found it, `false` otherwise. So, we have written a pseudocode to find a book name from our book list. But what about the other remaining books? How do we continue our search till all books are found and placed on the right shelf?:

```
Algorithm placeAllBooks
   Input: list of Ordered Books OL, List of received books L
   Output: nothing.


   for each book_name in OL, do
      if FindABook(L,book_name), then
         remove the book from the list L
         place it to the bookshelf
```

Now we have the complete pseudocode for our algorithm of solving the book organization problem. Here, we are going through the list of ordered books and finding the book in the delivered section. If the book is found, we are removing it from the list and placing it to the right shelf.

This simple approach of writing pseudocode can help us solve more complex problems in a structured manner. Since pseudocodes are independent of programming languages and platforms, algorithms are expressed as pseudocode most of the time.

Converting pseudocode to actual code

We are now going to convert our pseudocodes to actual PHP 7 codes as shown:

```
function findABook(Array $bookList, String $bookName) {
    $found = FALSE;

    foreach($bookList as $index => $book) {
        if($book === $bookName) {
            $found = $index;
            break;
        }
    }
    return $found;
}

function placeAllBooks(Array $orderedBooks, Array &$bookList) {
    foreach ($orderedBooks as $book) {
    $bookFound = findABook($bookList, $book);
    if($bookFound !== FALSE) {
        array_splice($bookList, $bookFound, 1);
    }
  }
}

$bookList = ['PHP','MySQL','PGSQL','Oracle','Java'];
$orderedBooks = ['MySQL','PGSQL','Java'];

placeAllBooks($orderedBooks, $bookList);
echo implode(",", $bookList);
```

Let us now understand what is happening in the preceding code. First we have defined a new function, findABook at the beginning of the code. The function is defined with two parameters. One is Array $bookList and the other is String $bookName. At the beginning of the function we are initializing the $found to FALSE, which means nothing has been found yet. The foreach loop iterates through the book list array $bookList and for each book, it matches with our provided book name $bookName. If the book name that we are looking for matches with the book in the $bookList, we are assigning the index (where we found the match) to our $found variable.

Since we have found it, there is no point in continuing the loop. So, we have used the `break` command to get out of the loop. Just out of the loop we are returning our `$found` variable. If the book was found, usually `$found` will return any integer value greater than 0, else it will return `false`:

```php
function placeAllBooks(Array $orderedBooks, Array &$bookList) {
    foreach ($orderedBooks as $book) {
    $bookFound = findABook($bookList, $book);
    if($bookFound !== FALSE) {
        array_splice($bookList, $bookFound, 1);
    }
  }
}
```

This particular function `placeAllBooks` actually iterates through our ordered books `$orderedBooks`. We are iterating our ordered book list and searching each book in our delivered list using the `findABook` function. If the book is found in the ordered list (`$bookFound !== FALSE`), we are removing that book from the delivered book list using the `array_splice()` function of PHP:

```php
$bookList = ['PHP','MySQL','PGSQL','Oracle','Java'];
$orderedBooks = ['MySQL','PGSQL','Java'];
```

These two lines actually shows two PHP arrays which are used for the list of books we have received, `$bookList` and the list of books we have actually ordered `$orderedBooks`. We are just using some dummy data to test our implemented code as shown:

```php
placeAllBooks($orderedBooks, $bookList);
```

The last part of our code actually calls the function `placeAllBooks` to perform the whole operation of checking each book searching for it in our received books and removing it, if it is in the list. So basically, we have implemented our pseudocode to an actual PHP code which we can use to solve our problem.

Algorithm analysis

We have completed our algorithm in the previous section. But one thing we have not done yet is the analysis of our algorithm. A valid question in the current scenario can be, why do we really need to have an analysis of our algorithm? Though we have written the implementation, we are not sure about how many resources our written code will utilize. When we say resource, we mean both time and storage resource utilized by the running application. We write algorithms to work with any length of the input.

In order to understand how our algorithm behaves when the input grows larger and how many resources have been utilized, we usually measure the efficiency of an algorithm by relating the input length to the number of steps (time complexity) or storage (space complexity). It is very important to do the analysis of algorithms in order to find the most efficient algorithm to solve the problem.

We can do algorithm analysis in two different stages. One is done before implementation and one after the implementation. The analysis we do before implementation is also known as *theoretical analysis* and we assume that other factors such as processing power and spaces are going to be constant. The after implementation analysis is known as *empirical analysis* of an algorithm which can vary from platform to platform or from language to language. In empirical analysis, we can get solid statistics from the system regarding time and space utilization.

For our algorithm to place the books and finding the books from purchased items, we can perform a similar analysis. At this time, we will be more concerned about the time complexity rather than the space complexity. We will explore space complexity in coming chapters.

Calculating the complexity

There are two types of complexity we measure in algorithmic analysis:

- **Time complexity**: Time complexity is measured by the number of key operations in the algorithm. In other words, time complexity quantifies the amount of time taken by an algorithm from start to finish.
- **Space complexity**: Space complexity defines the amount of space (in memory) required by the algorithm in its life cycle. It depends on the choice of data structures and platforms.

Now let us focus on our implemented algorithm and find about the operations we are doing for the algorithm. In our `placeAllBooks` function, we are searching for each of our ordered books. So if we have 10 books, we are doing the search 10 times. If the number is 1000, we are doing the search 1000 times. So simply, we can say if there is n number of books, we are going to search it n number of times. In algorithm analysis, input number is mostly represented by n.

For each item in our ordered books, we are doing a search using the `findABook` function. Inside the function, we are again searching through each of the received books with a name we received from the `placeAllBooks` function. Now if we are lucky enough, we can find the name of the book at the beginning of the list of received books. In that case, we do not have to search the remaining items. But what if we are very unlucky and the book we are searching for is at the end of the list? We then have to search each of the books and, at the end, we find it. If the number of received books is also *n*, then we have to run the comparison *n* times.

If we assume that other operations are fixed, the only variable should be the input size. We can then define a boundary or mathematical equation to define the situation to calculate its runtime performance. We call it *asymptotical analysis*. Asymptotical analysis is input bound which means if there is no input, other factors are constant. We use asymptotical analysis to find out the best case, worst case, and average case scenario of algorithms:

- **Best case**: Best case indicates the minimum time required to execute the program. For our example algorithm, the best case can be that, for each book, we are only searching the first item. So, we end up searching for a very little amount of time. We use Ω notation (Sigma notation) to indicate the best case scenario.
- **Average case**: It indicates the average time required to execute a program. For our algorithm the average case will be finding the books around the middle of the list most of the time, or half of the time they are at the beginning of the list and the remaining half are at the end of the list.
- **Worst case**: It indicates the maximum running time for a program. The worst case example will be finding the books at the end of the list all the time. We use the **O** (big oh) notation to describe the worst case scenario. For each book searching in our algorithm, it can take **O(n)** running time. From now on, we will use this notation to express the complexity of our algorithm.

Understanding the big O (big oh) notation

The big O notation is very important for the analysis of algorithms. We need to have a solid understanding of this notation and how to use this in the future. We are going to discuss the big O notation throughout this section.

Our algorithm for finding the books and placing them has *n* number of items. For the first book search, it will compare *n* number of books for the worst case situation. If we say time complexity is *T*, then for the first book the time complexity will be:

```
T(1) = n
```

As we are removing the founded book from the list, the size of the list is now *n-1*. For the second book search, it will compare *n-1* number of books for the worst case situation. Then for the second book, the time complexity will be *n-1*. Combining the both time complexities, for first two books it will be:

```
T(2) = n + (n - 1)
```

If we continue like this, after the *n-1* steps the last book search will only have *1* book left to compare. So, the total complexity will look like:

```
T(n) = n + (n - 1) + (n - 2) + . . . . . .  . . . . + 3 + 2 + 1
```

Now if we look at the preceding series, doesn't it look familiar? It is also known as the **sum of n numbers** equation as shown:

$$\sum_{k=1}^{n} k = \frac{n(n+1)}{2}.$$

So we can write:

```
T(n) = n(n + 1)/2
```

Or:

```
T(n) = n2/2 + n/2
```

For asymptotic analysis, we ignore low order terms and constant multipliers. Since we have *n2*, we can easily ignore the *n* here. Also, the 1/2 constant multiplier can also be ignored. Now we can express the time complexity with the big O notation as the order of *n* squared:

```
T(n) = O(n2)
```

Throughout the book, we will be using this big **O** notation to describe complexity of the algorithms or operations. Here are some common big **O** notations:

Type	Notation
Constant	**O (1)**
Linear	**O (n)**
Logarithmic	**O (log n)**
n log n	**O (n log n)**
Quadratic	**O (n^2)**

Cubic	$O(n^3)$
Exponential	$O(2^n)$

Standard PHP Library (SPL) and data structures

The **Standard PHP Library** (**SPL**), is one of the best possible features of the PHP language in last few years. SPL was created to solve common problems which were lacking in PHP. SPL extended the language in many ways but one of the striking features of SPL is its support of data structures. Though SPL is used for many other purposes, we are going to focus on the data structure part of SPL. SPL comes with core PHP installations and does not require any extension or change in configurations to enable it.

SPL provides a set of standard data structures through Object-Oriented Programming in PHP. The supported data structures are:

- **Doubly linked lists**: It is implemented in `SplDoublyLinkedList`.
- **Stack**: It is implemented in `SplStack` by using `SplDoublyLinkedList`.
- **Queue**: It is implemented in `SplQueue` by using `SplDoublyLinkedList`.
- **Heaps**: It is implemented in `SplHeap`. It also supports max heap in `SplMaxHeap` and min heap in `SplMinHeap`.
- **Priority queue**: It is implemented in `SplPriorityQueue` by using `SplHeap`.
- **Arrays**: It is implemented in `SplFixedArray` for a fixed size array.
- **Map**: It is implemented in `SplObjectStorage`.

In coming chapters, we are going to explore each of the SPL data structure implementations and know their pros and cons, along with their performance analysis with our implementation of corresponding data structures. But as these data structures are already built in, we can use them for a quick turnaround of features and applications.

After the release of PHP 7, everyone was happy with the performance boost of the PHP application in general. PHP SPL is not having the similar performance boost in many cases, but we are going to analyze those in upcoming chapters.

Summary

In this chapter, we have focused our discussion on basic data structures and their names. We have also learned about solving problems with defined steps, known as algorithms. We have also learned about analyzing the algorithms and the big O notation along with how to calculate the complexity. We had a simple brief about the built-in data structures in PHP in the form of SPL.

In the next chapter, we are going to focus on the PHP array, one of the most powerful, flexible data types in PHP. We are going to explore different uses of the PHP array to implement different data structures such as hash table, map, structs, and so on.

2
Understanding PHP Arrays

The PHP array is one of the most used data types in PHP. Most of the time we use it without considering the impact of PHP arrays in our developed code or application. It is so easy to use and dynamic in nature; we love to use PHP arrays for almost any purpose. Sometimes we do not even want to explore if there are other available solutions which can be used instead of PHP array. In this chapter, we are going to explore the positives and negatives of PHP arrays, along with how to use arrays in different data structure implementations along with boosting performances. We will start with explaining different types of arrays in PHP followed by creating fixed sized arrays. Then we are going to see the memory footprints for PHP array elements and how can we improve them along with some data structure implementations.

Understanding PHP arrays in a better way

PHP arrays are so dynamic and flexible that we have to think about whether it is a regular array, an associative array, or a multidimensional array, as in some other languages. We do not need to define the size and data type of the array we are going to use. How can PHP do that, while other languages like C and Java cannot do the same? The answer is very simple: the array concept in PHP is not actually the real array, it is actually a **HashMap**. In other words, a PHP array is not the plain and simple array concept we have from other languages. A simple array will look like this:

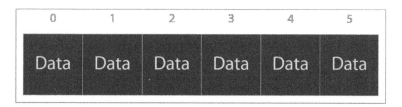

But, we can definitely do that with PHP. Let us check with an example:

```
$array = [1,2,3,4,5];
```

This line shows how a typical array should look. Similar types of data have a sequential index (starting from 0 to 4) to access the values. So who says a PHP array is not a typical array? Let us explore some more examples. Consider the following:

```
$mixedArray = [];
$mixedArray[0] = 200;
$mixedArray['name'] = "Mixed array";
$mixedArray[1] = 10.65;
$mixedArray[2] = ['I', 'am', 'another', 'array'];
```

It is a PHP array that we use on a daily basis; we do not define the size and we are storing integers, a floating point number, a string, and even another array. Does it sound odd or is it just a super power of PHP? We can look at the definition from `http://php.net`.

An array in PHP is actually an **ordered map**. A map is a type that associates values to keys. This type is optimized for several different uses; it can be treated as an array, list (vector), hash table (an implementation of a map), dictionary, collection, stack, queue, and probably more. As array values can be other arrays, trees and multidimensional arrays are also possible.

So a PHP array has got real super powers and it can be used for all possible data structures such as list/vector, hash table, dictionary, collection, stack, queue, doubly linked list, and so on. It seems that the PHP array has been built in such a way that it is either optimized for everything or it is not optimized for anything. We will explore that in this chapter.

If we want to categorize the array, then there are mainly three types of arrays:

- Numeric array
- Associative array
- Multidimensional array

We are going to explore each type of array with some examples and explanations.

Numeric array

A numeric array does not mean it only holds numeric data. In fact, it means the indexes will be numbers only. In PHP they can either be sequential or non-sequential but they have to be numeric. In numeric arrays, values are stored and accessed in a linear way. Here are some examples of PHP numeric array:

```
$array = [10,20,30,40,50];
$array[] = 70;
$array[] = 80;

$arraySize = count($array);
for($i = 0;$i<$arraySize;$i++) {
    echo "Position ".$i." holds the value ".$array[$i]."\n";
}
```

This will have the following output:

```
Position 0 holds the value 10
Position 1 holds the value 20
Position 2 holds the value 30
Position 3 holds the value 40
Position 4 holds the value 50
Position 5 holds the value 70
Position 6 holds the value 80
```

This is a very simple example where we have an array defined and indexes are autogenerated from 0 and incremented with the value of the array. When we add a new element in the array using `$array[]`, it actually increments the index and assigns the value in the new index. That is why value 70 has the index 5 and 80 has the index 6.

If our data is sequential, we can always use a `for` loop without any problem. When we say sequential, we do not mean just 0,1,2,3....,n. It can be 0,5,10,15,20,......,n where n is a multiple of 5. Or it can be 1,3,5,7,9......,n where n is odd. We can create hundreds of such sequences to make the array numeric.

A big question can be, if the indexes are not sequential, can't we construct a numeric array? Yes definitely we can. We just have to adopt a different way to iterate. Consider the following example:

```
$array = [];
$array[10] = 100;
$array[21] = 200;
$array[29] = 300;
$array[500] = 1000;
$array[1001] = 10000;
```

```
$array[71] = 1971;

foreach($array as $index => $value) {
    echo "Position ".$index." holds the value ".$value."\n";
}
```

If we look at the indexes, they are not sequential. They are having random indexes such as 10 followed by 21, 29, and so on. Even at the end we have the index 71, which is much smaller than the previous one of 1001. So, should the last index show in between 29 and 500? Here is the output:

```
Position 10 holds the value 100
Position 21 holds the value 200
Position 29 holds the value 300
Position 500 holds the value 1000
Position 1001 holds the value 10000
Position 71 holds the value 1971
```

Couple of things to notice here:

We are iterating the array the way we entered the data. There is no internal sorting of the indexes at all, though they are all numeric. Another interesting fact is that the size of the array $array is only 6. It is not 1002 like C++, Java, or other languages where we need to predefine the size of the array before using it, and the max index can be *n-1* where *n* is the size of the array.

Associative array

An associative array is accessed by a key which can be any string. In an associative array, values are stored against the key instead of a linear index. We can use an associative array to store any type of data, just like the numeric array. Let us create a student array where we will store student information:

```
$studentInfo = [];
$studentInfo['Name'] = "Adiyan";
$studentInfo['Age'] = 11;
$studentInfo['Class'] = 6;
$studentInfo['RollNumber'] = 71;
$studentInfo['Contact'] = "info@adiyan.com";

foreach($studentInfo as $key => $value) {
    echo $key.": ".$value."\n";
}
```

Here is the output of the code:

```
Name: Adiyan
Age: 11
Class: 6
RollNumber: 71
Contact: info@adiyan.com
```

Here we are using each key to hold one piece of data. We can add as many keys as we need without any problem. This gives us the flexibility to represent a data structure similar to structure, map, and dictionary using a PHP associative array.

Multidimensional array

A multidimensional array contains multiple arrays in it. In other words, it is an array of array(s). In this book, we will be using multidimensional arrays in different examples as they are one of the most popular and efficient ways of storing data for graphs and other tree-type data structures. Let us explore the PHP multidimensional array using an example:

```php
$players = [];
$players[] = ["Name" => "Ronaldo", "Age" => 31, "Country" => "Portugal",
"Team" => "Real Madrid"];
$players[] = ["Name" => "Messi", "Age" => 27, "Country" => "Argentina",
"Team" => "Barcelona"];
$players[] = ["Name" => "Neymar", "Age" => 24, "Country" => "Brazil",
"Team" => "Barcelona"];
$players[] = ["Name" => "Rooney", "Age" => 30, "Country" => "England",
"Team" => "Man United"];

foreach($players as $index => $playerInfo) {
    echo "Info of player # ".($index+1)."\n";
    foreach($playerInfo as $key => $value) {
        echo $key.": ".$value."\n";
    }
    echo "\n";
}
```

The example we just saw is an example of a two-dimensional array. As a result, we are using two `foreach` loops to iterate the two-dimensional array. Here is the output of the code:

```
Info of player # 1
Name: Ronaldo
Age: 31
Country: Portugal
```

```
Team: Real Madrid

Info of player # 2
Name: Messi
Age: 27
Country: Argentina
Team: Barcelona

Info of player # 3
Name: Neymar
Age: 24
Country: Brazil
Team: Barcelona

Info of player # 4
Name: Rooney
Age: 30
Country: England
Team: Man United
```

We can create n-dimensional arrays using PHP as per our needs, but we have to remember one thing: the more dimensions we add, the more complex the structure becomes. We as humans usually visualize three dimensions, so in order to have more than three-dimensional arrays, we must have a solid understanding of how an array works in multiple dimensions.

 We can use both a numeric array and an associative array as a single array in PHP. But in such a case, we have to be very cautious to choose the right way to iterate through the array elements. In such cases, `foreach` will be a better choice than a `for` or `while` loop.

Using an array as flexible storage

So far we have seen a PHP array as a dynamic, hybrid data structure for storing any type of data. This gives us a lot more freedom to utilize an array as a flexible storage container for our data. We can mix different data types and different dimensions of data in a single array. We do not have to even define the size or type of array we are going to use. We can grow, shrink, and modify data to and from an array whenever we need to.

Not only does PHP allows us to create dynamic arrays, but it also provides us with lots of built-in functionalities for arrays. For example: `array_intersect`, `array_merge`, `array_diff`, `array_push`, `array_pop`, `prev`, `next`, `current`, `end`, and many more.

Use of multi-dimensional arrays to represent data structures

In coming chapters, we will talk about many different data structures and algorithms. One of the key data structures we are going to focus is the graph. We already know the definition of graph data structures. Most of the time we will be using PHP multidimensional arrays to represent that data as an adjacency matrix. Let us consider the following graph diagram:

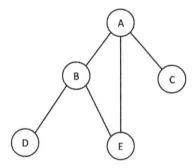

Now if we consider each node of the graph to be a value of an array, we can represent the nodes as:

```
$nodes = ['A', 'B', 'C', 'D', 'E'];
```

But this will only give us node names. We cannot connect or create a relationship between nodes. In order to do that, we need to construct a two-dimensional array where the node names will be keys, and values will be 0 or 1 based on the interconnectivity of two nodes. Since there is no direction provided in the graph, we do not know if *A* connects to *C* or if Connects to *A*. So we will assume both are connected to each other.

First, we need to create an array for the graph and initialize each node of the two-dimensional arrays as 0. The following code will exactly do that:

```
$graph = [];
$nodes = ['A', 'B', 'C', 'D', 'E'];
foreach ($nodes as $xNode) {
    foreach ($nodes as $yNode) {
        $graph[$xNode][$yNode] = 0;
    }
}
```

Let us print the array using the following code so that we see how it looks actually before defining the connectivity between nodes:

```
foreach ($nodes as $xNode) {
    foreach ($nodes as $yNode) {
        echo $graph[$xNode][$yNode] . "\t";
    }
    echo "\n";
}
```

As no connection between the nodes has been defined, all cells are showing 0. So the output looks like this:

0	0	0	0	0
0	0	0	0	0
0	0	0	0	0
0	0	0	0	0
0	0	0	0	0

Now we will define the connectivity of the nodes in such a way that a connection between the two nodes will be expressed as a value of 1, just like the following code:

```
$graph["A"]["B"] = 1;
$graph["B"]["A"] = 1;
$graph["A"]["C"] = 1;
$graph["C"]["A"] = 1;
$graph["A"]["E"] = 1;
$graph["E"]["A"] = 1;
$graph["B"]["E"] = 1;
$graph["E"]["B"] = 1;
$graph["B"]["D"] = 1;
$graph["D"]["B"] = 1;
```

As there is no direction given in the graph diagram, we will consider it as the undirected graph and hence we are setting two values to 1 for each connection. For the connection between *A* and *B*, we are setting both `$graph["A"]["B"]` and `$graph["B"]["A"]` to 1. We will learn more about defining connectivity between nodes and why we are doing it in later chapters. For now we are just focusing on how to use multidimensional arrays for data structures. We can reprint the matrix and this time, the output looks like this:

0	1	1	0	1
1	0	0	1	1
1	0	0	0	0
0	1	0	0	0
1	1	0	0	0

It will be much more fun and interesting to find out more about graphs and their operations in `Chapter 9`, *Putting Graphs into Action*.

Creating fixed size arrays with the SplFixedArray method

So far, we have explored PHP arrays and we know, we do not define the size of the arrays. PHP arrays can grow or shrink as per our demand. This flexibility comes with a great inconvenience regarding memory usage. We are going to explore that in this section. For now, let us focus on creating fixed size arrays using the SPL library.

Why do we need a fixed size array? Does it have any added advantage? The answer is that when we know we only need a certain number of elements in an array, we can use a fixed array to reduce the memory usage. Before going to the memory use analysis, let us have some examples of using the `SplFixedArray` method:

```
$array = new SplFixedArray(10);

for ($i = 0; $i < 10; $i++)
    $array[$i] = $i;

for ($i = 0; $i < 10; $i++)
    echo $array[$i] . "\n";
```

First, we are creating a new `SplFixedArray` object with a defined size of 10. The remaining lines actually follow the same principle which we use in regular PHP array value assignment and retrieval. If we want to access an index which is out of the range (here it is 10), it will throw an exception:

```
PHP Fatal error:  Uncaught RuntimeException: Index invalid or out of range
```

The basic difference between a PHP array and `SplFixedArray` are:

- `SplFixedArray` must have a fixed defined size
- The indexes of `SplFixedArray` must be integers and within the range of 0 to *n*, where *n* is the size of the array we defined

The `SplFixedArray` method can be very handy when we have a lot of defined arrays with known size or have an upper limit for the maximum required size of the array. But if we do not know the array size, then it is better to use a PHP array.

Performance comparison between a regular PHP array and SplFixedArray

One of the key questions we encountered in the last section was, why should we use `SplFixedArray` instead of PHP arrays? We are now ready to explore the answer. We came across the concept that PHP arrays are actually not arrays rather than hash maps. Let us run a small example code in PHP 5.x version to see the memory usage of a PHP array.

Let us create an array with 100,000 unique PHP integers. As I am running a 64 bit machine, I expect each integer to take 8 bytes each. So we will have around 800,000 bytes of memory consumed for the array. Here is the code:

```
$startMemory = memory_get_usage();
$array = range(1,100000);
$endMemory = memory_get_usage();
echo ($endMemory - $startMemory)." bytes";
```

If we run this code in our command prompt, we will see an output of 14,649,040 bytes. Yes, it is correct. The memory usage is almost 18.5 times more than what we have planned for. That means, for each element in the array an overhead of 144 bytes (18 * 8 bytes) for one PHP array. Now, where does this extra 144 bytes come from and why does PHP utilize so much extra memory for each array element? Here is an explanation of the extra bytes used by a PHP array:

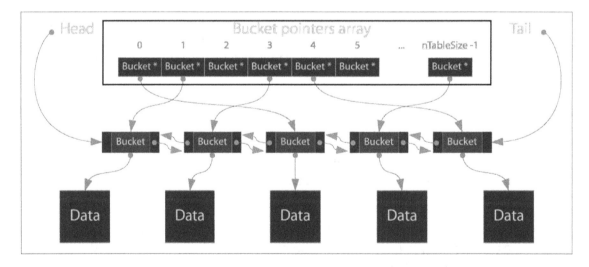

This diagram shows how a PHP array works internally. It stores data in a bucket to avoid collision and to accommodate more data. To manage this dynamic nature, it implements both a doubly linked list and hash table internally for array. Eventually, it costs lots of extra memory space for each individual elements in the array. Here is the breakdown of the memory consumption of each element based on the PHP array implementation code (C code):

	32 bit	64 bit
zval	16 bytes	24 bytes
+ cyclic GC info	4 bytes	8 bytes
+ allocation header	8 bytes	16 bytes
zval (value) total	28 bytes	48 bytes
bucket	36 bytes	72 bytes
+ allocation header	8 bytes	16 bytes
+ pointer	4 bytes	8 bytes
bucket (array element) total	48 bytes	96 bytes
Grand total (bucket+zval)	76 bytes	144 bytes

In order to understand the internal structure of a PHP array, we need to study in depth about PHP internals. It is beyond the scope of this particular book. A good recommended read is:
`https://nikic.github.io/2011/12/12/How-big-are-PHP-arrays-really -Hint-BIG.html`

With the new PHP 7 version, there is a very big improvement in the PHP array and how it is constructed internally. As a result, the 144 bytes overhead on each element has come down to 36 bytes only. That is a big improvement and it is applicable for both 32 bit and 64 bit OS. A comparison chart, having a range of 100,000 items in an array, is shown as follows:

$array = Range(1,100000)	32 bit	64 bit
PHP 5.6 or below	7.4 MB	14 MB
PHP 7	3 MB	4 MB

So, in other words, PHP 7 has an improvement factor of 2.5 times for 32 bit and 3.5 times for 64 bit system for array storage. That is a really good improvement. But this was all about a PHP array, what about `SplFixedArray`? Let us run the same example using `SplFixArray` in both PHP 7 and PHP 5.x:

```
$items = 100000;
$startMemory = memory_get_usage();
$array = new SplFixedArray($items);
for ($i = 0; $i < $items; $i++) {
    $array[$i] = $i;
}
$endMemory = memory_get_usage();

$memoryConsumed = ($endMemory - $startMemory) / (1024*1024);
$memoryConsumed = ceil($memoryConsumed);
echo "memory = {$memoryConsumed} MB\n";
```

We have written the memory consumption functionality of a `SplFixedArray` here. If we just change the line `$array = new SplFixedArray($items);` to `$array = [];`, we will have the same code running as for a PHP array.

 The benchmark result can vary from machine to machine as there can be different OS, memory size, debugger on/off, and so on. It is always suggested to run the codes in your own machines to generate a similar benchmark for comparisons.

Here is a comparison of memory consumption of a PHP array and `SplFixedArray` for an array with 100,000 integers in a 64 bit system:

100,000 items	Using PHP array	SplFixedArray
PHP 5.6 or below	14 MB	6 MB
PHP 7	5 MB	2 MB

Not only in memory usage, `SplFixedArray` is also faster in execution compared to general PHP array operations such as accessing value, assigning value, and so on.

Though we use the `SplFixedArray` object with [] just like the array, PHP array functions will not be applicable for `SplFixedArray`. We cannot directly apply any PHP array functions such as `array_sum`, `array_filter`, and so on.

More examples using SplFixedArray

Since `SplFixedArray` has a good performance boost indicator, we can utilize it instead of a regular PHP array in most of our data structures and algorithms. Now we will explore some more examples of using `SplFixedArray` in different scenarios.

Changing from a PHP array to SplFixedArray

We have seen how we can create a `SplFixedArray` with a fixed length. What if I want to create an array to `SplFixedArray` during runtime? The following code block shows how to achieve it:

```
$array =[1 => 10, 2 => 100, 3 => 1000, 4 => 10000];
$splArray = SplFixedArray::fromArray($array);
print_r($splArray);
```

Here we are constructing a `SplFixedArray` from an existing array `$array` using the static method `fromArray` of the `SplFixedArray` class. Then we are printing the array using the PHP `print_r` function. It will show an output like this:

```
SplFixedArray Object
(
    [0] =>
    [1] => 10
    [2] => 100
    [3] => 1000
    [4] => 10000
)
```

We can see the array has been now converted to an `SplFixedArray` and it maintained the index number exactly as it was in the actual array. Since the actual array did not have 0 index defined, here index 0 is kept as null. But if we want to ignore the indexes from the previous array and assign them new indexes, then we have to change the second line of the previous code to this:

```
$splArray = SplFixedArray::fromArray($array,false);
```

Now if we print the array again, we will have the following output:

```
SplFixedArray Object
(
    [0] => 10
    [1] => 100
    [2] => 1000
    [3] => 10000
)
```

> If we want to convert an array to a fixed array during runtime, it is a better idea to unset the regular PHP array if it is not being used later on. It will save memory usage if it is a big array.

Converting a SplFixedArray to a PHP array

We might also need to convert a `SplFixedArray` to a regular PHP array to apply some predefined array functions from PHP. Like the previous example, this is also a very simple thing to do:

```
$items = 5;
$array = new SplFixedArray($items);
for ($i = 0; $i < $items; $i++) {
    $array[$i] = $i * 10;
}

$newArray = $array->toArray();
print_r($newArray);
```

This will produce the following output:

```
Array
(
    [0] => 0
    [1] => 10
    [2] => 20
    [3] => 30
    [4] => 40
)
```

Changing the SplFixedArray size after declaration

As we are defining the array size at the beginning, we may require changing the size later on. In order to do that, we have to use the setSize() method of the SplFixedArray class. An example is shown as follows:

```
$items = 5;
$array = new SplFixedArray($items);
for ($i = 0; $i < $items; $i++) {
    $array[$i] = $i * 10;
}

$array->setSize(10);
$array[7] = 100;
```

Creating a multidimensional array using SplFixedArray

We might also require creating two or more dimensional arrays using SplFixedArray. In order to do that, it is recommended to follow this example:

```
$array = new SplFixedArray(100);
for ($i = 0; $i < 100; $i++)
$array[$i] = new SplFixedArray(100);
```

We are actually creating another SplFixedArray inside each array indexes. We can add as many dimensions as we want. But we have to remember that, with dimensions, we are multiplying the size of the array. So it can grow really big very quickly.

Understanding hash tables

In programming language, a hash table is a data structure which is used to make an array associative. It means we can use keys to map values instead of using an index. A hash table must use a hash function to compute an index into an array of buckets or slots, from which the desired value can be found:

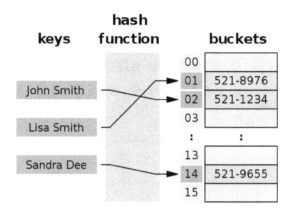

As we have mentioned several times, a PHP array is actually a hash table and hence it supports associative arrays. We need to remember one thing: that we do not need to define a hash function for the associative array implementation. PHP does it internally for us. As a result, when we create an associative array in PHP, we are actually creating a hash table. For example, the following code can be considered as the hash table:

```
$array = [];
$array['Germany'] = "Position 1";
$array['Argentina'] = "Position 2";
$array['Portugal'] = "Position 6";
$array['Fifa_World_Cup'] = "2018 Russia";
```

As a matter of fact, we can directly invoke any keys with only **O(1)** complexity. The key will always refer to the same index inside the bucket, as PHP will use the same hash function to calculate the index.

Implementing struct using a PHP array

As we already know, a struct is a complex data type where we define multiple properties as a group so that we can use it as a single data type. We can write a struct using a PHP array and class. Here is an example of a struct using a PHP array:

```php
$player = [
    "name" => "Ronaldo",
    "country" => "Portugal",
    "age" => 31,
    "currentTeam" => "Real Madrid"
];
```

It is simply an associative array with keys as string. A complex struct can be constructed using single or more constructs as its properties. For example using the player struct, we can use a team struct:

```php
$ronaldo = [
    "name" => "Ronaldo",
    "country" => "Portugal",
    "age" => 31,
    "currentTeam" => "Real Madrid"
];

$messi = [
    "name" => "Messi",
    "country" => "Argentina",
    "age" => 27,
    "currentTeam" => "Barcelona"
];

$team = [
    "player1" => $ronaldo,
    "player2" => $messi
];

The same thing we can achieve using PHP Class. The example will look like:
Class Player {

    public $name;
    public $country;
    public $age;
    public $currentTeam;

}

$ronaldo = new Player;
```

```php
$ronaldo->name = "Ronaldo";
$ronaldo->country = "Portugal";
$ronaldo->age = 31;
$ronaldo->currentTeam = "Real Madrid";
```

Since we have seen both ways of defining a struct, we have to choose either one of them to implement a struct. While creating an object might look more convenient, it is slower compared to array implementation. Where an array has an added advantage of speed, it also has a disadvantage as it takes more memory space compared to an object. Now we have to make the decision based on our preference.

Implementing sets using a PHP array

A set is a simply a collection of values without any particular order. It can contain any data type and we can run different set operations such as union, intersection, complement, and so on. As a set only contains values, we can construct a basic PHP array and assign values to it so that it grows dynamically. The following example shows two sets that we have defined; one contains some odd numbers and the other one has some prime numbers:

```php
$odd = [];
$odd[] = 1;
$odd[] = 3;
$odd[] = 5;
$odd[] = 7;
$odd[] = 9;

$prime = [];
$prime[] = 2;
$prime[] = 3;
$prime[] = 5;
```

In order to check the existence of a value inside the set along with union, intersection, and complement operation, we can use the following example:

```php
if (in_array(2, $prime)) {
    echo "2 is a prime";
}

$union = array_merge($prime, $odd);
$intersection = array_intersect($prime, $odd);
$compliment = array_diff($prime, $odd);
```

PHP has many built-in functions for such operations and we can utilize them for our set operations. But we have to consider one fact: since the set is not ordered in any particular way, searching using the `in_array()` function might have the complexity of **O(n)** in worst case scenario. Same goes for the `array_merge()` function, as it will check each value from one array with another array. In order to speed things up, we can modify our code a little bit and make it efficient:

```
$odd = [];
$odd[1] = true;
$odd[3] = true;
$odd[5] = true;
$odd[7] = true;
$odd[9] = true;

$prime = [];
$prime[2] = true;
$prime[3] = true;
$prime[5] = true;

if (isset($prime[2])) {
    echo "2 is a prime";
}

$union = $prime + $odd;
$intersection = array_intersect_key($prime, $odd);
$compliment = array_diff_key($prime, $odd);
```

If we analyze this code, we can see that we are using an index or key to define the set. Since a PHP array index or key lookup have a complexity of **O(1),** it makes the searching much faster. As a result, all the lookup, union, intersect, and complement operations will take lesser time compared to the previous example.

Best usage of a PHP array

Though a PHP array consumes more memory, the flexibility of using a PHP array is much more important for many data structures. As a result, we will use a PHP regular array as well as `SplFixedArray` in many of our data structure implementations and algorithms. If we just consider a PHP array as a container for our data, it will be easier for us to utilize its immensely powerful features in many data structure implementations. Along with built-in functions, a PHP array is definitely a must use data structure for programming and developing applications using PHP.

PHP has some built-in sorting functions for an array. It can sort using keys and values along with keeping association while sorting. We are going to explore these built-in functions in `Chapter 7`, *Using Sorting Algorithms*.

PHP array, is it a performance killer?

We have seen in this chapter how each element in a PHP array has a very big overhead of memory. Since it is done by the language itself, there is very little we can do over here, except that we use `SplFixedArray` instead of a regular array where it is applicable. But if we move from our PHP 5.x version to the new PHP 7, then we can have a huge improvement in our application, whether we use regular PHP array or `SplFixedArray`.

In PHP 7, the internal implementation of a hash table has been changed drastically and it is not built for efficiency. As a result, the overhead memory consumption for each element has gone down significantly. Though we can argue that less memory consumption does not make a code speedy, we can have a counter argument that if we have less memory to manage, we can focus more on execution rather than memory management. As a result, we have some impact on the performance.

So far from the discussion, we can easily say the newly improved array in PHP 7 is definitely a recommended choice for developers to solve complex and memory efficient applications.

Summary

In this chapter, we have focused our discussion on PHP arrays and what can be done using a PHP array as a data structure. We are going to continue our exploration of array features in the coming chapters. In the next chapter, we are going to focus on linked list data structures and different variants of linked list. We are also going to explore different types of practical examples regarding linked lists and their best usages.

3
Using Linked Lists

We know a lot about arrays already. Now, we are going to shift our focus to a new type of data structure known as a *list*. It is one of the most used data structures in the programming world. In most of the programming languages, the array is a fixed size structure. As a result, it cannot grow dynamically, and shrinking or removing an item from a fixed size array is also problematic since we have to shift the array's items to fill up the gap. For this reason, many developers prefer lists instead of arrays. Considering the fact that each array element can have an overhead of some extra bytes, linked lists can be used where memory efficiency is a big factor. In this chapter, we will explore the different types of linked lists in PHP and their implementation. We will also look at real-world problems that can be solved using linked lists.

What is a linked list?

A linked list is a collection of objects known as nodes. Each node is connected to the next node with a link, which is nothing but an object reference. If we consider the following image, each box represents a node. The arrow indicates the link between the nodes. This is an example of a singly linked list. The last node contains the next link of a NULL, so that it marks the end of the list:

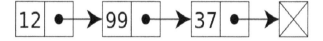

A node is an object, meaning it can store any data type as simple as a string, integer, or float, or complex, such as an array, array of arrays, objects, or object arrays. We can store anything as per our need.

We can also perform a wide variety of operations on a linked list, such as the following ones:

- Checking whether the list is empty
- Displaying all items in the list
- Searching an item in the list
- Getting the size of the list
- Inserting a new item at the beginning or end of the list
- Removing an item from the beginning or end of the list
- Inserting a new item at a specific place or before/after an item
- Reversing a list

These are only some of the operations that can be performed on a linked list.

Let's write a simple linked list to store some names:

```
class ListNode {
    public $data = NULL;
    public $next = NULL;

    public function __construct(string $data = NULL) {
        $this->data = $data;
    }
}
```

We mentioned earlier that a linked list consists of nodes. We have created a simple class for our node. The `ListNode` class has two properties: one that will store the data and the other for the link called `next`. Now, we are going to implement a linked list using the `ListNode` class. For simplicity, we will just have two operations: `insert` and `display`:

```
class LinkedList {
    private $_firstNode = NULL;
    private $_totalNodes = 0;

    public function insert(string $data = NULL) {
        $newNode = new ListNode($data);

        if ($this->_firstNode === NULL) {
            $this->_firstNode = &$newNode;
        } else {
            $currentNode = $this->_firstNode;
            while ($currentNode->next !== NULL) {
```

```
                $currentNode = $currentNode->next;
            }
            $currentNode->next = $newNode;
        }
        $this->_totalNode++;
        return TRUE;
    }

    public function display() {
        echo "Total book titles: ".$this->_totalNode."\n";
        $currentNode = $this->_firstNode;
        while ($currentNode !== NULL) {
            echo $currentNode->data . "\n";
            $currentNode = $currentNode->next;
        }
    }
}
```

The preceding code actually implements our two basic operations for `insert` and `display` nodes. In the `LinkedList` class, we have two private properties: `$_firstNode` and `$_totalNodes`. Both have the default value of `NULL` and `0`, respectively. We need to mark the head node or first node, so that we always know where we have to start from. We can also call it the front node. Whatever name we provide, it will be mainly used to indicate the start of the linked list. Now, let's move to the `insert` operation code.

The insert method takes one argument, which is the data itself. We will create a new node with the data using the `ListNode` class. Before inserting a book title in our linked list, we have to consider two possibilities:

- The list is empty and we are inserting the first title
- The list is not empty and the title is going to be added at the end

Why do we need to consider both cases? The answer is pretty simple. If we do not know whether the list is empty or not, we might get different results for our operations. We might also create invalid linking between the nodes. So, the idea is if the list is empty, our insert item is going to be the first item of the list. This is what the first part of the code is doing:

```
$newNode = new ListNode($data);

if ($this->_firstNode === NULL) {
        $this->_firstNode = &$newNode;
}
```

We can see from the preceding code segment that we are creating a new node with the data and naming the node object $newNode. After that, it checks whether $_firstNode is NULL or not. If it is NULL, then the list is empty. If it is empty, then we assign the $newNode object to the $_firstNode property. Now, the remaining part of the insert method represents our second condition, which is that the list is not empty, and we have to add the new item at the end of the list:

```
$currentNode = $this->_firstNode;
while ($currentNode->next !== NULL) {
  $currentNode = $currentNode->next;
}
$currentNode->next = $newNode;
```

Here, we get the first node of the list from the $_firstNode property. Now, we are going to iterate from the first node until the end of the list. We will ensure this by checking the condition that the next link for the current node is not NULL. If it is NULL, then we have reached the end of the list. In order to make sure that we are not looping to the same node all the time, we set the next node on from the current node as the current item during the iteration process. The while loop code implements the logic. Once we get out of the while loop, we set the last node of the linked list as $currentNode. Now, we have to assign the next link of the current last node to the newly created node named $newNode, so we simply put the object to the next link of the node. This object reference will work as a link between two node objects. At the end, we also increment the total node count value by 1 by post-incrementing the $_totalNode property.

We could have easily created another property for the list that would track the last node. It could have saved us from looping the whole list every time we are inserting a new node. We ignored this option intentionally to work through the basic understanding of the linked list. Later in this chapter, we will implement that for faster operations.

If we look at our display method, we can see that we are using almost similar logic to iterate through each of the nodes and displaying its content. We first get the head item for the linked list. Then, we iterate through the list until the list item is NULL. Inside the loop, we display the node data by showing its $data property. Now, we have a node class ListNode to create individual nodes for the linked list, and we have the LinkedList class to do basic insert and display operations. Let's write a small code to utilize the LinkedList class to create a linked list for book titles:

```
$BookTitles = new LinkedList();
$BookTitles->insert("Introduction to Algorithm");
$BookTitles->insert("Introduction to PHP and Data structures");
```

```
$BookTitles->insert("Programming Intelligence");
$BookTitles->display();
```

Here, we create a new object for `LinkedList` and name it `$BookTitles`. Then, we insert new book items using the `insert` method. We add three books, and then, we are displaying the book names using the `display` method. If we run the preceding code, we will see following output:

```
Total book titles: 3
Introduction to Algorithm
Introduction to PHP and Data structures
Programming Intelligence
```

As we can see, there is a counter at the first line that shows that we have three book titles, along with their names. If we look carefully, we will see that the book titles are displayed the same way that we entered them. This means our implemented linked list is actually maintaining the order. This is because we have always entered the new node at the end of the list. We could have done this differently if we wanted. As our first example, we have covered a lot about linked lists and how to construct them. In the upcoming sections, we will explore more about how to create different types of linked lists, and with more complex examples. For now, we are going to focus on the different types of linked lists.

Different types of linked list

So far, we have dealt with the kind of list known as a singly linked list, or linear linked list. However, there are also several different types of linked lists based on the operations involved:

- Doubly linked list
- Circular linked list
- Multi-linked list

Doubly linked lists

In a doubly linked list, there are two links on each node: one to point to the next node and another one to the previous node. Where the singly linked list is unidirectional, the doubly linked list is bidirectional. We can move forward or backward in the list without any problem. The following image shows a sample doubly linked list. Later, in the *Implementing a doubly linked list in PHP* section, we will explore how to implement a doubly linked list:

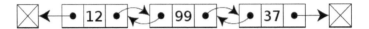

Circular linked lists

In a singly or doubly linked list, there is no node after the last node, so the last node does not have any subsequent node to iterate on. If we allow the last node to point to the first node, we are making a circle. Such linked lists are known as circular linked lists. We can have both singly and doubly linked lists as circular linked lists. We will also implement a circular linked list in this chapter. The following image depicts a circular linked list:

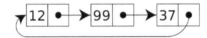

Multi-linked lists

A multi-linked list, or multiply linked list, is a special type of linked list that has two or more links linking each node to another node. It can grow multi-directionally based on the purpose of the linked list. For example, if we take the example of a list of students with each student being a node with the properties of name, age, gender, department, major, and so on, then we can link each student's node not only with the next and previous nodes, but also with age, gender, department, and major. Though the usage of such a linked list requires a good understanding of the linked list concept, we can use such special linked lists whenever we need. The following image depicts a multi-linked list:

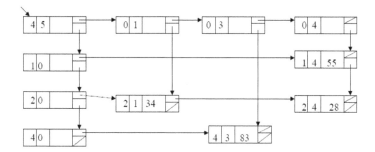

Inserting, deleting, and searching for an item

So far, we have seen only the operations for inserting a node and displaying all node contents. Now, we will explore the other operations available in a linked list. We will mainly focus on the following operations:

- Inserting at the first node
- Searching for a node
- Inserting before a specific node
- Inserting after a specific node
- Deleting the first node
- Deleting the last node
- Searching for and deleting one node
- Reversing a linked list
- Getting Nth position element

Inserting at the first node

When we add a node in the front, or head, we have to consider two simple possibilities. The list can be empty and as a result the new node is the head. This possibility is as simple as it can get. However, if the list already has a head, then we have to do the following:

1. Create the new node.
2. Make the new node as first node or head.
3. Assign the previous head or first node as the next to follow for the newly created first node.

Here is the code for this:

```
public function insertAtFirst(string $data = NULL) {
    $newNode = new ListNode($data);
    if ($this->_firstNode === NULL) {
        $this->_firstNode = &$newNode;
    } else {
        $currentFirstNode = $this->_firstNode;
        $this->_firstNode = &$newNode;
        $newNode->next = $currentFirstNode;
    }
    $this->_totalNode++;
    return TRUE;
}
```

Searching for a node

Searching for a node is pretty simple. We need to iterate through each node and check whether the target data matches with the node data. If the data is found, the node will be returned; otherwise, it will return FALSE. The implementation looks like this:

```
public function search(string $data = NULL) {
    if ($this->_totalNode) {
        $currentNode = $this->_firstNode;
        while ($currentNode !== NULL) {
            if ($currentNode->data === $data) {
                return $currentNode;
            }
            $currentNode = $currentNode->next;
        }
    }
    return FALSE;
}
```

Inserting before a specific node

This process is similar to the first operation that we looked at. The main difference is that we need to find out the specific node and then insert a new node before it. When we find the target node, we can change the next node so that it points to the newly created node, and then we can change the node following the newly created node so that it points to the node that we searched for. This is shown in the following image:

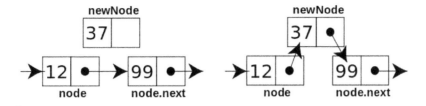

Here is the code to implement the logic shown earlier:

```
public function insertBefore(string $data = NULL, string $query = NULL) {
    $newNode = new ListNode($data);

    if ($this->_firstNode) {
        $previous = NULL;
        $currentNode = $this->_firstNode;
        while ($currentNode !== NULL) {
            if ($currentNode->data === $query) {
                $newNode->next = $currentNode;
                $previous->next = $newNode;
                $this->_totalNode++;
                break;
            }
            $previous = $currentNode;
            $currentNode = $currentNode->next;
        }
    }
}
```

If we inspect the preceding code, we can see that the logic is pretty straightforward. We have two parameters in this method: one is the data and one is the query. We iterate through each node. While doing this, we also track the current node and previous node. It is important to track the previous node as we will set the next of previous node to a newly created node when our target node is found.

Inserting after a specific node

This process is similar to the inserted a node before a target node. The difference is that we need to insert the new node after the target node. Here, we need to consider the target node as well as the next node, to which it's pointing. When we find the target node, we can change the next node so that it points to the newly created node, and then we can change node following the newly created node so that it points to the next node following the target node. Here is the code used to implement this:

```
public function insertAfter(string $data = NULL, string $query =
  NULL) {
    $newNode = new ListNode($data);

    if ($this->_firstNode) {
        $nextNode = NULL;
        $currentNode = $this->_firstNode;
        while ($currentNode !== NULL) {
            if ($currentNode->data === $query) {
                if($nextNode !== NULL) {
                    $newNode->next = $nextNode;
                }
                $currentNode->next = $newNode;
                $this->_totalNode++;
                break;
            }
            $currentNode = $currentNode->next;
            $nextNode = $currentNode->next;
        }
    }
}
```

Deleting the first node

Deleting a node simply means taking out the node and rearranging the previous and subsequent node links. If we just remove a node and connect the previous node's next link with the node following the deleted node, we are done with the delete operation. Just have a look at the following example:

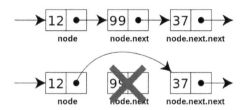

When we delete the first node, we just have to make the second node our head or first node. We can achieve that very easily by using the following code:

```
public function deleteFirst() {
        if ($this->_firstNode !== NULL) {
            if ($this->_firstNode->next !== NULL) {
                $this->_firstNode = $this->_firstNode->next;
            } else {
                $this->_firstNode = NULL;
            }
            $this->_totalNode--;
            return TRUE;
        }
        return FALSE;
    }
```

Now, we have to consider one special case, namely decreasing the total node count by one.

Deleting the last node

Deleting the last node will require us to assign the second from last node's next link to NULL. We will iterate until the last node and track the previous node as we go. Once we hit the last node, the previous node property of the next will be set to NULL, as shown in the following example:

```
public function deleteLast() {
    if ($this->_firstNode !== NULL) {
        $currentNode = $this->_firstNode;
        if ($currentNode->next === NULL) {
            $this->_firstNode = NULL;
        } else {
            $previousNode = NULL;

            while ($currentNode->next !== NULL) {
                $previousNode = $currentNode;
                $currentNode = $currentNode->next;
            }
```

```
                $previousNode->next = NULL;
                $this->_totalNode--;
                return TRUE;
            }
        }
        return FALSE;
    }
```

At first, we check whether the list is empty or not. After that, we check whether the list has more than one node. Based on the answer, we iterate to the the last node and tracking the previous node. Then, we assign the previous node's next link as NULL, just to omit the very last node from the list.

Searching for and deleting a node

We can delete any node from our list using a search and delete operation. First, we search for the node from the list and then remove the node by removing references from the node. Here is the code to achieve this:

```
public function delete(string $query = NULL) {
    if ($this->_firstNode) {
        $previous = NULL;
        $currentNode = $this->_firstNode;
        while ($currentNode !== NULL) {
            if ($currentNode->data === $query) {
                if ($currentNode->next === NULL) {
                    $previous->next = NULL;
                } else {
                    $previous->next = $currentNode->next;
                }

                $this->_totalNode--;
                break;
            }
            $previous = $currentNode;
            $currentNode = $currentNode->next;
        }
    }
}
```

Reversing a list

There are many approaches to reversing a linked list. We will work on a simple approach to reverse the list, which is known as in place reverse. We iterate through the nodes and change the next node to the previous, previous to the current, and the current to the next. A pseudo algorithm for the logic will look like this:

```
prev    = NULL;
current = first_node;
next = NULL;
while (current != NULL)
{
  next  = current->next;
  current->next = prev;
  prev = current;
  current = next;
}
first_node = prev;
```

If we implement our reverse function based on this pseudocode, it will look like this:

```
public function reverse() {
    if ($this->_firstNode !== NULL) {
        if ($this->_firstNode->next !== NULL) {
            $reversedList = NULL;
            $next = NULL;
            $currentNode = $this->_firstNode;
            while ($currentNode !== NULL) {
                $next = $currentNode->next;
                $currentNode->next = $reversedList;
                $reversedList = $currentNode;
                $currentNode = $next;
            }
            $this->_firstNode = $reversedList;
        }
    }
}
```

Getting the Nth position element

As lists are different from arrays, it is not easier to get elements from their positions directly. In order to get an element in the Nth position, we have to iterate to that position and get the element. Here is the code sample for this method:

```
public function getNthNode(int $n = 0) {
    $count = 1;
    if ($this->_firstNode !== NULL) {
        $currentNode = $this->_firstNode;
        while ($currentNode !== NULL) {
            if ($count === $n) {
                return $currentNode;
            }
            $count++;
            $currentNode = $currentNode->next;
        }
    }
}
```

We have now written all the required operations for our `LinkedList` class. Now, let's run the program with different operations. If we run the following program, we will mostly cover all the operations we have written:

```
$BookTitles = new LinkedList();
$BookTitles->insert("Introduction to Algorithm");
$BookTitles->insert("Introduction to PHP and Data structures");
$BookTitles->insert("Programming Intelligence");
$BookTitles->insertAtFirst("Mediawiki Administrative tutorial guide");
$BookTitles->insertBefore("Introduction to Calculus", "Programming
Intelligence");
$BookTitles->insertAfter("Introduction to Calculus", "Programming
Intelligence");
$BookTitles->display();
$BookTitles->deleteFirst();
$BookTitles->deleteLast();
$BookTitles->delete("Introduction to PHP and Data structures");
$BookTitles->reverse();
$BookTitles->display();
echo "2nd Item is: ".$BookTitles->getNthNode(2)->data;
```

The output of the preceding code will look like this:

```
Total book titles: 6
Mediawiki Administrative tutorial guide
Introduction to Algorithm
Introduction to PHP and Data structures
Introduction to Calculus
Programming Intelligence
Introduction to Calculus
Total book titles: 3
Programming Intelligence
Introduction to Calculus
Introduction to Algorithm
2nd Item is: Introduction to Calculus
```

Now we have a complete implementation of a linked list using PHP 7. One thing we have understood so far is that unlike the implementation of arrays, we have to do lots of operations manually by writing codes. We also have to remember one thing: This is not the only way we can implement a linked list. Many prefer to track both the first and last nodes of the list for a better insert operation. Now, we will look at the complexity of linked list operations in average and worst-case scenarios.

Understanding complexity for linked lists

Here is the best, worst, and average-case complexity for linked list operations:

Operation	Time Complexity: Worst Case	Time Complexity: Average Case
Insert at beginning or end	O(1)	O(1)
Delete at beginning or end	O(1)	O(1)
Search	O(n)	O(n)
Access	O(n)	O(n)

We can achieve the O(1) insert complexity at the end of the linked list by keeping a track of the last node, as we did for the first node in our examples. This will help us jump directly to the last node of the linked list without any iteration.

Making the linked list iterable

So far, we have seen that we can traverse each node of the linked list using a `while` loop inside the methods. What if we need to iterate from outside using just the linked list object? It is very much possible to achieve this. PHP has a very intuitive iterator interface that allows any external iterators to iterate through an object internally. The `Iterator` interface provides the following methods:

- **Current**: Return the current element
- **Next**: Move forward to the next element
- **Key**: Return the key of the current element
- **Rewind**: Rewind the `Iterator` to the first element
- **Valid**: Checks whether the current position is valid

We will now implement these methods in our `LinkedList` class to make our object iterate through the nodes from the object directly. In order to track the current node and the current position within the list during iteration, we will require two new properties for our `LinkedList` class:

```
private $_currentNode = NULL;
private $_currentPosition = 0;
```

The `$_currentNode` property will track the current node during the iteration, and `$_currentPosition` will track the current position during the iteration. We also need to make sure that our class `LinkedList` class is also implementing the `Iterator` interface. It will look like this:

```
class LinkedList implements Iterator{

}
```

Now, let's implement those five new methods to make our linked list object iterable. These five methods are very straightforward and simple to implement. Here is the code for that:

```
public function current() {
    return $this->_currentNode->data;
}

public function next() {
    $this->_currentPosition++;
    $this->_currentNode = $this->_currentNode->next;
}

public function key() {
```

```
            return $this->_currentPosition;
        }

        public function rewind() {
            $this->_currentPosition = 0;
            $this->_currentNode = $this->_firstNode;
        }

        public function valid() {
            return $this->_currentNode !== NULL;
        }
```

Now, we have a list that is iterable. This means that now we can iterate through our linked list object using the `foreach` loop or any other iteration process we wish to follow. So, now, if we write the following code, we will see all the book titles:

```
foreach ($BookTitles as $title) {
    echo $title . "\n";
}
```

Another approach can be using the `rewind`, `valid`, `next`, and `current` methods from the iterable interface. It will have the same output as the preceding code:

```
for ($BookTitles->rewind(); $BookTitles->valid();
  $BookTitles->next()) {
    echo $BookTitles->current() . "\n";
}
```

Building circular linked list

Building a circular linked list is not at as hard as it sounds from the name. So far, we have seen that adding a new node at the end is pretty simple; we set the next reference of the last node to NULL. In a circular linked list, the last node's next reference will actually point to the first node, thereby creating a circular list. Let's write a simple circular linked list where the nodes will be inserted at the end of the list:

```
class CircularLinkedList {

    private $_firstNode = NULL;
    private $_totalNode = 0;

    public function insertAtEnd(string $data = NULL) {
        $newNode = new ListNode($data);
        if ($this->_firstNode === NULL) {
            $this->_firstNode = &$newNode;
```

```
        } else {
            $currentNode = $this->_firstNode;
            while ($currentNode->next !== $this->_firstNode) {
                $currentNode = $currentNode->next;
            }
            $currentNode->next = $newNode;
        }
        $newNode->next = $this->_firstNode;
        $this->_totalNode++;
        return TRUE;
    }
}
```

If we look closely look at the preceding code, it looks exactly like our singly linked list implementation. The only difference is that we do not check the end of the list, rather than making sure the current node is not the same as the first node. Also, in the following line, we assign the next reference of the newly created node to the first node of the list:

```
$newNode->next = $this->_firstNode;
```

As we are implementing this, the new nodes are added to the back of the list. All we need to do is set the new node's next reference to our first node in the list. By doing so, we have actually created a circular linked list. We have to make sure that we do not run- in an infinite loop. That is why we are comparing `$currentNode->next` to `$this->_firstNode`. The same principle will apply when we are displaying all elements in the circular linked list. We need to ensure that we do not fall in an infinite loop while displaying the titles. Here is the code that will display all titles from a circular linked list:

```
public function display() {
    echo "Total book titles: " . $this->_totalNode . "\n";
    $currentNode = $this->_firstNode;
    while ($currentNode->next !== $this->_firstNode) {
        echo $currentNode->data . "\n";
        $currentNode = $currentNode->next;
    }

    if ($currentNode) {
        echo $currentNode->data . "\n";
    }
}
```

So far, we have built a singly linked list and implemented a circular linked list. Now, we will implement a doubly linked list with PHP.

Implementing a doubly linked list in PHP

We already know from the definition of a doubly linked list that a doubly linked list node will have two links: one to point to the next node and another to point to the previous node. Also, when we add a new node or delete a new node, we need to set both the next and previous references for each affected nodes. We saw a different approach in the singly linked list implementation where we did not track the last node, and as a result, we had to use an iterator to reach the last node each time. This time, we will track the last node, along with our insert and delete operations, to make sure our insert, and delete, and end operations have O(1) complexity.

Here is how the new node class will look with two link pointers followed by our barebones structure of a doubly linked list class:

```php
class ListNode {

    public $data = NULL;
    public $next = NULL;
    public $prev = NULL;

    public function __construct(string $data = NULL) {
        $this->data = $data;
    }

}


class DoublyLinkedList {

    private $_firstNode = NULL;
    private $_lastNode = NULL;
    private $_totalNode = 0;

}
```

In the next section, we will explore the different operations of a doubly linked list so that we understand the basic difference between a singly linked list and a doubly linked list.

Doubly linked list operations

We will explore the following operations in our doubly linked list implementation. Though they sound similar to those used in singly linked lists, they have a major difference in their implementations:

- Inserting at the first node
- Inserting at the last node
- Inserting before a specific node
- Inserting after a specific node
- Deleting the first node
- Deleting the last node
- Searching for and deleting one node
- Displaying the list forward
- Displaying the list backward

Inserting at first the node

When we add a node at the front or head, we have to check whether the list is empty or not. If the list is empty, both the first and last node will point to the newly created node. However, if the list already has a head, then we have to do the following:

1. Create the new node.
2. Make the new node as the first node or head.
3. Assign the previous head or first node as the next, to follow the newly created first node.
4. Assign the previous first node's previous link to the new first node.

Here is the code for that:

```php
public function insertAtFirst(string $data = NULL) {
    $newNode = new ListNode($data);
    if ($this->_firstNode === NULL) {
        $this->_firstNode = &$newNode;
        $this->_lastNode = $newNode;
    } else {
        $currentFirstNode = $this->_firstNode;
        $this->_firstNode = &$newNode;
        $newNode->next = $currentFirstNode;
        $currentFirstNode->prev = $newNode;
    }
```

```
    $this->_totalNode++;
    return TRUE;
}
```

Inserting at the last node

Since we are now tracking the last node, it will be easier to insert a new node at the end. First, we need to check that the list is not empty. If it is empty, then the new node becomes both the first and last node. However, if the list already has a last node, then we have to do the following:

1. Create the new node.
2. Make the new node the last node.
3. Assign the previous last node as the previous link of the current last node.
4. Assign the previous last node's next link to the new last node's previous link.

Here is the code for that:

```php
public function insertAtLast(string $data = NULL) {
    $newNode = new ListNode($data);
    if ($this->_firstNode === NULL) {
        $this->_firstNode = &$newNode;
        $this->_lastNode = $newNode;
    } else {
        $currentNode = $this->_lastNode;
        $currentNode->next = $newNode;
        $newNode->prev = $currentNode;
        $this->_lastNode = $newNode;
    }
    $this->_totalNode++;
    return TRUE;
}
```

Inserting before a specific node

Inserting before a specific node requires us to find the node first, and based on its position, we need to change the next and previous nodes for the new node, the target node, and the node before the target node, as follows:

```php
public function insertBefore(string $data = NULL, string $query =
    NULL) {
    $newNode = new ListNode($data);
```

```
        if ($this->_firstNode) {
            $previous = NULL;
            $currentNode = $this->_firstNode;
            while ($currentNode !== NULL) {
                if ($currentNode->data === $query) {
                    $newNode->next = $currentNode;
                    $currentNode->prev = $newNode;
                    $previous->next = $newNode;
                    $newNode->prev = $previous;
                    $this->_totalNode++;
                    break;
                }
                $previous = $currentNode;
                $currentNode = $currentNode->next;
            }
        }
    }
}
```

Inserting after a specific node

Inserting after a specific node is similar to the method we just discussed. Here, we need to change the next and previous nodes for the new node, the target node, and the node following the target node. Here is the code for that:

```
public function insertAfter(string $data = NULL, string $query =
    NULL) {
    $newNode = new ListNode($data);

    if ($this->_firstNode) {
        $nextNode = NULL;
        $currentNode = $this->_firstNode;
        while ($currentNode !== NULL) {
            if ($currentNode->data === $query) {
                if ($nextNode !== NULL) {
                    $newNode->next = $nextNode;
                }
                if ($currentNode === $this->_lastNode) {
                    $this->_lastNode = $newNode;
                }
                $currentNode->next = $newNode;
                $nextNode->prev = $newNode;
                $newNode->prev = $currentNode;
                $this->_totalNode++;
                break;
            }
            $currentNode = $currentNode->next;
```

```
            $nextNode = $currentNode->next;
        }
    }
}
```

Deleting the first node

When we remove the first node from a doubly linked list, we just need to make the second node the first node. Set the new first node's previous node to NULL and reduce the total node count, just like the following code:

```
public function deleteFirst() {
    if ($this->_firstNode !== NULL) {
        if ($this->_firstNode->next !== NULL) {
            $this->_firstNode = $this->_firstNode->next;
            $this->_firstNode->prev = NULL;
        } else {
            $this->_firstNode = NULL;
        }
        $this->_totalNode--;
        return TRUE;
    }
    return FALSE;
}
```

Deleting the last node

Deleting the last node requires us to set a second to last node as the new last node. Also, the newly created last node should not have any next reference. The code sample is shown here:

```
public function deleteLast() {
    if ($this->_lastNode !== NULL) {

        $currentNode = $this->_lastNode;
        if ($currentNode->prev === NULL) {
            $this->_firstNode = NULL;
            $this->_lastNode = NULL;
        } else {
            $previousNode = $currentNode->prev;
            $this->_lastNode = $previousNode;
            $previousNode->next = NULL;
            $this->_totalNode--;
```

```
                return TRUE;
            }
        }
        return FALSE;
    }
```

Searching for and deleting one node

When we are deleting a node from the middle of the list, we have to readjust the previous and the following node of the item we are looking for. First, we will find the intended node. Get the previous node of the target node, along with the next node. Then, assign the node following the previous node to point to the next node after the target node, and the same applies for the previous node in a reverse manner. Here is the code for that:

```
public function delete(string $query = NULL) {
    if ($this->_firstNode) {
        $previous = NULL;
        $currentNode = $this->_firstNode;
        while ($currentNode !== NULL) {
            if ($currentNode->data === $query) {
                if ($currentNode->next === NULL) {
                    $previous->next = NULL;
                } else {
                    $previous->next = $currentNode->next;
                    $currentNode->next->prev = $previous;
                }

                $this->_totalNode--;
                break;
            }
            $previous = $currentNode;
            $currentNode = $currentNode->next;
        }
    }
}
```

Displaying the list forward

Doubly linked lists gives us the opportunity to display the list in both directions. So far, we have seen that we can display the list in a unidirectional way while working in a singly linked list. Now, we will see the list from both directions. Here is the code used to display the list forward:

```
public function displayForward() {
```

```
        echo "Total book titles: " . $this->_totalNode . "\n";
        $currentNode = $this->_firstNode;
        while ($currentNode !== NULL) {
            echo $currentNode->data . "\n";
            $currentNode = $currentNode->next;
        }
    }
```

Displaying the list backward

To display the list backward, we have to start from the last node and continue to move backward using the previous link until we reach the end of the list. This gives us a unique way of moving in any direction we need during operations. Here is the code for that:

```
    public function displayBackward() {
        echo "Total book titles: " . $this->_totalNode . "\n";
        $currentNode = $this->_lastNode;
        while ($currentNode !== NULL) {
            echo $currentNode->data . "\n";
            $currentNode = $currentNode->prev;
        }
    }
```

Complexity for doubly linked lists

Here is the best, worst, and average-case complexity for doubly linked list operations. It is similar to that of singly linked list operations:

Operation	Time Complexity: Worst Case	Time Complexity: Average Case
Insert at beginning or end	O(1)	O(1)
Delete at beginning or end	O(1)	O(1)
Search	O(n)	O(n)
Access	O(n)	O(n)

Using PHP SplDoublyLinkedList

The PHP **Standard PHP Library** (**SPL**) has an implementation of a doubly linked list, which is known as SplDoublyLinkedList. If we are using the built-in class, we do not need to implement the doubly linked list ourselves. The doubly linked list implementation actually works as a stack and queue as well. The PHP implementation of the doubly linked list has lots of additional functionalities. Here are some of the common features of SplDoublyLinkedList:

Method	Description
Add	Adds a new node in a specified index
Bottom	Peeks a node from beginning of the list
Count	Returns the size of the list
Current	Returns the current node
getIteratorMode	Returns the mode of iteration
setIteratorMode	Sets the mode of iteration. For example, LIFO, FIFO, and so on
Key	Returns the current node index
next	Moves to the next node
pop	Pops a node from the end of the list
prev	Moves to the previous node
push	Adds a new node at the end of the list
rewind	Rewinds the iterator back to the top
shift	Shifts a node from the beginning of the linked list
top	Peeks a node from the end of the list
unshift	Prepends an element in the list
valid	Checks whether there are any more nodes in the list

Now, let's write a small program using `SplDoublyLinkedList` for our book titles applications:

```
$BookTitles = new SplDoublyLinkedList();

$BookTitles->push("Introduction to Algorithm");
$BookTitles->push("Introduction to PHP and Data structures");
$BookTitles->push("Programming Intelligence");
$BookTitles->push("Mediawiki Administrative tutorial guide");
$BookTitles->add(1,"Introduction to Calculus");
$BookTitles->add(3,"Introduction to Graph Theory");

for($BookTitles->rewind();$BookTitles->valid();$BookTitles->next()){
    echo $BookTitles->current()."\n";
}
```

The preceding code will have the following output:

```
Introduction to Algorithm
Introduction to Calculus
Introduction to PHP and Data structures
Introduction to Graph Theory
Programming Intelligence
Mediawiki Administrative tutorial guide
```

Summary

The linked list is one of the most popular data structures that are used to solve different problems. Whether it's regarding for a stack, queue, priority queue, or for implementing complex graph algorithms, the linked list is a very handy data structure to solve any problems you might find. In this chapter, we explored all possible details regarding the singly linked list, doubly linked list, and circular linked list, along with their complexity analysis. In the upcoming chapters, we will utilize linked lists to implement different data structures and writing algorithms.

4
Constructing Stacks and Queues

In everyday life, we use two of the most common data structures. We can assume that these data structures are inspired by the real-world, but they have very important effects in the computing world. We are talking about stack and queue data structures. We stack our books, files, plates, and clothes on a daily basis, whereas we maintain queues for ticket counters, bus stops, and shopping checkouts. Also, we have heard about message queue in PHP, one of the most used features in high-end applications. In this chapter, we are going to explore the different implementations of popular stack and queue data structures. We are going to learn about queues, priority queues, circular queues, and double-ended queues in PHP.

Understanding stack

The stack is a linear data structure that follows the **Last-In**, **First-Out** (**LIFO**) principle. This means that there is only one end for the stack, which is used to add items and remove items from the structure. The addition of new items in the stack is known as push, and push whilst removing an item is known as pop. Since we only have one end to operate, we are always going to push an item at that end, and when we pop, the last item from that end will be popped up. The top most elements in the stack that are also at the very beginning of the stack end are known as the top.

If we consider the following image, we can see that after each pop and push operation, the top changes. Also, we are performing the operation at the top of the stack, not at the beginning or middle of the stack. We have to be careful about popping an element when the stack is empty, as well as pushing an element when the stack is full. We might have a stack overflow if we want to push more elements than its capacity.

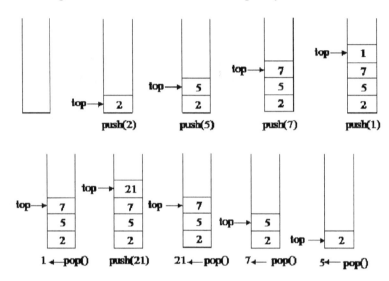

From our earlier discussion, we now know that we have four basic operations in a stack:

- **Push**: add an item at the top of the stack.
- **Pop**: remove the top item of the stack.
- **Top**: returns the top item of the stack. It is not the same as pop, as it does not remove the item, it just gets the value for us.
- **isEmpty**: checks whether the stack is empty or not.

Now let us implement the stack using PHP, but in different ways. First, we will try to implement the stack using PHP's built-in array function. Then we will look at how to build a stack without using PHP's built-in functions, but by using some other data structures, such as linked lists.

Implementing a stack using PHP array

First, we will create an interface for the stack so that we can use it in different implementations, and can ensure that all implementations have some similarity to each other. Let us write the simple interface for the stack:

```
interface Stack {

    public function push(string $item);

    public function pop();

    public function top();

    public function isEmpty();

}
```

As we can see from the preceding interface, we kept all stack functions inside the interface because the class that it is implementing must have all these mentioned functions, otherwise, else a fatal error will be thrown during runtime. Since we are implementing the stack using a PHP array, we are going to use some existing PHP functions for push, pop, and top operations. We are going to implement the stack in such a way that we can define the size of the stack. If there is no item in the array and we still want to pop, it will throw an underflow exception, and if we try to push more items than its capacity allows, then an overflow exception will be thrown. Here is the code for a stack implementation using an array:

```
class Books implements Stack {

    private $limit;
    private $stack;

    public function __construct(int $limit = 20) {
        $this->limit = $limit;
        $this->stack = [];
    }

    public function pop(): string {

        if ($this->isEmpty()) {
            throw new UnderflowException('Stack is empty');
        } else {
            return array_pop($this->stack);
        }
    }
}
```

```
    public function push(string $newItem) {

      if (count($this->stack) < $this->limit) {
          array_push($this->stack, $newItem);
      } else {
          throw new OverflowException('Stack is full');
      }
    }

    public function top(): string {
      return end($this->stack);
    }

    public function isEmpty(): bool {
      return empty($this->stack);
    }
  }
```

Now let us go through the code we have written for the stack. We named the stack implementation Books, but we can name it anything we want as long as it's a valid class name. First, we construct the stack using the __construct() method with an option to limit the number of items we can store in the stack. The default value is set at 20. The next method defines the pop operation:

```
public function pop():  string {

  if ($this->isEmpty()) {
      throw new UnderflowException('Stack is empty');
  } else {
      return array_pop($this->stack);
  }
  }
```

The pop method will return a string if the stack is not empty. We use the empty method we defined in the stack class for this purpose. If the stack is empty, we throw an UnderFlowException from SPL. If there is no item to pop, we can prevent that operation from taking place. If the stack is not empty, we use the array_pop function from PHP to return the last item from the array.

In the push method, we do the opposite of pop. First, we check whether or not the stack is full. If it is not, we add the string item at the end of the stack using the array_push function of PHP. If the stack is full, we throw an OverFlowException from SPL. The top method returns the top most element of the stack. The isEmpty method checks whether or not the stack is empty.

Since we are following PHP 7, we are using both scalar type declarations at method level and return types for methods.

In order to use our just implemented stack class, we have to think of an example where we can use all these operations. Let us write a small program to make a book stack. Here is the code for this:

```
try {
    $programmingBooks = new Books(10);
    $programmingBooks->push("Introduction to PHP7");
    $programmingBooks->push("Mastering JavaScript");
    $programmingBooks->push("MySQL Workbench tutorial");
    echo $programmingBooks->pop()."\n";
    echo $programmingBooks->top()."\n";
} catch (Exception $e) {
    echo $e->getMessage();
}
```

We have created an instance for our book stack, and for keeping our programming book titles in it. We have three push operations. The last inserted book name is "MySQL workbench tutorial". If we pop after three push operations, we will have this title name as the return. After that, the top will return "Mastering JavaScript", which will become the top item once the pop operation has been performed. We are nesting the whole code in a try...catch block so that we can handle the exception thrown by the overflow and underflow. The preceding code will have the following output:

```
MySQL Workbench tutorial
Mastering JavaScript
```

Now let us focus on the complexities of the different stack operations we have just completed.

Understanding complexity of stack operations

Here is the time complexity of different stack operations. For the worst case, the time complexities for stack operations are as follows:

Operation	Time Complexity
pop	O(1)
push	O(1)
top	O(1)
isEmpty	O(1)

Since the stack operates at one end that remembers the top of the stack all the time, if we want to search for an item in the stack, it means we have to search through the whole list. It is the same for accessing a particular item in the stack. Although it is not good practice to use stack for these sorts of operations, if we want to do so, we have to remember that the time complexity is based on more than general stack operations.

Operation	Time Complexity
Access	O(n)
Search	O(n)

 The space complexity for stack is always O(n).

So far, we have seen how to implement stack using a PHP array and it's built-in function line `array_pop` and `array_push`. But we could have ignored the built-in functions and implemented it with manual array operations, or we could have used the `array_shift` and `array_unshift` built-in functions.

Implementing stack using linked list

In Chapter 3, *Using Linked Lists*, we learned how to implement linked lists. We saw that in a linked list we can insert a node at the end, remove it from the end, insert it into the middle of the list, at the beginning, and so on. If we consider the insert at the end and remove at the end operations of a single linked list data structure, we can easily perform something similar with stack. So let us use our LinkedList class from the previous chapter to implement with the stack. This is how the code will look:

```php
class BookList implements Stack {

    private $stack;

    public function __construct() {
      $this->stack = new LinkedList();
    }

    public function pop(): string {

      if ($this->isEmpty()) {
          throw new UnderflowException('Stack is empty');
      } else {
          $lastItem = $this->top();
          $this->stack->deleteLast();
          return $lastItem;
      }
    }

    public function push(string $newItem) {

      $this->stack->insert($newItem);
    }


public function top(): string {
  return $this->stack->getNthNode($this->stack->getSize())->data;
}

    public function isEmpty(): bool {
      return $this->stack->getSize() == 0;
    }
}
```

Let us go through each of the code blocks to understand what is happening here. If we start from the top, we can see that in the constructor method, we are creating a new LinkedList object and assigning it to our stack property instead of the array in the previous example. We are assuming that the LinkedList class is autoloaded, or the file is included in the script. Let us now focus on the push operation. The push operation is as simple as it can get. We just need to insert a new node in the linked list. Since we do not have any size limit for the linked list, we are not checking any overflow here.

In our linked list implementation, there was no method for displaying the last node. We had inserted a new last node and removed the previous last node, but here, we need to get the value of the last node without deleting it. In order to achieve that functionality, which is exactly the top operation for our stack, we can utilize the getNthNode method along with getSize from the LinkedList implementation. This way, we can get the node. But we have to remember one thing: we want the string value of the node, not the full node object. That is why we return the data property of the returned node.

Similar to the top operation, the pop operation also needs to return the last node's data before removing it from the list. In order to achieve that, we use the top() method and then the deleteLast() method from the LinkedList class. Now let us run a sample code to use this newly implemented BookList class for stack operations. Here is the code:

```
try {
    $programmingBooks = new BookList();
    $programmingBooks->push("Introduction to PHP7");
    $programmingBooks->push("Mastering JavaScript");
    $programmingBooks->push("MySQL Workbench tutorial");
    echo $programmingBooks->pop()."\n";
    echo $programmingBooks->pop()."\n";
    echo $programmingBooks->top()."\n";
} catch (Exception $e) {
    echo $e->getMessage();
}
```

It looks quite similar to the last example we ran, but here we are trying to do two pop operations and then the top one. So the output will look like the following:

```
MySQL Workbench tutorial
Mastering JavaScript
Introduction to PHP7
```

If we know the basic behavior of the stack and how to achieve it, we can use an array, linked list, doubly linked list to implement stack. Since we have already seen the array and linked list implementations, we are now going to explore the SPL implementation of a stack, which actually uses a doubly linked list.

Using SplStack class from SPL

If we are not interested in implementing our own version of a stack, we can use the existing SPL implementation for stacks. It is very easy to use and requires minimal code to write. As we already know, `SplStack` uses `SplDoublyLinkedList`. It has all possible operations to push, pop, move forward, backward, shift, unshift, and so on. In order to implement the same example we saw previously, we have to write the following lines:

```
$books = new SplStack();
$books->push("Introduction to PHP7");
$books->push("Mastering JavaScript");
$books->push("MySQL Workbench tutorial");
echo $books->pop() . "\n";
echo $books->top() . "\n";
```

Yes, it is this simple to build a stack using the `SplStack` class. It is up to us to decide whether we want to implement it using a PHP array, a linked list, or a built-in class, such as `SplStack`.

Real life usage of stack

Stack has many usages in modern day applications. Whether in browser histories or in the popular development term stack trace, stack is used everywhere. Now we are going to try to solve a real-world problem using stack.

Nested parentheses matching

When we are solving mathematical expressions, the first thing we need to consider is the correctness of nested parentheses. If the parentheses are not nested properly, then calculation might not be possible, or may be wrong. Let us look at some examples:

```
8 * (9 -2) + { (4 * 5) / ( 2 * 2) }
5 * 8 * 9 / ( 3 * 2 ) )
[{ (2 * 7) + ( 15 - 3) ]
```

From the preceding expressions, only the first one is correct; the other two are incorrect, as the parentheses are not nested properly. In order to identify whether or not the parentheses are nested, we can use stack to implement the solution. Here is the pseudo algorithm for the implementation:

```
valid = true
s = empty stack
for (each character of the string) {
    if(character = ( or { or [ )
        s.push(character)
  else if (character = ) or } or ] ) {
    if(s is empty)
valid = false

    last = s.pop()
   if(last is not opening parentheses of character)
        valid = false
  }
}
if(s is not empty)
valid = false
```

If we look at the pseudocode, it looks very simple. The goal is to ignore any numbers, operands, or empty spaces from the string and only consider the parentheses, curly braces, and brackets. If they are opening brackets, we will push into the stack. If they are closing brackets, we are going to pop the stack. If the popped parenthesis is not the opening one we are trying to match, then it is not valid. At the end of the loop, the stack should be empty if the string is valid. But if the stack is not empty, then there are extra parentheses, so the string is not valid. Now let us convert this to a program:

```
function expressionChecker(string $expression): bool {
    $valid = TRUE;
    $stack = new SplStack();

    for ($i = 0; $i < strlen($expression); $i++) {
    $char = substr($expression, $i, 1);

    switch ($char) {
      case '(':
      case '{':
      case '[':
      $stack->push($char);
      break;

      case ')':
      case '}':
      case ']':
```

```
        if ($stack->isEmpty()) {
            $valid = FALSE;
        } else {
          $last = $stack->pop();
          if (($char == ")" && $last != "(")
              || ($char == "}" && $last != "{")
              || ($char == "]" && $last != "[")) {

        $valid = FALSE;
            }
      }
    break;
  }

  if (!$valid)
      break;
    }

    if (!$stack->isEmpty()) {
    $valid = FALSE;
    }

    return $valid;
}
```

Now let us run the three examples we discussed earlier:

```
$expressions = [];
$expressions[] = "8 * (9 -2) + { (4 * 5) / ( 2 * 2) }";
$expressions[] = "5 * 8 * 9 / ( 3 * 2 ) )";
$expressions[] = "[{ (2 * 7) + ( 15 - 3) ]";

foreach ($expressions as $expression) {
    $valid = expressionChecker($expression);

    if ($valid) {
    echo "Expression is valid \n";
    } else {
    echo "Expression is not valid \n";
    }
}
```

This will produce the following output, which is exactly what we wanted:

```
Expression is valid
Expression is not valid
Expression is not valid
```

Understanding queue

The queue is another special linear data structure that follows the **First-In, First-Out (FIFO)** principle. There are two ends for the operation: one to append to the queue and one to remove from the queue. This is different from a stack, where we used one end for both the add and remove operations. The insertion will always be at the back or rear section. The removal of an element will take place from the frontend. The process of adding a new element to the queue is known as enqueue and the process of removing an element is known as dequeue. The process of looking at the front element of the queue without removing the element is known as a peek, similar to the top operation of a stack. The following figure depicts a representation of a queue:

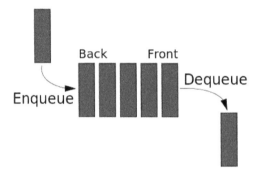

Now, if we define an interface for a queue, it will look like this:

```
interface Queue {

    public function enqueue(string $item);

    public function dequeue();

    public function peek();

    public function isEmpty();
}
```

Now we can implement the queue using different methods, as we did for the stack. First, we are going to implement the queue using a PHP array, followed by `LinkedList`, and then `SplQueue`.

Implementing a queue using PHP array

We are now going to implement the queue data structure using a PHP array. We have already seen that we can use the `array_push()` function to add an element at the end of the array. In order to remove the first element of the array, we can use the `array_shift()` function of PHP, and for the peek function, we can use the `current()` function of PHP. Here is how the code will look, based on our discussion:

```php
class AgentQueue implements Queue {

    private $limit;
    private $queue;

    public function __construct(int $limit = 20) {
        $this->limit = $limit;
        $this->queue = [];
    }

    public function dequeue(): string {

        if ($this->isEmpty()) {
            throw new UnderflowException('Queue is empty');
        } else {
            return array_shift($this->queue);
        }
    }

    public function enqueue(string $newItem) {

        if (count($this->queue) < $this->limit) {
            array_push($this->queue, $newItem);
        } else {
            throw new OverflowException('Queue is full');
        }
    }

    public function peek(): string {
        return current($this->queue);
    }

    public function isEmpty(): bool {
        return empty($this->queue);
    }

}
```

Here, we are maintaining the same principle we did for the stack. We want to define a fixed-size queue, with checking of overflow and underflow. In order to run the queue implementation, we can consider using it as an agent queue for a call center application. Here is the code to utilize our queue operations:

```
try {
    $agents = new AgentQueue(10);
    $agents->enqueue("Fred");
    $agents->enqueue("John");
    $agents->enqueue("Keith");
    $agents->enqueue("Adiyan");
    $agents->enqueue("Mikhael");
    echo $agents->dequeue()."\n";
    echo $agents->dequeue()."\n";
    echo $agents->peek()."\n";
} catch (Exception $e) {
    echo $e->getMessage();
}
```

This will produce the following output:

```
Fred
John
Keith
```

Implementing a queue using linked list

As we did with the stack implementation, we are going to use our linked list implementation in Chapter 3, *Using Linked Lists*, to implement the queue here. We can use the `insert()` method to ensure that we are always inserting at the end. We can use `deleteFirst()` for a dequeue operation and `getNthNode()` for a peek operation. Here is the sample implementation of a queue using a linked list:

```
class AgentQueue implements Queue {

    private $limit;
    private $queue;

    public function __construct(int $limit = 20) {
        $this->limit = $limit;
        $this->queue = new LinkedList();
    }

    public function dequeue(): string {
```

```
    if ($this->isEmpty()) {
        throw new UnderflowException('Queue is empty');
    } else {
        $lastItem = $this->peek();
        $this->queue->deleteFirst();
        return $lastItem;
    }
}

public function enqueue(string $newItem) {

    if ($this->queue->getSize() < $this->limit) {
        $this->queue->insert($newItem);
    } else {
        throw new OverflowException('Queue is full');
    }
}

public function peek(): string {
    return $this->queue->getNthNode(1)->data;
}

public function isEmpty(): bool {
    return $this->queue->getSize() == 0;
}

}
```

Using SplQueue class from SPL

If we do not want any hard time implementing queue functionalities, and are happy with a built-in solution, we can use the SplQueue class for any of our basic queue needs. We have to remember one thing: that there is no peek function available in the SplQueue class. We have to use the bottom() function to get the first element of the queue. Here is the simple queue implementation for our AgentQueue using SplQueue:

```
$agents = new SplQueue();
$agents->enqueue("Fred");
$agents->enqueue("John");
$agents->enqueue("Keith");
$agents->enqueue("Adiyan");
$agents->enqueue("Mikhael");
echo $agents->dequeue()."\n";
echo $agents->dequeue()."\n";
echo $agents->bottom()."\n";
```

Understanding priority queue

A priority queue is a special type of queue where items are inserted and removed based on their priority. In the programming world, the use of the priority queue is immense. For example, say that we have a very large e-mail queue system where we send a monthly newsletter through a queue system. What if we need to send an urgent email to a user using the same queue functionality? Since the general queue principle is to add the item at the end, the process of sending that message will be very much delayed. In order to solve the problem, we can use the priority queue. In such a case, we assign a priority to each node and sort them based on that priority. An item with higher priority will go to the top of the list and will be dequeued earlier.

We can take two approaches in building a priority queue.

Ordered sequence

If we plan an ordered sequence for a priority queue, it can have either an ascending or a descending order. The positive side of having an order sequence is that we can quickly find the maximum or remove the maximum priority item, as we can find it using O(1) complexity. But the insertion will take more time, as we have to check each element in the queue to place the item in the right position based on its priority.

Unordered sequence

The unordered sequence does not require us to go through each queue element in order to place the newly added element. It is always added to the rear as a general queue principle. As a result, we can achieve the enqueue operation with O(1) complexity. But if we want to find or remove the highest priority element, then we have to go through each element to find the right one. As a result, it is not very search-friendly.

Now we are going to write code to implement the priority queue using an ordered sequence with a linked list.

Implementing priority queue using linked list

So far, we have seen a linked list using only one value, which is the node data. Now we need to pass another value that will be the priority. In order to achieve that, we need to change our `ListNode` implementation:

```
class ListNode {

    public $data = NULL;
    public $next = NULL;
    public $priority = NULL;

    public function __construct(string $data = NULL, int $priority =
      NULL) {
      $this->data = $data;
      $this->priority = $priority;
    }

}
```

Now we have both the data and the priority as part of the node. In order to allow this priority to be considered during the insert operation, we also need to change our `insert()` implementation inside the `LinkedList` class. Here is the modified implementation:

```
public function insert(string $data = NULL, int $priority = NULL) {
    $newNode = new ListNode($data, $priority);
    $this->_totalNode++;

    if ($this->_firstNode === NULL) {
        $this->_firstNode = &$newNode;
    } else {
        $previous = $this->_firstNode;
        $currentNode = $this->_firstNode;
        while ($currentNode !== NULL) {
        if ($currentNode->priority < $priority) {

            if ($currentNode == $this->_firstNode) {
            $previous = $this->_firstNode;
            $this->_firstNode = $newNode;
            $newNode->next = $previous;
            return;
            }
            $newNode->next = $currentNode;
            $previous->next = $newNode;
            return;
        }
        $previous = $currentNode;
```

```
    $currentNode = $currentNode->next;
    }
}

return TRUE;
}
```

As we can see, our `insert` method has been changed to take both the data and the priority during the insert operation. As usual, the first process is to create a new node and increment the node count. There can be three possibilities for insertion, shown as follows:

- The list is empty, so the new node is the first node.
- The list is not empty, but the new item has the highest priority, so. So it becomes the first node and the previous first node follows it.
- The list is not empty and the priority is not the highest, so it inserts the new node inside the list, or maybe at the end of the list.

In our implementation, we have considered all three possibilities, three facts. As a result, we always have the highest priority item at the beginning of the list. Now let us run the `AgentQueue` implementation with this new code, as shown in the following example:

```
try {
    $agents = new AgentQueue(10);
    $agents->enqueue("Fred", 1);
    $agents->enqueue("John", 2);
    $agents->enqueue("Keith", 3);
    $agents->enqueue("Adiyan", 4);
    $agents->enqueue("Mikhael", 2);
    $agents->display();
    echo $agents->dequeue()."\n";
    echo $agents->dequeue()."\n";
} catch (Exception $e) {
    echo $e->getMessage();
}
```

If there was no priority, then the queue should have been Fred, John, Keith, Adiyan, and Mikhael. But since we have added priorities to the list, the output is:

Adiyan
Keith
John
Mikhael
Fred

Since Adiyan has the highest priority, it is placed at the beginning of the queue, even though it was inserted in the fourth place in the queue.

Implement a priority queue using SplPriorityQueue

PHP already has a built-in support for implementing a priority queue using SPL. We can use the SplPriorityQueue class to implement our priority queues. Here is the sample previous example using a linked list, but this time we are choosing SPL:

```php
class MyPQ extends SplPriorityQueue {

    public function compare($priority1, $priority2) {
    return $priority1 <=> $priority2;
    }

}

$agents = new MyPQ();

$agents->insert("Fred", 1);
$agents->insert("John", 2);
$agents->insert("Keith", 3);
$agents->insert("Adiyan", 4);
$agents->insert("Mikhael", 2);

//mode of extraction
$agents->setExtractFlags(MyPQ::EXTR_BOTH);

//Go to TOP
$agents->top();

while ($agents->valid()) {
    $current = $agents->current();
    echo $current['data'] . "\n";
    $agents->next();
}
```

This will produce the same result as the linked list example. The added advantage of extending to our own MyPQ class is that we can define whether we want to sort it in ascending or descending order. Here, we are choosing a descending order, sorting using a PHP combined comparison operator, or the spaceship operator.

 Most of the time, priority queues are implemented using heap. When we move on to the heap chapter, we will also implement a priority queue using heap.

Implementing a circular queue

When we use a standard queue, every time we dequeue an item, we have to re-buffer the whole queue. In order to solve this problem, we can use a circular queue, where the rear is followed by the front, forming a circle. This special type of queue requires a special calculation for the enqueue and dequeue operations, with consideration of the rear, front, and limit of the queue. Circular queues are always fixed queues, and are also known as circular buffers, or ring buffers. The following figure shows a representation of a circular queue:

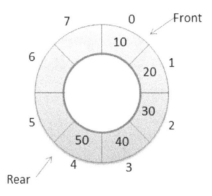

We can implement a circular queue using a PHP array. Since we have to calculate the positions of the rear and front part, the array can be used efficiently for this purpose. Here is an example of a circular queue:

```
class CircularQueue implements Queue {

    private $queue;
    private $limit;
    private $front = 0;
    private $rear = 0;

    public function __construct(int $limit = 5) {
        $this->limit = $limit;
        $this->queue = [];
    }

    public function size() {
        if ($this->rear > $this->front)
            return $this->rear - $this->front;
        return $this->limit - $this->front + $this->rear;
    }
}
```

```php
public function isEmpty() {
  return $this->rear == $this->front;
}

public function isFull() {
  $diff = $this->rear - $this->front;
  if ($diff == -1 || $diff == ($this->limit - 1))
      return true;
  return false;
}

public function enqueue(string $item) {
  if ($this->isFull()) {
      throw new OverflowException("Queue is Full.");
  } else {
      $this->queue[$this->rear] = $item;
      $this->rear = ($this->rear + 1) % $this->limit;
  }
}

public function dequeue() {
  $item = "";
  if ($this->isEmpty()) {
      throw new UnderflowException("Queue is empty");
  } else {
      $item = $this->queue[$this->front];
      $this->queue[$this->front] = NULL;
      $this->front = ($this->front + 1) % $this->limit;
  }
  return $item;
}

public function peek() {
  return $this->queue[$this->front];
}

}
```

 Since we are considering 0 as a front marker, the total size of the queue will be of the limit -1.

Creating a double - ended queue (deque)

So far, we have implemented queues where one end is used for enqueuer, and is known as the rear, and the other end is used for dequeuer, and is known as the front. So, in general, each end should be used for a specific purpose. But what if we need to enqueuer and dequeuer from both ends? This is possible by using a concept called the double-ended queue or deque. In deque, both ends can be used for enqueue and dequeue operations. If we look at our queue implementation using linked list, we find that we can insert at last, insert at first, delete at last, and delete at first using our linked list implementation. If we implement a new deque class based on that, we can easily achieve our desired goals. The following figure depicts a double-ended queue:

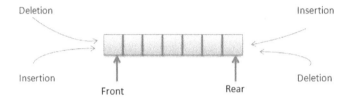

Here is the implementation of a deque:

```
class DeQueue {

    private $limit;
    private $queue;

    public function __construct(int $limit = 20) {
        $this->limit = $limit;
        $this->queue = new LinkedList();
    }

    public function dequeueFromFront(): string {

        if ($this->isEmpty()) {
            throw new UnderflowException('Queue is empty');
        } else {
            $lastItem = $this->peekFront();
            $this->queue->deleteFirst();
            return $lastItem;
        }
    }
}
```

```php
   public function dequeueFromBack(): string {

      if ($this->isEmpty()) {
         throw new UnderflowException('Queue is empty');
      } else {
         $lastItem = $this->peekBack();
         $this->queue->deleteLast();
         return $lastItem;
      }
   }

   public function enqueueAtBack(string $newItem) {

      if ($this->queue->getSize() < $this->limit) {
         $this->queue->insert($newItem);
      } else {
         throw new OverflowException('Queue is full');
      }
   }

   public function enqueueAtFront(string $newItem) {

      if ($this->queue->getSize() < $this->limit) {
         $this->queue->insertAtFirst($newItem);
      } else {
         throw new OverflowException('Queue is full');
      }
   }

   public function peekFront(): string {
      return $this->queue->getNthNode(1)->data;
   }

   public function peekBack(): string {
      return $this->queue->getNthNode($this->queue->getSize())->data;
   }

   public function isEmpty(): bool {
      return $this->queue->getSize() == 0;
   }

}
```

Now we are going to use this class to check the operations of a double-ended queue:

```
try {
    $agents = new DeQueue(10);
    $agents->enqueueAtFront("Fred");
    $agents->enqueueAtFront("John");
    $agents->enqueueAtBack("Keith");
    $agents->enqueueAtBack("Adiyan");
    $agents->enqueueAtFront("Mikhael");
    echo $agents->dequeueFromBack() . "\n";
    echo $agents->dequeueFromFront() . "\n";
    echo $agents->peekFront() . "\n";
} catch (Exception $e) {
    echo $e->getMessage();
}
```

If we look at the preceding code example, first we add Fred at the front, then we add John at the front again. So the sequence is now John, Fred. Then we add Keith at the back, followed by Adiyan at the back. So now we have the sequence John, Fred, Keith, Adiyan. Lastly, we add Mikhael at the beginning. So the final sequence is Mikhael, John, Fred, Keith, Adiyan.

Since we are performing a dequeue from the back first, Adiyan will be out first, and then Mikhael from the front. The new peek at the front will be John. Here is the output when you run the code:

```
Adiyan
Mikhael
John
```

Summary

Stacks and queues are one of the most used data structures. In future algorithms and data structures, we can use these abstract data types in different ways. In this chapter, we learned of the different ways of implementing stacks and queues, along with the different types of queues. In the next chapter, we are going to talk about recursion - a special way to solve bigger problems by dividing them into smaller instances.

5
Applying Recursive Algorithms - Recursion

Solving complex problems is always hard. Even for programmers, solving complex problems can prove tougher, and sometimes, a special solution is required. Recursion is one such special approach that computer programmers follow to solve complex problems. In this chapter, we will go through the definition of recursion, properties, different types of recursions, and lots of examples. Recursion is not a new concept; in nature, we see lots of recursive elements. Fractals show recursive behavior. The following image shows natural recursion:

Understanding recursion

Recursion is a way to solve larger problems by dividing them into smaller problems. In other words, recursion is breaking the big problem into smaller similar problems to solve them and get the actual results. Often, recursion is termed as a function calling itself. It might sound strange, but the fact is the function must call itself when it is in recursion. What does this look like? Let's look at an example,

In mathematics, the term "factorial" is very popular. A factorial of a number N is defined as multiplication of all positive integers less than and equal to N. It is always denoted with $!$ (an exclamation mark). So, a factorial of 5 can be written as follows:

5! = 5 X 4 X 3 X 2 X 1

Similarly, we can write the following factorials of the given number::

4! = 4 X 3 X 2 X 1

3! = 3 X 2 X 1

2! = 2 X 1

1! = 1

If we look closely at our example, we can see that we can write factorial of 5 in terms of factorials of 4 like this:

5! = 5 X 4!

Similarly, we can write:

4! = 4 X 3!

3! = 3 X 2!

2! = 2 X 1!

1! = 1 X 0!

0! = 1

Alternatively, we can simply say in general terms that:

n! = n * (n-1)!

This represents recursion. We are breaking each of the steps into smaller ones and solving the actual big problem. Here is an image to show how a factorial of 3 is calculated:

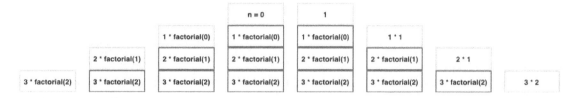

So, the steps are as follows:

1. *3! = 3 X 2!*
2. *2! = 2 X 1!*
3. *1! = 1 X 0!*
4. *0! = 1*
5. *1! = 1 X 1 = 1*
6. *2! = 2 X 1 = 2*
7. *3! = 3 X 2 = 6*

Properties of recursive algorithms

Now, the question can be, "If a function calls itself, then how does it stop or know when to finish the recursive call?" When we are writing a recursive solution, we have to make sure it has the following properties:

1. Each recursive call should be on a smaller subproblem. Like the factorial example, a factorial of 6 is solved with 6 and multiplication of a factorial of 5 and so it goes on.
2. It must have a base case. When the base case is reached, there will be no further recursion, and the base case must be able to solve the problem without any further recursive call. In our factorial example, we did not go any further down from 0. So, in this case, 0 is our base case.
3. There should not be any cycle. If each recursive call makes a call to the same problem, then there will be a never-ending cycle. After some repetitions, the computer will show a stack overflow error.

So, if we now write our factorial program using PHP 7, then it will look like this:

```
function factorial(int $n): int {
    if ($n == 0)
      return 1;

    return $n * factorial($n - 1);
}
```

In the preceding example code, we can see that we have a base condition where we are returning 1 when the value of $n is 0. If this condition is not met, then we are returning a multiplication of $n and a factorial of $n-1. So, it satisfies property to both numbers, 1 and 3. We are avoiding cycles and also making sure each recursive call is creating a subproblem of the bigger one. We will write the recursive behavior like this algorithm:

$$n! = \begin{cases} 1 & \text{if } n = 0 \\ (n-1)! \times n & \text{if } n > 0 \end{cases}$$

Recursion versus iterative algorithms

If we analyze our factorial function, we can see that it could be written using a simple iterative approach with a for or while loop, as shown here:

```
function factorial(int $n): int {
    $result = 1;

    for ($i = $n; $i > 0; $i--) {
      $result *= $i;
    }

    return $result;
}
```

If this can be written as a simple iterative one, then why should we use recursion? Recursion is used to solve more complex problems. Not all problems can be solved iteratively so easily. For example, we need to show all the files in a certain directory. We can simply do this by running a loop to list all the files. However, what if there is another directory inside it? Then, we have to run another loop to get all those files inside that directory. What if there is another directory inside that directory and it goes on and on? In such a situation, an iterative approach might not help at all or might create a complex solution. It is better to choose a recursive approach here.

Recursion manages a call stack for managing function calls. As a result, recursion will take more memory and time to complete compared to iteration. Also, in iteration, in each step, we can have a result, but for recursion, we have to wait until the base case to execute to get any result. If we consider both iterative and recursive examples for a factorial, we can see that there is a local variable called `$result` to store the calculation of each step. However, in recursion, there is no need for local variables or assignment.

Implementing Fibonacci numbers using recursion

In mathematics, Fibonacci numbers are special integer sequences where a number is composed from summation of the past two numbers, as shown in the following the expression:

$$F(n) := \begin{cases} 0 & \text{if } n = 0; \\ 1 & \text{if } n = 1; \\ F(n-1) + F(n-2) & \text{if } n > 1. \end{cases}$$

If we implement this using PHP 7, it will look like this:

```
function fibonacci(int $n): int {
    if ($n == 0) {
    return 1;
    } else if ($n == 1) {
    return 1;
    } else {
    return fibonacci($n - 1) + fibonacci($n - 2);
    }
}
```

If we consider the preceding implementation, we can see it is a bit different from the previous examples. Now, we are calling two functions from one function call. We will discuss different types of recursions shortly.

Implementing GCD calculation using recursion

Another common use of recursion is implementing **Greatest Common Division (GCD)** of two numbers. In GCD calculation, we will continue until a remainder becomes 0. It can be expressed as follows:

$$\gcd(a, b) = \begin{cases} a & \text{if } b = 0 \\ \gcd(b, a \bmod b) & \text{else} \end{cases}$$

Now, if we implement recursively using PHP 7, it will look like this:

```
function gcd(int $a, int $b): int {
    if ($b == 0) {
     return $a;
    } else {
     return gcd($b, $a % $b);
    }
}
```

Another interesting part of this implementation is that unlike a factorial, we are not returning from a base case to other steps in the call stack. The base case will return the calculated value. This is one of the optimized ways to do recursion.

Different types of recursions

So far, we have seen some example cases of recursion and how it is being used. Though the term says recursion, there are different types of recursions. We will explore them one by one.

Linear recursion

One of the most commonly used recursions in the programming world is linear recursion. When a function calls itself once in each run, we will call it a linear recursion. Just like our factorial example, when we are breaking the big calculation to smaller ones until the base condition is reached, we call it winding. When we are returning from the base condition to the first recursive call, we call it unwinding. We will work on different linear recursions in the upcoming section in this chapter.

Binary recursion

In binary recursion, the function calls itself twice in each run. As a result, the calculation depends on two results from two different recursive calls to itself. If we look at our Fibonacci sequence generation recursive function, we can easily find that it is a binary recursion. Other than this, we have many commonly used binary recursions in the programming world, such as binary search, divide and conquer, merge sort, and so on. The following image shows a binary recursion:

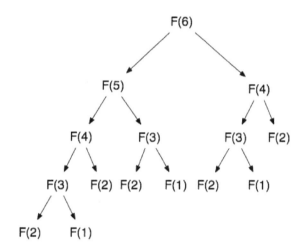

Tail recursion

A recursive method is tail recursive when there is no pending operation to be performed on return. For example, in our factorial code, the returned value is used to multiply with the previous value to calculate the factorial. So, this is not tail recursive. The same goes for the Fibonacci series recursion. If we look at our GCD recursion, we can find that there is no operation to do after the return. So, the final return or base case return is actually the answer. So, GCD is an example of tail recursion. Tail recursion is also a form of linear recursion.

Mutual recursion

It might be the case that we may require to call two different methods recursively from two different methods in an alternate fashion. For example, function A() calls function B() and function B() calls function A() in each call. This is known as mutual recursion.

Nested recursion

When a recursive function call has itself as the parameter, then it is called nested recursion. One of the common examples of nested recursion is the Ackermann function. Look at the following equation:

$$A(m,n) = \begin{cases} n+1 & \text{if } m = 0 \\ A(m-1, 1) & \text{if } m > 0 \text{ and } n = 0 \\ A(m-1, A(m, n-1)) & \text{if } m > 0 \text{ and } n > 0. \end{cases}$$

If we look at the last line, we can see that function A () is called recursively, but the second parameter itself is another recursive call. So, this is one of the examples of nested recursions.

Though there are different types of recursions available, we will only use those that are required based on our needs. Now, we will see some real-life usage of recursion in our projects.

Building an N-level category tree using recursion

Building a multilevel nested category tree or menu is always a problem. Many CMS and sites only allow a certain level of nesting. In order to save performance issues due to multiple joins, some only allow 3-4 levels of nesting at maximum. Now, we will explore how we can create an N-level nested category tree or menu with the help of recursion, without compromising on performance. Here is our approach for the solution:

1. We will define the table structure for the category in the database.

2. We will get all categories in the table without the use of any join or multiple queries. It will be a single database query with a simple select statement.

3. We will build an array of categories such that we can utilize the recursion with that to display the nested categories or menu.

Let's assume that we have a simple table structure in our database to store our categories and it looks like this:

```
CREATE TABLE `categories` (
  `id` int(11) NOT NULL,
  `categoryName` varchar(100) NOT NULL,
  `parentCategory` int(11) DEFAULT 0,
  `sortInd` int(11) NOT NULL
) ENGINE=InnoDB DEFAULT CHARSET=utf8;
```

For simplicity, we are assuming that there is no other field required in the table. Also, we have some data in the table like this:

Id	categoryName	parentCategory	sortInd
1	First	0	0
2	Second	1	0
3	Third	1	1
4	Fourth	3	0
5	Fifth	4	0
6	Sixth	5	0
7	Seventh	6	0
8	Eight	7	0
9	Ninth	1	0
10	Tenth	2	1

Now, we have created a table structured for our database, and we have assumingly also entered some sample data. Let's build a query to retrieve this data so that we can move to our recursive solution:

```
$dsn = "mysql:host=127.0.0.1;port=3306;dbname=packt;";
$username = "root";
$password = "";
$dbh = new PDO($dsn, $username, $password);

$result = $dbh->query("Select * from categories order by parentCategory
asc, sortInd asc", PDO::FETCH_OBJ);

$categories = [];

foreach($result as $row) {
    $categories[$row->parentCategory][] = $row;
}
```

The core part of the preceding code is how we are storing our categories in an array. We are storing the results based on their parent category. This will help us show child categories of a category recursively. This looks pretty simple. Now, based on the categories array, let's write the recursive function to show the categories hierarchically:

```
function showCategoryTree(Array $categories, int $n) {
    if(isset($categories[$n])) {

      foreach($categories[$n] as $category) {
          echo str_repeat("-", $n)."".$category->categoryName."\n";
          showCategoryTree($categories, $category->id);
      }
    }
    return;
}
```

The preceding code actually shows all the categories and their child categories recursively. We take a level and first print the category on that level. Immediately, we will check whether it has any child level categories or not with the code `showCategoryTree($categories, $category->id)`. Now, if we call the recursive function with a root level (level 0), then we will have the following output:

```
showCategoryTree($categories, 0);
```

The output for this will be as follows:

```
First
-Second
--Tenth
-Third
---Fourth
----fifth
-----Sixth
------seventh
-------Eighth
-Nineth
```

As we can see, without thinking about the depth of the category level or multiple queries, we can build nested categories or menus with just a simple query and recursive function. We can use `<ul>` and `<li>` to create a nested menu if we want it with dynamic show and hide functionality. This can be vital for having an efficient solution to the problem without getting into implementation blocks, such as having a fixed level of joins or fixed level of categories. The preceding example is a perfect display of tail recursion where we are not waiting for the recursion to return anything, and as we move forward, the results are already displayed.

Building a nested comment reply system

Quite often, we face the challenge to display comment replies in a proper way. Showing them chronologically does not fit our need sometimes. We may require showing them in such a way that the reply for each comment is below the actual comment itself. In other words, we can say we need a nested comment reply system or threaded comments.

We want to build something similar to the following screenshot:

Comment by
Lorem ipsum dolor sit amet, consectetur adipiscing elit, sed do
eiusmod tempor incididunt ut labore et dolore magna aliqua.
Ut enim ad minim veniam, quis nostrud exercitation ullamco
laboris nisi ut aliquip ex ea commodo consequat.

Read More

Comment Reply
Lorem ipsum dolor sit amet, consectetur adipiscing elit, sed do
eiusmod tempor incididunt ut labore et dolore magna aliqua.

Read More

Comment Reply
Lorem ipsum dolor sit amet, consectetur adipiscing elit, sed do
eiusmod tempor incididunt ut labore et dolore magna aliqua.

Read More

Comment Reply
Lorem ipsum dolor sit amet, consectetur adipiscing elit, sed do
eiusmod tempor incididunt ut labore et dolore magna aliqua.

Read More

Comment Reply
Lorem ipsum dolor sit amet, consectetur adipiscing elit, sed do
eiusmod tempor incididunt ut labore et dolore magna aliqua.

Read More

Comment By
Lorem ipsum dolor sit amet, consectetur adipiscing elit, sed do
eiusmod tempor incididunt ut labore et dolore magna aliqua.
Ut enim ad minim veniam, quis nostrud exercitation ullamco
laboris nisi ut aliquip ex ea commodo consequat.

Read More

Comment Reply
Lorem ipsum dolor sit amet, consectetur adipiscing elit, sed do
eiusmod tempor incididunt ut labore et dolore magna aliqua.

Read More

We can follow the same steps we did in the nested category section. However, this time, we will have some UI elements to give it a more realistic look. Let's assume that we have a table named `comments` with the following data and columns. For simplicity, we are not going into multiple table relationships. We are assuming that the usernames are stored in the same table with the comments:

Id	comments	username	Datetime	parentID	postID
1	First comment	Mizan	2016-10-01 15:10:20	0	1
2	First reply	Adiyan	2016-10-02 04:09:10	1	1
3	Reply of first reply	Mikhael	2016-10-03 11:10:47	2	1
4	Reply of reply of first reply	Arshad	2016-10-04 21:22:45	3	1
5	Reply of reply of reply of first reply	Anam	2016-10-05 12:01:29	4	1
6	Second comment	Keith	2016-10-01 15:10:20	0	1
7	First comment of second post	Milon	2016-10-02 04:09:10	0	2
8	Third comment	Ikrum	2016-10-03 11:10:47	0	1
9	Second comment of second post	Ahmed	2016-10-04 21:22:45	0	2
10	Reply of second comment of second post	Afsar	2016-10-18 05:18:24	9	2

Let's now write a prepared statement to fetch all the comments from a post. Then, we can construct an array similar to the nested category one:

```
$sql = "Select * from comments where postID = :postID order by parentID
asc, datetime asc";
$stmt = $dbh->prepare($sql, array(PDO::ATTR_CURSOR =>
PDO::CURSOR_FWDONLY));
$stmt->setFetchMode(PDO::FETCH_OBJ);
$stmt->execute(array(':postID' => 1));
$result = $stmt->fetchAll();

$comments = [];

foreach ($result as $row) {
    $comments[$row->parentID][] = $row;
}
```

Now, we have the array and all required data in it; we can now write a function that will call recursively to display the comment with proper indentations:

```php
function displayComment(Array $comments, int $n) {
    if (isset($comments[$n])) {
        $str = "<ul>";
        foreach ($comments[$n] as $comment) {
            $str .= "<li><div class='comment'><span class='pic'>
              {$comment->username}</span>";
            $str .= "<span class='datetime'>{$comment->datetime}</span>";
            $str .= "<span class='commenttext'>" . $comment->comment . "
              </span></div>";

            $str .= displayComment($comments, $comment->id);
            $str .= "</li>";
        }

        $str .= "</ul>";

        return $str;
    }
    return "";
}

echo displayComment($comments, 0);
```

Since we have added some HTML elements in the PHP code, we need some basic CSS to make it work. Here is the CSS code we have written to make it a clean design. Nothing fancy, but pure CSS to create the cascading effects and some basic styling for each section of the comment:

```css
ul {
    list-style: none;
    clear: both;
}

li ul {
    margin: 0px 0px 0px 50px;
}

.pic {
    display: block;
    width: 50px;
    height: 50px;
    float: left;
```

```
        color: #000;
        background: #ADDFEE;
        padding: 15px 10px;
        text-align: center;
        margin-right: 20px;
    }

.comment {
        float: left;
        clear: both;
        margin: 20px;
        width: 500px;
    }

.datetime {
        clear: right;
        width: 400px;
        margin-bottom: 10px;
        float: left;
    }
```

As mentioned earlier, we are not trying to make something complex here, just responsive, device friendly, and so on. We are assuming that you can integrate the logic in different parts of your application without any problem.

Here is the output from the data and the preceding code:

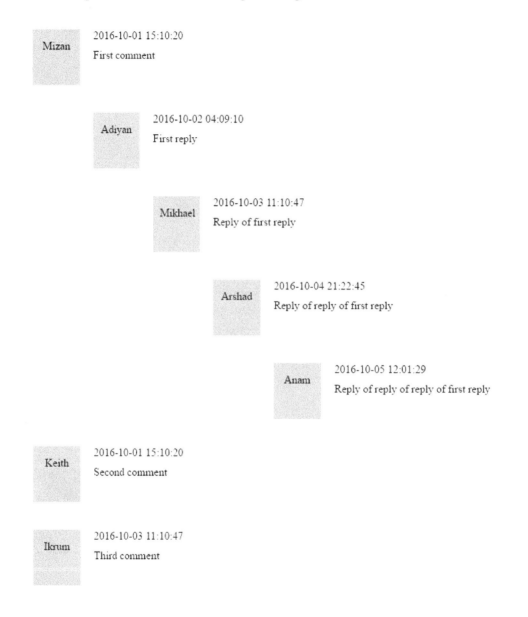

From the preceding two examples, we can see that it is very easy to create nested contents without having multiple queries or having a limitation of join statements for nesting. We do not even require a self-join to generate the nested data.

Finding files and directories using recursion

Quite often, we need to find all the files inside a directory. This includes all subdirectories inside it and also directories inside those subdirectories. As a result, we need a recursive solution to find the list of files from the given directory. The following example will show a simple recursive function to list all the files in a directory:

```php
function showFiles(string $dirName, Array &$allFiles = []) {
    $files = scandir($dirName);

    foreach ($files as $key => $value) {
      $path = realpath($dirName . DIRECTORY_SEPARATOR . $value);
      if (!is_dir($path)) {
          $allFiles[] = $path;
      } else if ($value != "." && $value != "..") {
          showFiles($path, $allFiles);
          $allFiles[] = $path;
      }
    }
    return;
}

$files = [];

showFiles(".", $files);
```

The `showFiles` function actually takes a directory and first scans the directory to list all the files and directories under it. Then, with a `foreach` loop, it iterates through each file and directory. If it is a directory, we recall the . function again to list the files and directories under it. This continues until we traverse all the files and directories. Now, we have all the files under the `$files` array. Now, let's show the files using a `foreach` loop sequentially:

```php
foreach($files as $file) {
    echo $file."\n";
}
```

This will have the following output in the command line:

```
/home/mizan/packtbook/chapter_1_1.php
/home/mizan/packtbook/chapter_1_2.php
/home/mizan/packtbook/chapter_2_1.php
/home/mizan/packtbook/chapter_2_2.php
/home/mizan/packtbook/chapter_3_.php
/home/mizan/packtbook/chapter_3_1.php
/home/mizan/packtbook/chapter_3_2.php
/home/mizan/packtbook/chapter_3_4.php
```

```
/home/mizan/packtbook/chapter_4_1.php
/home/mizan/packtbook/chapter_4_10.php
/home/mizan/packtbook/chapter_4_11.php
/home/mizan/packtbook/chapter_4_2.php
/home/mizan/packtbook/chapter_4_3.php
/home/mizan/packtbook/chapter_4_4.php
/home/mizan/packtbook/chapter_4_5.php
/home/mizan/packtbook/chapter_4_6.php
/home/mizan/packtbook/chapter_4_7.php
/home/mizan/packtbook/chapter_4_8.php
/home/mizan/packtbook/chapter_4_9.php
/home/mizan/packtbook/chapter_5_1.php
/home/mizan/packtbook/chapter_5_2.php
/home/mizan/packtbook/chapter_5_3.php
/home/mizan/packtbook/chapter_5_4.php
/home/mizan/packtbook/chapter_5_5.php
/home/mizan/packtbook/chapter_5_6.php
/home/mizan/packtbook/chapter_5_7.php
/home/mizan/packtbook/chapter_5_8.php
/home/mizan/packtbook/chapter_5_9.php
```

 These were solutions for some common challenges we face during development. However, there are other places where we will use recursion heavily, such as binary search, trees, divide and conquer algorithm, and so on. We will discuss them in the upcoming chapters.

Analyzing recursive algorithms

Analysis of recursive algorithms depends on the type of recursion we are using. If it is linear, the complexity will be different; if it is binary, it will have a different complexity. So, we do not have a generic complexity for the recursive algorithms. We have to analyze it on a case-by-case basis. Here, we will analyze factorial series. First, let's focus on the factorial part. If we recall from this section, we had something like this for factorial recursion:

```
function factorial(int $n): int {
    if ($n == 0)
    return 1;

    return $n * factorial($n - 1);
}
```

Let's assume that it will take `T(n)` to compute factorial (`$n`). We will focus on how to use this `T(n)` in terms of the Big O notation. Each time we call the factorial function, there are certain steps involved:

1. Every time, we are checking the base case.
2. Then, we call factorial (`$n-1`) on each loop.
3. We do a multiplication with `$n` on each loop.
4. Then, we return the result.

Now, if we represent this using `T(n)`, then we can say:

$T(n) = a$ *when n = 0*

$T(n) = T(n-1) + b$ *when n > 0*

Here, both *a* and *b* are some constants. Now, let's generate a relationship between *a* and *b* with *n*. We can easily write the equation as follows:

$T(0) = a$

$T(1) = T(0) + b = a + b$

$T(2) = T(1) + b = a + b + b = a + 2b$

$T(3) = T(2) + b = a + 2b + b = a + 3b$

$T(4) = T(3) + b = a + 3b + b = a + 4b$

We can see that a pattern is emerging here. So, we can establish that:

$T(n) = a + (n) b$

Alternatively, we can also say in simple terms that `T(n) = O(n)`.

So, the factorial recursion has a linear complexity of `O(n)`.

A fibonacci sequence with recursion has approximately `O(2`^{n}`)` complexity. The calculation is very elaborative as we have to consider both the lower bound and upper bound for the Big O notation. In the upcoming chapters, we will also analyze binary recursion such as binary search and merge sorts. We will focus more on recursive analysis in those chapters.

Maximum recursion depth in PHP

Since recursion is the process when a function calls itself, we can have a valid question in mind such as "how deep can we go with this recursion?". Let's do a small program for this:

```
function maxDepth() {
    static $i = 0;
    print ++$i . "\n";
    maxDepth();
}

maxDepth();
```

Can we guess the max depth level? The depth reached 917,056 levels before exhausting the memory limit. If **XDebug** is enabled, then the limit will be much less compared to this. It also depends on your memory, OS, and PHP settings such as memory limit and max execution time.

Though we have the option to go very deep with our recursion, it is always important to remember that we must have control with our recursive function. We should know the base conditions and where the recursion must end. Otherwise, it might create some wrong results or end abruptly.

Using SPL recursive iterators

The Standard PHP Library SPL has many built-in iterators for recursion purposes. We can use them as per our need, without taking the pain of implementing them from scratch. Here is the list of iterators and their functionality:

- **RecursiveArrayIterator**: This recursive iterator allows iterating over any type of array or objects and modifying the key or values or unsetting them. It also allows iterating over the current iterator entry.

- **RecursiveCallbackFilterIterator**: If we are looking forward to applying a callback recursively to any array or objects, this iterator can be very helpful.

- **RecursiveDirectoryIterator**: This iterator allows iterating any directory or filing systems. It makes the directory listing very easy. For example, we can rewrite the directory listing program we wrote in this chapter easily using this iterator:

```
$path = realpath('.');
```

```
$files = new RecursiveIteratorIterator(
    new RecursiveDirectoryIterator($path),
RecursiveIteratorIterator::SELF_FIRST);
foreach ($files as $name => $file) {
    echo "$name\n";
}
```

- **RecursiveFilterIterator:** If we are looking for a filter option in our iteration recursively, we can use this abstract iterator to implement the filtering part.

- **RecursiveIteratorIterator:** If we want to iterate over any recursive iterator, we can use this one. It is already built-in, and we can easily apply it. An example of how it is used is shown in the directory iterator section in the RecursiveDirectoryIterator section.

- **RecursiveRegexIterator:** If you want to apply a regular expression to filter an iterator, we can use this iterator along with other iterators.

- **RecursiveTreeIterator:** The recursive tree iterator allows us to create a graphical representation like a tree for any directory or multidimensional array. For example, the following football team list array will produce a tree structure:

```
$teams = array(
    'Popular Football Teams',
    array(
  'La Lega',
  array('Real Madrid', 'FC Barcelona', 'Athletico Madrid',
'Real
    Betis', 'Osasuna')
    ),
    array(
  'English Premier League',
  array('Manchester United', 'Liverpool', 'Manchester City',
'Arsenal',
    'Chelsea')
    )
);


$tree = new RecursiveTreeIterator(
  new RecursiveArrayIterator($teams), null, null,
RecursiveIteratorIterator::LEAVES_ONLY
);
```

```
        foreach ($tree as $leaf)
            echo $leaf . PHP_EOL;
```

The output will look like this:

```
|-Popular Football Teams
| |-La Lega
|   |-Real Madrid
|   |-FC Barcelona
|   |-Athletico Madrid
|   |-Real Betis
|   \-Osasuna
  |-English Premier League
    |-Manchester United
    |-Liverpool
    |-Manchester City
    |-Arsenal
    \-Chelsea
```

Using the PHP built-in function array_walk_recursive

The `array_walk_recursive` can be a very handy built-in function for PHP as it can traverse any size of array recursively and apply a callback function. Whether we want to find whether an element is in a multidimensional array or not, or get the total sum of the array of the multidimensional array, we can use this function without any problem.

The following code sample will produce an output of **136** when executed:

```
function array_sum_recursive(Array $array) {
    $sum = 0;
    array_walk_recursive($array, function($v) use (&$sum) {
      $sum += $v;
    });

    return $sum;
}

$arr =
[1, 2, 3, 4, 5, [6, 7, [8, 9, 10, [11, 12, 13, [14, 15, 16]]]]];

echo array_sum_recursive($arr);
```

The other two built-in recursive array functions in PHP are `array_merge_recursive` and `array_replace_recursive`. We can use them to merge multiple arrays to one or replace from multiple arrays, respectively.

Summary

So far, we discussed different properties and practical usage of recursion. We have seen how to do the analysis of recursive algorithms. Computer programming and recursion are two inseparable parts. The usage of recursion is almost everywhere in the programming world. In the upcoming chapters, we will explore it more and apply wherever it's applicable. In the next chapter, we will discuss another special data structure called "tree".

6
Understanding and Implementing Trees

Our exploration of data structures has so far touched the linear parts only. Whether we used arrays, linked lists, stacks, or queues, all are linear data structures. We have seen the complexities of linear data structure operations, and most of the time, the insertion and deletion can be performed with $O(1)$ complexity. However, the searching is a little complicated and takes $O(n)$ complexity. The only exception is a PHP array, which, in fact, works as a hash table and can be searched in $O(1)$ if the index or keys are managed in such a way. In order to solve this problem, we can use a hierarchical data structure instead of the linear one. Hierarchical data can solve many issues that a linear data structure cannot solve easily. Whenever we are talking about family tree, organization structure, and network connectivity diagrams, we are actually talking about hierarchical data. Trees are a special **Abstract Data Type** (**ADT**) that represents hierarchical data. Unlike a linked list, which is also an ADT, trees are hierarchical compared to the linear nature of linked lists. In this chapter, we will explore the world of trees. A perfect example of a tree structure can be a family tree, just like the following image:

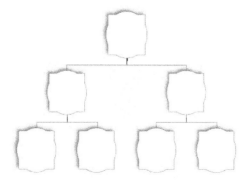

Tree definition and properties

A tree is a hierarchical collection of nodes or vertices connected by edges. Trees cannot have cycles, and only edges will exist between a node and its descended nodes or child nodes. Two child nodes of a same parent cannot have any edges in between them. Each node can have a parent other than the top node, which is also known as the root node. There can be only one root node per tree. Each node can have zero or more child nodes. In the following diagram, **A** is the root node, and **B**, **C**, and **D** are the child nodes of **A**. We can also say that A is the parent node of **B**, **C**, and **D**. **B**, **C**, and **D** are known as siblings as they are child nodes from the same parent, **A**:

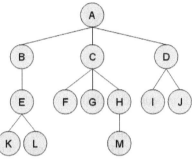

The node that does not have any children is known as a leaf. In the preceding diagram, **K**, **L**, **F**, **G**, **M**, **I**, and **J** are leaf nodes. Leaf nodes are also known as external nodes or terminal nodes. A node, other than the root, having at least one child, is known as an internal node. Here, **B**, **C**, **D**, **E**, and **H** are internal nodes. Here are some other common terms we use when describing tree data structure:

- **Descendent**: This is a node that can be reached from a parent node by repeated proceedings. For example, **M** is a descendent of **C** in the previous diagram.
- **Ancestor**: This is a node that can be reached from a child node to a parent node by a repeated way. For example, **B** is the ancestor of **L**.
- **Degree**: The total number of child nodes of a particular parent node is known as its degree. In our example, **A** has degree 3, **B** has degree 1, **C** has degree 3, and **D** has degree 2.

- **Path**: The sequence of nodes and edges from a source node to a target node is known as the path between two nodes. The length of the path is the number of nodes in the path. In our example, the path between **A** to **M** is **A-C-H-M**, and the length of the path is 4:

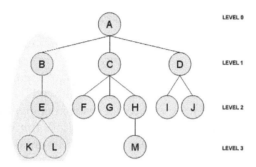

- **Height of node**: The height of a node is defined by the number of edges between the node and the deepest level of the descendent node. For example, the height of node **B** is 2.
- **Level**: The level represents the generation of nodes. If a parent node is in level *n*, its child node will be in the *n+1* level. So, the level is defined by 1+ number of edges between the node and the root. Here:
  - Root **A** is in **Level 0**
  - **B**, **C**, and **D** are in **Level 1**
  - **E**, **F**, **G**, **H**, **I**, and **J** are in **Level 2**
  - **K**, **L**, and **M** are in **Level 3**
- **Height of tree**: The height of a tree is defined by the height of its root node. Here, the height of the tree is 3.
- **Subtree**: In a tree structure, each child forms a subtree recursively. In other words, a tree consists of many subtrees. For example, **B** forms a subtree with **E**, **K**, and **L**, whereas **E** forms a subtree with **K** and **L**. In the preceding example, we have identified each in the left-hand side in different shades. We can do the same for **C** and **D** and their subtrees as well.
- **Depth**: The depth of a node is determined by the number of edges between the node and the root node. For example, in our tree image, the depth of **H** is 2 and the depth of **L** is 3.
- **Forest**: A forest is a set of zero or more disjoint trees.

- **Traverse**: This indicates the process of visiting nodes in a specific order. We will use this term often in the upcoming sections.
- **Keys**: A key is a value from the node that is used for searching purposes.

Implementing a tree using PHP

So far, you have learned about different properties of a tree data structure. If we compare a tree data structure with a real-life example, we can consider our organization structure or family tree to represent the data structure. For an organization structure, there is one root node that can be the CEO of the company, followed by CXO-level employees, followed by other level employees. Here, we are not restricting any degree for a particular node. This means a node can have multiple children. So, let's think of a node structure where we can define the node property, its parent node, and its children nodes. It might look something like this:

```php
class TreeNode {

    public $data = NULL;
    public $children = [];

    public function __construct(string $data = NULL) {
      $this->data = $data;
    }

    public function addChildren(TreeNode $node) {
      $this->children[] = $node;
    }

}
```

If we look at the preceding code, we can see that we have declared two public properties for data and children. We also have a method to add children to a particular node. Here, we are just appending the new child node at the end of the array. This will give us an option to add multiple nodes as children for a particular node. As a tree is a recursive structure, it will help us build a tree recursively and also traverse the tree in a recursive manner.

Now, we have the node; let's build a tree structure that will define the root node of the tree and also a method to traverse the whole tree. So, the basic tree structure will look like this:

```php
class Tree {

    public $root = NULL;
    public function __construct(TreeNode $node) {
```

```
        $this->root = $node;
    }

    public function traverse(TreeNode $node, int $level = 0) {

        if ($node) {
            echo str_repeat("-", $level);
            echo $node->data . "\n";

            foreach ($node->children as $childNode) {
                $this->traverse($childNode, $level + 1);
            }
        }
    }

}
```

The preceding code shows a simple tree class where we can store the root node reference and also traverse the tree from any node. In the traverse part, we are visiting each child node and then immediately recursively calling the traverse method to get the children of the current node. We are passing a level to print out a dash (-) at the beginning of the node name so that we can understand the child level data easily.

Let's now create the root node and assign it to the tree as a root. The code will look like this:

```
        $ceo = new TreeNode("CEO");
        $tree = new Tree($ceo);
```

Here, we created the first node as CEO, and then created the tree and assigned the CEO node as the root node of the tree. Now, it is time to grow our tree from the root node. Since we choose the example of the CEO, we will now add CXOs and other employees under the CEO. Here is the code for this:

```
$cto       = new TreeNode("CTO");
$cfo       = new TreeNode("CFO");
$cmo       = new TreeNode("CMO");
$coo       = new TreeNode("COO");

$ceo->addChildren($cto);
$ceo->addChildren($cfo);
$ceo->addChildren($cmo);
$ceo->addChildren($coo);

$seniorArchitect = new TreeNode("Senior Architect");
$softwareEngineer = new TreeNode("Software Engineer");
$userInterfaceDesigner     = new TreeNode("User Interface Designer");
$qualityAssuranceEngineer = new TreeNode("Quality Assurance Engineer");
```

```
$cto->addChildren($seniorArchitect);
$seniorArchitect->addChildren($softwareEngineer);
$cto->addChildren($qualityAssuranceEngineer);
$cto->addChildren($userInterfaceDesigner);

$tree->traverse($tree->root);
```

Here we are creating four new nodes (CTO, CFO, CMO, and COO) at the beginning and assigning them as child nodes of the CEO node. Then we are creating Senior Architect and here is the Software engineer node followed by the user interface designer and Quality assurance engineer. We have assigned the senior software engineer node to be a child node of the senior architect node and senior architect to be a child node of CTO, along with user interface engineer and quality assurance engineer. The last line is to display the tree from the root. This will output the following lines in our command line:

```
CEO
-CTO
--Senior Architect
---Software Engineer
--Quality Assurance Engineer
--User Interface Designer
-CFO
-CMO
-COO
```

If we consider the preceding output, we have CEO at level 0. CTO, CFO, CMO, and COO are at level 1. Senior Architect, User Interface Designer, and Quality Assurance Engineer are at level 2 and Software Engineer is at level 3.

We have constructed a basic tree data structure using PHP. Now, we will explore the different types of trees we have.

Different types of tree structures

There are many types of tree data structures present in the programming world. We will explore some of the most used tree structures here.

Binary tree

Binary is the most basic form of tree structure where each node has a maximum of two child nodes. The child nodes are known as left and right nodes. A binary tree will look like the one shown in the following diagram:

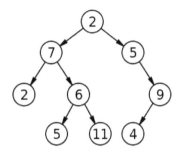

Binary search tree

A binary search tree (BST) is a special type of binary tree where the nodes are stored in a sorted manner. It is sorted in such a way that at any given point, a node value must be greater than or equal to the left child node value and smaller than the right child node value. Each node has to satisfy this property to consider it as a binary search tree. Since the nodes are sorted in a particular order, the binary search algorithm can be applied to search items in a BST in logarithmic time. It is always better than linear searching, which takes **O(n)** time, and we will explore it in the next chapter. Here is an example of a binary search tree:

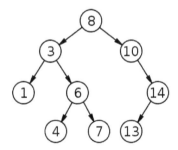

Self-balanced binary search tree

A self-balanced binary search tree or height-balance binary search tree is a special type of binary search tree that attempts to keep the height or number of levels of the tree as small as possible all the time by adjusting automatically. For example, the following diagram shows a binary search tree on the left and a the self-balanced binary search tree on the right:

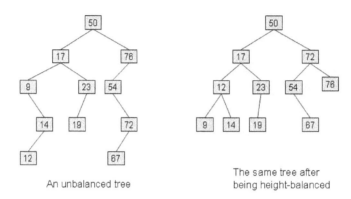

An unbalanced tree   The same tree after being height-balanced

A height-balanced binary tree is always better as it helps search operations faster compared to a regular BST. There are different implementations of self-balanced or height-balanced binary search trees. Some of the popular ones are as follows:

- AA tree
- AVL tree
- Red-black tree
- Scapegoat tree
- Splay tree
- 2-3 tree
- Treap

We will discuss few of the height-balanced trees in the following sections.

AVL tree

An AVL tree is a self-balancing binary search tree where the heights of two child subtrees of a node will differ by a maximum of 1. If the height increases, in any case, there will be a rebalance to make the height difference to 1. This gives the AVL tree an added advantage of logarithmic complexity for different operations. Here is an example of an AVL tree:

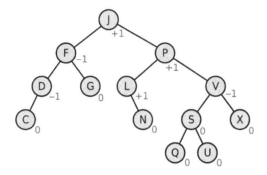

Red-black tree

A red-black tree is a self-balanced binary search tree with some extra properties, which is the color. Each node in the binary tree stores one extra bit of information, which is known as color and can have either red or black as values. Like an AVL tree, a red-black tree is also used for real-time applications as the average and worst case complexity is also logarithmic. A sample red-black tree looks like this:

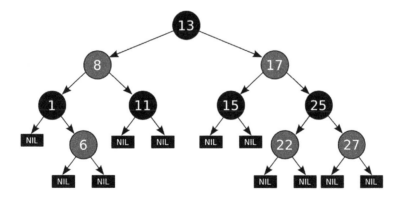

B-tree

A B-tree is a special type of binary tree, which is self-balanced. This is not the same as a self-balanced binary search tree. The key difference is that in a B-tree, we can have any number of nodes as child nodes, not just two. A B-tree is used for a large set of data and is mainly used in filesystems and databases. The complexity of different operations in a B-tree is logarithmic.

N-ary Tree

An N-ary tree is a special type of tree where a node can have maximum N children. This is also known as a k-way tree or M-ary tree. A binary tree is an N-ary tree where the value of N is 2.

Understanding a binary tree

We always get confused with binary trees and binary search trees. As we have seen in the definition, BST is a sorted binary tree. If it is sorted, then we can have the performance improvement compared to a regular binary tree. Each binary tree node can have a maximum of two child nodes, which are known as the left child node and right child node. However, based on the type of binary tree, there can be zero, one, or two child nodes.

We can also classify binary trees into different categories:

- **Full binary tree:** A full binary tree is a tree that has either zero or two child nodes on each node. A full binary tree is also known as a proper tree or a plane binary tree.
- **Perfect binary tree**: A perfect binary tree is a binary tree in which all internal nodes have exactly two child nodes and all leaves have the same level or depth.
- **Complete binary tree:** A complete binary tree is a binary tree in which all levels, except the last level, are completely filled and all nodes are as far left as possible. The following diagram shows the full binary tree, complete binary tree, and perfect binary tree:

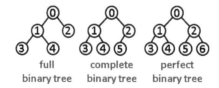

full
binary tree

complete
binary tree

perfect
binary tree

Implementing a binary tree

We will now create a binary tree (not a binary search tree). The key factor to have in a binary tree is that we must have two placeholders for the left child node and the right child node, along with the data we want to store in the node. A simple implementation of a binary node will look like this:

```
class BinaryNode {

    public $data;
    public $left;
    public $right;

    public function __construct(string $data = NULL) {
      $this->data = $data;
      $this->left = NULL;
      $this->right = NULL;
    }

    public function addChildren(BinaryNode $left, BinaryNode $right) {
      $this->left = $left;
      $this->right = $right;
    }

}
```

The preceding code shows that we have a class with tree properties to store data, left and right. When we are constructing a new node, we are adding the node value to the data property, and left and right is kept NULL as we are not sure if we need those or not. We also have an addChildren method to add left children and right children to a particular node.

Now, we will create a binary tree class where we can define the root node as well as the traversal method similar to our basic tree implementation earlier in this chapter. The difference between two implementations is the traversal process. In our previous example, we used foreach to traverse each child node as we did not know how many nodes are there. Since each node in the binary tree can have a maximum of two nodes and they are named as left and right, we can only traverse the left node and then the right node for each particular node visit. The changed code will look like this:

```
class BinaryTree {

    public $root = NULL;

    public function __construct(BinaryNode $node) {
    $this->root = $node;
    }
```

```
    public function traverse(BinaryNode $node, int $level
      = 0) {

    if ($node) {
        echo str_repeat("-", $level);
        echo $node->data . "\n";

        if ($node->left)
          $this->traverse($node->left, $level + 1);

        if ($node->right)
          $this->traverse($node->right, $level + 1);
    }
  }

}
```

It looks very similar to the basic tree class we had earlier in this chapter. Now, let's fill up the binary tree with some nodes. Usually, in any football or cricket tournament, we have knockout rounds where two teams play with each other, the winner moves forward, and it continues to the final. We can have a similar structure as a binary tree for our example. So, let's create some binary nodes and structure them in a hierarchy:

```
$final = new BinaryNode("Final");

$tree = new BinaryTree($final);

$semiFinal1 = new BinaryNode("Semi Final 1");
$semiFinal2 = new BinaryNode("Semi Final 2");
$quarterFinal1 = new BinaryNode("Quarter Final 1");
$quarterFinal2 = new BinaryNode("Quarter Final 2");
$quarterFinal3 = new BinaryNode("Quarter Final 3");
$quarterFinal4 = new BinaryNode("Quarter Final 4");

$semiFinal1->addChildren($quarterFinal1, $quarterFinal2);
$semiFinal2->addChildren($quarterFinal3, $quarterFinal4);

$final->addChildren($semiFinal1, $semiFinal2);

$tree->traverse($tree->root);
```

First, we created a node called final and made it as a root node. Then, we created two semifinal nodes and four quarter final nodes. Two semifinal nodes each have two quarter final nodes as left and right child nodes. The final node has two semifinal nodes as left and right child nodes. The `addChildren` method is doing the children assignment job for the nodes. In the last line, we traversed the tree and displayed the data hierarchically. If we run this code in the command line, we will see the following output:

```
Final
-Semi Final 1
--Quarter Final 1
--Quarter Final 2
-Semi Final 2
--Quarter Final 3
--Quarter Final 4
```

Creating a binary tree using a PHP array

We can implement a binary tree using a PHP array. Since a binary tree has a maximum of zero to two child nodes, we can use the maximum child nodes as 2 and construct a formula to find the child nodes of a given node. Let's number the nodes in a binary tree from top to bottom and left to right. So, the root node will have number **0**, the left child **1**, and right child **2**, and this will follow until each node is numbered, just like the following diagram:

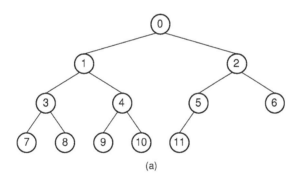

(a)

We can easily see that for node **0**, the left child is **1**, and the right child **2**. For node **1**, the left child is **3**, and the right child is **4**, and it goes on. We can easily put this in a formula:

If *i* is our node number, then:

Left node = 2 X i + 1

Right node = 2 X (i + 1)

Let's now create our example for the match schedule part using a PHP array. If we rank it as per our discussion, then it will look like this:

```php
$nodes = [];
$nodes[] = "Final";
$nodes[] = "Semi Final 1";
$nodes[] = "Semi Final 2";
$nodes[] = "Quarter Final 1";
$nodes[] = "Quarter Final 2";
$nodes[] = "Quarter Final 3";
$nodes[] = "Quarter Final 4";
```

Basically, we will create an array with auto-indexing, starting from 0. This array will be used as a binary tree representation. Now, we will modify our `BinaryTree` class to use this array instead of our node class, with left and right child nodes as well as the traversal method. Now, we will traverse based on the node number instead of the actual node reference:

```php
class BinaryTree {

    public $nodes = [];

    public function __construct(Array $nodes) {
      $this->nodes = $nodes;
    }

    public function traverse(int $num = 0, int $level = 0) {

      if (isset($this->nodes[$num])) {
          echo str_repeat("-", $level);
          echo $this->nodes[$num] . "\n";

          $this->traverse(2 * $num + 1, $level+1);
          $this->traverse(2 * ($num + 1), $level+1);
      }
    }

}
```

As we can see from preceding implementation, the traverse part uses the node positioning instead of a reference. This node position is nothing but the array indexes. So, we can directly access the array index and check whether it's empty or not. If not, we can continue to go deeper using the recursive way. If we want to create the binary tree using the array and print the array values, we have to write the following code:

```
$tree = new BinaryTree($nodes);
$tree->traverse(0);
```

If we run this code in the command line, we will see following output:

```
Final
-Semi Final 1
--Quarter Final 1
--Quarter Final 2
-Semi Final 2
--Quarter Final 3
--Quarter Final 4
```

We can use a simple `while` loop to iterate through the array and visit each node instead of proceeding recursively. In all our recursive examples, we will see that some are more efficient if we use them the iterative way. We can also just use them directly instead of creating a class for the binary tree.

Understanding the binary search tree

A BST is a binary tree that is built in such way that the tree is always sorted. This means the left child node has a value less than or equal to the parent node value, and right child node will have the value greater than the parent node value. So, whenever we need to search a value, either we will search left or search right. As it is sorted, we have to search one part of the tree, not both, and this continues recursively. For its dividing nature, the searching becomes very fast, and we can achieve logarithmic complexity for the search. For example, if we have *n* number of nodes, we will search either the first half or second half of the nodes. Once we are in the first or second half, we can divide it again into two halves, which means our half now becomes a quarter, and it goes on and on until we reach the final node. As we are not moving to each node to search, it is not going to take `O(n)` complexity for the operation. In the next chapter, we will do the complexity analysis of a binary search and will see why the binary search tree has a search complexity of `O(log n)`. Unlike the binary tree, we cannot add any node to or remove any node from the tree without reconstructing the BST properties.

If node **X** has two children, then the successor of node **X** is the smallest value that belongs to the tree, which is greater than the value of **X**. In other words, the successor is the minimum value of the right subtree. On the other hand, the predecessor is the maximum value of the left subtree. Now, we will focus more on the different operations of a BST and the steps we need to consider to perform those operations correctly.

Here are the operations of a BST.

Inserting a new node

When we are inserting a new node in the binary search tree, we have to consider the following steps:

1. Create a new node as a leaf (no left child or right child).
2. Start with the root node and set it as the current node.
3. If the node is empty, make the new node as the root.
4. Check whether the new value is less than the current node or more.
5. If less, go to the left and set the left as the current node.
6. If more, go to the right and set the right as the current node.
7. Continue to *step 3* until all the nodes are visited and the new node is set.

Searching a node

When we are searching a new node in a binary search tree, we have to consider the following steps:

1. Start with the root node and set it as the current node.
2. If the current node is empty, return false.
3. If the current node value is the search value, return true.
4. Check whether the searching value is less than the current node or more.
5. If less, go to the left and set the left as the current node.
6. If more, go to the right and set the right as the current node.
7. Continue to *step 3* until all the nodes are visited.

Finding the minimum value

As a binary search tree stores data in a sorted way, we can always find the smaller data in the left nodes and the bigger ones in the right node. So, finding the minimum value will require us to visit all the left nodes from the root node until we find the left-most node and its value. Here are the steps for finding the minimum value:

1. Start with the root node and set it as the current node.
2. If the current node is empty, return false.
3. Go to the left and set the left as the current node.
4. If the current node does not have a left node, go to *step 5*; otherwise, continue to *step 4*.
5. Continue to *step 3* until all the left nodes are visited.
6. Return the current node.

Finding the maximum value

Here are the steps for finding the maximum value:

1. Start with the root node and set it as the current node.
2. If the current node is empty, return false.
3. Go to the right and set the right as the current node.
4. If the current node does not have a right node, go to *step 5*; otherwise, continue to *step 4*.
5. Continue to *step 3* until all the right nodes are visited.
6. Return the current node.

Deleting a node

When we are deleting a node, we have to consider that the node can be an internal node or a leaf. If it's a leaf, it has zero children. However, if the node is internal, it can have one or two children. In such a case, we need to take extra steps to make sure the tree is constructed right after the deletion. That is why deleting a node from BST is always a challenging job compared to other operations. Here are the things to consider for a node deletion:

1. If the node has no child, make the node NULL.

2. If the node has only one child, make the child take node's place.
3. If the node has two children, then find the successor of the node and replace it to the current node's place. Remove the successor node.

We have discussed most of the possible operations for a binary search tree. Now, we will implement the binary search tree step-by-step, starting with insert, search, finding minimum and maximum, and at the end, the delete operation. Let's get started with the implementations.

Constructing a binary search tree

As we know, a node can have two children and itself can represent a tree in a recursive manner. We will define our node class to be more functional and have all the required functionalities to find the maximum value, minimum value, predecessors, and successors. Later on, we will add the delete functionality as well for a node. Let's check the following code for a node class for a BST:

```
class Node {

    public $data;
    public $left;
    public $right;

    public function __construct(int $data = NULL) {
        $this->data = $data;
        $this->left = NULL;
        $this->right = NULL;
    }

    public function min() {
        $node = $this;

        while($node->left) {
            $node = $node->left;
        }
        return $node;
    }

    public function max() {
        $node = $this;

        while($node->right) {
            $node = $node->right;
        }
```

```
            return $node;
    }

    public function successor() {
        $node = $this;
        if($node->right)
                return $node->right->min();
        else
                return NULL;
    }

    public function predecessor() {
        $node = $this;
        if($node->left)
                return $node->left->max();
        else
                return NULL;
    }

}
```

The node class looks straightforward and matches with our steps defined in the previous section. Each new node is a leaf and hence, does not have a left or right node at the moment of creation. As we know that we can find the smaller value at the left of the node to find the minimum, we are reaching to the left-most node and right-most node for the maximum value. For a successor, we are finding the minimum value of a node from the right subtree of a given node and the maximum value of a node from the left subtree for the predecessor part.

Now, we need a BST structure to add new nodes in the tree so that we can follow the insert principle:

```
class BST {

    public $root = NULL;

    public function __construct(int $data) {
        $this->root = new Node($data);
    }

    public function isEmpty(): bool {
        return $this->root === NULL;
    }

    public function insert(int $data) {

        if($this->isEmpty()) {
```

```php
                $node = new Node($data);
                $this->root = $node;
                return $node;
            }

        $node = $this->root;

        while($node) {
          if($data > $node->data) {
              if($node->right) {
                $node = $node->right;
              } else {
                $node->right = new Node($data);
                $node = $node->right;
                break;
              }

          } elseif($data < $node->data) {
              if($node->left) {
                $node = $node->left;
              } else {
                $node->left = new Node($data);
                $node = $node->left;
                break;
              }
          } else {
                break;
          }
        }
        return $node;

    }

    public function traverse(Node $node) {
      if ($node) {
          if ($node->left)
            $this->traverse($node->left);
          echo $node->data . "\n";
          if ($node->right)
            $this->traverse($node->right);
      }
    }

}
```

If we look at the preceding code, we have only one property for the BST class, which will mark the root node. During the construction of the BST object, we are passing a single value, which will be used as the root of the tree. The `isEmpty` method checks whether the tree is empty or not. The `insert` method allows us to add a new node in the tree. The logic checks whether the value is greater than or less than the root node and follows the principle of the BST to insert the new node in the right position. If the value is already inserted, we will ignore it and avoid adding to the tree.

We also have a `traverse` method to go through the nodes and see the data in an ordered format (first left, then the node, and then the right node value). It has a designated name, and we will explore that in the next section. For now, let's prepare a sample code to use the BST class and add a few numbers and check whether the numbers are stored in a proper way. If the BST is working, then the traverse will show a sorted list of numbers, no matter how we insert them:

```
$tree = new BST(10);

$tree->insert(12);
$tree->insert(6);
$tree->insert(3);
$tree->insert(8);
$tree->insert(15);
$tree->insert(13);
$tree->insert(36);

$tree->traverse($tree->root);
```

If we look at the preceding code, `10` is our root node, and then, we added new nodes randomly. At the end, we invoked the traverse method to show the nodes and how they are stored in the binary search tree. Here is the output of the preceding code:

```
3
6
8
10
12
13
15
36
```

The actual tree will look like this visually, which looks exactly like what is expected from the BST implementation:

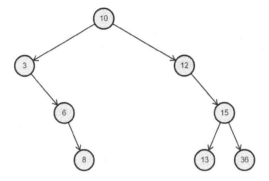

Now, we will add the search part in our BST class. We want to find whether the value exists in the tree or not. If the value is not in our BST, it will return false and the node otherwise. Here is the simple search functionality:

```
public function search(int $data) {
    if ($this->isEmpty()) {
        return FALSE;
    }

    $node = $this->root;

    while ($node) {
        if ($data > $node->data) {
          $node = $node->right;
        } elseif ($data < $node->data) {
          $node = $node->left;
        } else {
          break;
        }
    }

    return $node;
}
```

In the preceding code, we can see that we are searching a value in the tree from the node and following either left or right of the tree iteratively. If no node is found with the value, the leaf of the node is returned, which is NULL. We can test the code like this:

```
echo $tree->search(14) ? "Found" : "Not Found";
echo "\n";
echo $tree->search(36) ? "Found" : "Not Found";
```

This will produce the following output. Since 14 is not in our list, it will say Not Found, and for 36, it will show Found:

```
Not Found
Found
```

Now, we will move to our most complex part of the coding, the deletion of a node. We need to implement each of the cases where a node can have zero, one, or two child nodes. The following image shows us the three conditions we need to satisfy for deleting a node and making sure the binary search tree remains a binary search tree after the operation. We have to be careful when we are dealing with a node that has two child nodes. Since we need to go back and forth between nodes, we need to know which node is the parent node for the current node. As a result, we need to add an additional property to track the parent node for any node:

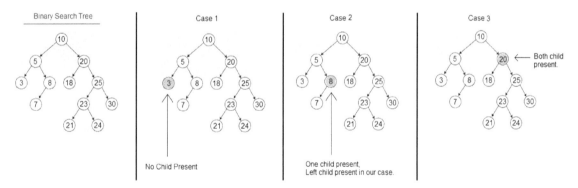

Here is the change of code we are adding to our Node class:

```
public $data;
public $left;
public $right;
public $parent;

public function __construct(int $data = NULL, Node $parent = NULL)
  {
    $this->data = $data;
```

```
            $this->parent = $parent;
            $this->left = NULL;
            $this->right = NULL;
        }
```

This code block now also creates a parent relationship with the newly created node to its immediate parent. We also want to attach our delete functionality with the individual node so that we can find a node and then just remove it using the delete method. Here is the code for the delete functionality:

```
public function delete() {
    $node = $this;
    if (!$node->left && !$node->right) {
        if ($node->parent->left === $node) {
            $node->parent->left = NULL;
        } else {
            $node->parent->right = NULL;
        }
    } elseif ($node->left && $node->right) {
        $successor = $node->successor();
        $node->data = $successor->data;
        $successor->delete();
    } elseif ($node->left) {
        if ($node->parent->left === $node) {
            $node->parent->left = $node->left;
            $node->left->parent = $node->parent->left;
        } else {
            $node->parent->right = $node->left;
            $node->left->parent = $node->parent->right;
        }
        $node->left = NULL;
    } elseif ($node->right) {

        if ($node->parent->left === $node) {
            $node->parent->left = $node->right;
            $node->right->parent = $node->parent->left;
        } else {
            $node->parent->right = $node->right;
            $node->right->parent = $node->parent->right;
        }
        $node->right = NULL;
    }
}
```

The first condition checks whether the node is a leaf or not. If the node is a leaf, then we are just making the parent node to remove the reference of the child node (either the left or right one). That way, the node will be disconnected from the tree, which satisfies our first condition of having zero children.

The next conditions actually checks our third condition where we are having two children of a node. In such a case, we are getting the successor of the node, assigning the successor value to the node itself, and removing the successor node. It is simply a copy-paste of the data from the successor.

The next two condition check whether the node has a single child, as shown in our *Case 2* diagram earlier. Since the node has only one child, it can be either the left child or the right child. So, the condition checks whether the single child is the left child of the node. If so, we need to point the left child to the node's parent left or right reference based on the position of the node itself with its parent. The same rule is applied for the right node. Here, the right node reference is set to its parent's left or right child, not to a reference based on the position of the node.

As we have updated our node class, we need to make some changes to our BST class for insertion and also for removal of a node. The insertion code will look like this:

```
function insert(int $data)
{
    if ($this->isEmpty()) {
        $node = new Node($data);
        $this->root = $node;
        return $node;
    }

    $node = $this->root;
    while ($node) {
        if ($data > $node->data) {
            if ($node->right) {
                $node = $node->right;
            }
            else {
                $node->right = new Node($data, $node);
                $node = $node->right;
                break;
            }
        }
        elseif ($data < $node->data) {
            if ($node->left) {
                $node = $node->left;
            }
            else {
```

```
                    $node->left = new Node($data, $node);
                    $node = $node->left;
                    break;
                }
            }
            else {
                break;
            }
        }
    }

    return $node;
}
```

The code looks similar to the one we used previously, with one minor change. Now, we are sending the current node reference when we are creating a new node. This current node will be used as a parent node for the new node. The new `Node($data, $node)` code actually does the trick.

For removing a node, we can first do a search and then delete the searched node using our `delete` method in the node class. As a result, the `remove` function itself is going to be very small, just like the code here:

```
public function remove(int $data) {
    $node = $this->search($data);
    if ($node) $node->delete();
}
```

As the code shows, we are first searching the data. If the node exists, we are removing it using the `delete` method. Now, let's run our previous example with a `remove` call and see if it works:

```
$tree->remove(15);
$tree->traverse($tree->root);
```

We are just removing 15 from our tree and then traversing the tree from the root. We will now see the following output:

```
3
6
8
10
12
13
36
```

We can see that 15 is not a part of our BST anymore. In such a way, we can remove any node, and if we traverse using the same method, we will see a sorted list. If we look at our preceding output, we can see that the output is shown in the ascending order. There is a reason behind it, and we will explore it in the next topic-different tree traversal way.

 You can find a great tool for visualized binary search tree operations at `http://btv.melezinek.cz/binary-search-tree.html`. It is a good starting for learners to understand the different operations visually.

Tree traversal

Tree traversal refers to the way we visit each node in a given tree. Based on how we do the traversing, we can follow three different ways of traversing. These traversals are very important in many different ways. Polish notation conversion for expression evaluation is one of the most popular examples of using tree traversals.

In-order

In-order tree traversal visits the left node first, then the root node, and followed by the right node. This continues recursively for each node. The left node stores a smaller value compared to the root node value and right node stores a bigger value than the root node. As a result, when we are applying in-order traversing, we are obtaining a sorted list. That is why, so far, our binary tree traversal was showing a sorted list of numbers. That traversal part is actually the example of an in-order tree traversal. The in-order tree traversal follows these principles:

1. Traverse the left subtree by recursively calling the in-order function.
2. Display the data part of the root (or current node).

3. Traverse the right subtree by recursively calling the in-order function.

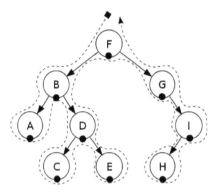

The preceding tree will show A, B, C, D, E, F, G, H, and I as output since it is being traversed in-order.

Pre-order

In pre-order traversal, the root node is visited first, followed by the left node and then the right node. The principles of pre-order traversal are as follows:

1. Display the data part of the root (or current node).
2. Traverse the left subtree by recursively calling the pre-order function.
3. Traverse the right subtree by recursively calling the pre-order function.

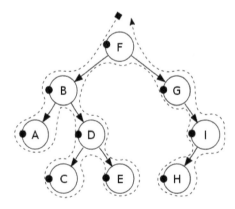

The preceding tree will have F, B, A, D, C, E, G, I, and H as output as it is being traversed in pre-order.

Post-order

In post-order traversal, the root node is visited last. The first left node is visited and then the right node. The principles of post-order traversal are as follows:

1. Traverse the left subtree by recursively calling the post-order function.
2. Traverse the right subtree by recursively calling the post-order function.
3. Display the data part of the root (or current node).

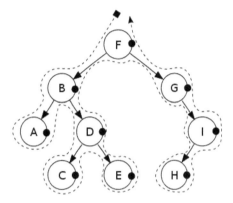

The preceding tree will have the output A, C, E, D, B, H, I, G, and F since it is traversed in a post-order way.

Now, let's implement the traversal logic in our BST class:

```
public function traverse(Node $node, string $type="in-order") {

switch($type) {
    case "in-order":
      $this->inOrder($node);
    break;

    case "pre-order":
      $this->preOrder($node);
    break;

    case "post-order":
      $this->postOrder($node);
    break;
  }
}
```

```php
public function preOrder(Node $node) {
  if ($node) {
      echo $node->data . " ";
      if ($node->left) $this->traverse($node->left);
      if ($node->right) $this->traverse($node->right);
  }
}

public function inOrder(Node $node) {
  if ($node) {
      if ($node->left) $this->traverse($node->left);
      echo $node->data . " ";
      if ($node->right) $this->traverse($node->right);
  }
}

public function postOrder(Node $node) {
  if ($node) {
      if ($node->left) $this->traverse($node->left);
      if ($node->right) $this->traverse($node->right);
      echo $node->data . " ";
  }
}
```

Now, if we run the three different traversal methods for our previous binary search tree, here is the code to run the traversal part:

```php
$tree->traverse($tree->root, 'pre-order');
echo "\n";
$tree->traverse($tree->root, 'in-order');
echo "\n";
$tree->traverse($tree->root, 'post-order');
```

This will produce the following output in our command line:

```
10 3 6 8 12 13 15 36
3 6 8 10 12 13 15 36
3 6 8 12 13 15 36 10
```

Complexity of different tree data structures

So far, we have seen different tree types and their operations. It is not possible to go through each of the tree types and their different operations, as this will be out of the scope of the book. We want to get the minimal idea about the other tree structures and their operation complexities. Here is a chart with average and worst case complexities of different operations and spaces for different types of trees. We might need to choose different tree structures based on our requirements:

Tree type		Average	Worst
Binary search tree	Space	$\Theta(n)$	$O(n)$
	Insert	$\Theta(\log n)$	$O(n)$
	Search	$\Theta(\log n)$	$O(n)$
	Delete	$\Theta(\log n)$	$O(n)$
Red black tree	Space	$O(n)$	$O(n)$
	Insert	$O(\log n)$	$O(\log n)$
	Search	$O(\log n)$	$O(\log n)$
	Delete	$O(\log n)$	$O(\log n)$
AVL tree	Space	$O(n)$	$O(n)$
	Insert	$O(\log n)$	$O(\log n)$
	Search	$O(\log n)$	$O(\log n)$
	Delete	$O(\log n)$	$O(\log n)$
B-tree	Space	$O(n)$	$O(n)$

Summary

In this chapter, we discussed the non-linear data structure in detail. You learned that trees are hierarchical data structures and that there are different tree types, operations, and complexities. We have also seen how to define a binary search tree. This will be very useful for implementing different searching techniques and data storage. In our next chapter, we will shift our focus from data structures to algorithms. We will focus on the first type of algorithm--the sorting algorithms.

7
Using Sorting Algorithms

Sorting is one of the most used algorithms in computer programming. Even in our everyday life, if things are not sorted, we can have a hard time with them. Sorting can pave the way for faster searching or ordering of items in a collection. Sorting can be done in many different ways, such as in ascending order or descending order. Sorting can also be based on the type of data. For example, sorting a collection of names will require lexicographical sorting rather than numerical sorting. As sorting can play an important role for other data structures and their efficiencies, there are many different sorting algorithms available. We will explore a few of the most popular sorting algorithms in this chapter, along with their complexity and usages.

Understanding sorting and their types

Sorting means a sorted order of the data. Often, our data is unsorted, which means we need a way to sort it. Usually, sorting is done by comparing different elements with each other and coming up with the ranking. In most cases, without the comparison, we cannot decide on the sorting part. After the comparison, we also need to swap the elements so that we can reorder them. A good sorting algorithm has the characteristics of making a minimum number of comparisons and swapping. There is also non-comparison based sorting, where no comparison is required to sort a list of items. We will also explore those algorithms in this chapter.

Sorting can be classified into different types based on the type of data set, direction, computational complexities, memory usage, space usage, and so on. Here are few of the sorting algorithms we will explore in this chapter:

- Bubble sort
- Insertion sort
- Selection sort
- Quick sort
- Merge sort
- Bucket sort

We will keep our discussion limited to the preceding list, as they are the most commonly used sorting algorithms and can be grouped and classified under different criteria such as simple sorting, efficient sorting, distribution sorting, and so on. We will now explore each of the sorting functionalities, their implementations, and complexity analysis, along with their pros and cons. Let's get started with the most commonly used sorting algorithm - bubble sort.

Understanding bubble sort

Bubble sort is the most commonly used sorting algorithm in the programming world. Most of the programmers start learning about sorting with this algorithm. It is a comparison-based sorting algorithm, which is always referred to as one of the most inefficient sorting algorithms. It requires maximum number of comparisons, and the average, and worst case complexity are the same.

In bubble sort, each item of the list is compared with the rest of the items and swapped if required. This continues for each item in the list. We can sort either in ascending or descending order. Here is the pseudo algorithm for bubble sort:

```
procedure bubbleSort( A : list of sortable items )
    n = length(A)
    for i = 0 to n inclusive do
      for j = 0 to n-1 inclusive do
        if A[j] > A[j+1] then
          swap( A[j], A[j+1] )
        end if
      end for
    end for
end procedure
```

As we can see from the preceding pseudocode, we are running one loop to ensure that we iterate each item of the list. The inner loop ensures that, once we point to an item, we are comparing the item with other items in the list. Based on our preference, we can swap the two items. The following image shows a single iteration to sort one item of the list. Let's assume our list has the following items: **20**, **45**, **93**, **67**, **10**, **97**, **52**, **88**, **33**, **92**. For the first pass (iteration) to sort out the first item, the following steps will be taken:

20	45	93	67	10	97	52	88	33	92	No exchange
20	45	93	67	10	97	52	88	33	92	No exchange
20	45	93	67	10	97	52	88	33	92	Exchange
20	45	67	93	10	97	52	88	33	92	Exchange
20	45	67	10	93	97	52	88	33	92	No exchange
20	45	67	10	93	97	52	88	33	92	Exchange
20	45	67	10	93	52	97	88	33	92	Exchange
20	45	67	10	93	52	88	97	33	92	Exchange
20	45	67	10	93	52	88	33	97	92	Exchange
20	45	67	10	93	52	88	33	92	97	97 is stored at the top after first pass

If we check the preceding image, we can see that we are comparing two numbers and then deciding whether we are going to swap/exchange the item. The items with background color shows the two items we are comparing. As we can see, the first iteration of the outer loop causes the topmost items to be stored in the topmost places in the list. This will continue until we iterate through each of the items in the list.

Let's now implement the bubble sort algorithm using PHP.

Implementing bubble sort using PHP

Since we are assuming the unsorted number will be in a list, we can use a PHP array to represent the list of unsorted numbers. Since the array has both index and values, we can utilize the array to easily iterate through each item, based on position, and swap them where it is applicable. The code will look like this, based on our pseudocodes:

```
function bubbleSort(array $arr): array {
    $len = count($arr);

    for ($i = 0; $i < $len; $i++) {
        for ($j = 0; $j < $len - 1; $j++) {
            if ($arr[$j] > $arr[$j + 1]) {
```

```
                    $tmp = $arr[$j + 1];
                    $arr[$j + 1] = $arr[$j];
                    $arr[$j] = $tmp;
                }
            }
        }
        return $arr;
    }
```

As we can see, we are using two `for` loops to iterate each item and comparing with the rest of the items. The swapping is done in the lines:

```
$tmp = $arr[$j + 1];
$arr[$j + 1] = $arr[$j];
$arr[$j] = $tmp;
```

First, we assigned the second value to a temporary variable named `$tmp`. Then, we assigned the first value to the second value and reassigned the temporary value to the first value. This is known as swapping two variables using a third or temporary variable.

We are only swapping if the first value is greater than the second value. Else, we are just ignoring. The comment on the right-hand side of the image shows whether an exchange occurred or not. If we want to sort it in a descending order (bigger number first), then we can just modify the `if` condition as follows:

```
if ($arr[$j] < $arr[$j + 1]) {
}
```

Now, let's run the code as follows:

```
$arr = [20, 45, 93, 67, 10, 97, 52, 88, 33, 92];
$sortedArray = bubbleSort($arr);
echo implode(",", $sortedArray);
```

This will produce the following output:

10,20,33,45,52,67,88,92,93,97

So, we can see that the array is sorted using the bubble sort algorithm. Now, let's discuss the complexity of the algorithm.

Complexity of bubble sort

For the first pass, in the worst case, we have to do *n-1* comparison and swapping. For the *n-1th* pass, in the worst case, we have to do only one comparison and swapping. So, if we write it step by step then we will see:

*Complexity = n - 1 + n - 2 + ... + 2 + 1 = n * (n - 1)/2 = O(n²)*

Thus, the complexity of bubble sort is $O(n^2)$. However, there is some constant time required to assign a temporary variable, swapping, go through inner loops, and so on. We can ignore them since they are constant.

Here is the time complexity table for bubble sort, for best, average, and worst case scenarios:

Best time complexity	$\Omega(n)$
Worst time complexity	$O(n^2)$
Average time complexity	$\Theta(n^2)$
Space complexity (worst case)	$O(1)$

Though the time complexity is $O(n^2)$ for bubble sort, we can still apply some improvements to reduce the number of comparison and swaps. Let's now explore those options. The best time is $\Omega(n)$ since we need at least one inner loop to run to find out that the array is already sorted.

Improving bubble sort algorithm

One of the most important aspects of bubble sort is that, for each iteration in the outer loop, there will be at least one swapping. If there is no swapping, then the list is already sorted. We can utilize this improvement in our pseudocode and redefine it like this:

```
procedure bubbleSort( A : list of sortable items )
    n = length(A)
    for i = 1 to n inclusive do
      swapped = false
      for j = 1 to n-1 inclusive do
        if A[j] > A[j+1] then
          swap( A[j], A[j+1] )
          swapped = true
        end if
      end for
```

```
        if swapped is false
            break
        end if

    end for
end procedure
```

As we can see that we now have a flag set for each iteration to be `false`, and we are expecting that, inside the inner iteration, the flag will be set to `true`. If the flag is still false after the inner loop is done, then we can break the loop so that we can mark the list as sorted. Here is the implementation of the improved version of the algorithm:

```
function bubbleSort(array $arr): array {
    $len = count($arr);

    for ($i = 0; $i < $len; $i++) {
      $swapped = FALSE;
      for ($j = 0; $j < $len - 1; $j++) {
          if ($arr[$j] > $arr[$j + 1]) {
              $tmp = $arr[$j + 1];
              $arr[$j + 1] = $arr[$j];
              $arr[$j] = $tmp;
              $swapped = TRUE;
          }
      }
        if(! $swapped) break;
    }
    return $arr;
}
```

Another observation is that, in the first iteration, the top item is placed to the right of the array. In the second loop, the second top item will be in the second to the right of the array. If we can visualize that after each iteration, the ith cell has already stored the sorted items, there is no need to visit that index and do a comparison. As a result, we can reduce the outer iteration number from the inner iteration and reduce the comparisons by a good margin. Here is the pseudocode for the second improvement we are proposing:

```
procedure bubbleSort( A : list of sortable items )
    n = length(A)
    for i = 1 to n inclusive do
      swapped = false
      for j = 1 to n-i-1 inclusive do
        if A[j] > A[j+1] then
          swap( A[j], A[j+1] )
          swapped = true
        end if
      end for
```

```
      if swapped is false
         break
      end if

   end for
end procedure
```

Now, let's implement the final improved version with PHP:

```php
function bubbleSort(array $arr): array {
    $len = count($arr);

    for ($i = 0; $i < $len; $i++) {
      $swapped = FALSE;
      for ($j = 0; $j < $len - $i - 1; $j++) {
          if ($arr[$j] > $arr[$j + 1]) {
             $tmp = $arr[$j + 1];
             $arr[$j + 1] = $arr[$j];
             $arr[$j] = $tmp;
             $swapped = TRUE;
          }
      }
      if(! $swapped) break;
    }
    return $arr;
}
```

If we look at the inner loop in the preceding code, the only difference is `$j < $len - $i - 1`; other parts are the same as the first improvement. So, basically, for our **20**, **45**, **93**, **67**, **10**, **97**, **52**, **88**, **33**, **92** list, we can easily say that after the first iteration, the top number **97** will not be considered for second iteration comparison. The same goes for **93**, which will not be considered for the third iteration, just like the following image:

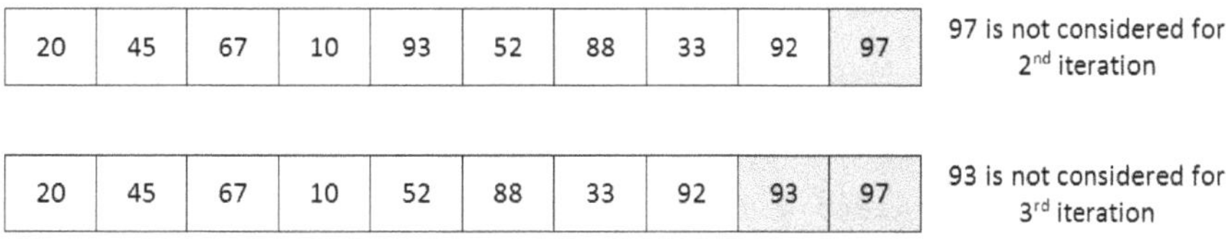

| 20 | 45 | 67 | 10 | 93 | 52 | 88 | 33 | 92 | 97 |

97 is not considered for 2nd iteration

| 20 | 45 | 67 | 10 | 52 | 88 | 33 | 92 | 93 | 97 |

93 is not considered for 3rd iteration

If we look at the preceding image, the immediate question that strikes our mind is "Isn't **92** already sorted? Do we need to again compare all numbers and mark that **92** is already sorted in its place?" Yes, we are right. It is a valid question. This means that we can know, in which position we did the last swap in the inner loop; after that, the array is already sorted. So, we can set a bound for the next loop to go, until then, and only compare until the boundary we set. Here is the pseudocode for this:

```
procedure bubbleSort( A : list of sortable items )
   n = length(A)
   bound = n -1
   for i = 1 to n inclusive do
     swapped = false
     newbound = 0
     for j = 1 to bound inclusive do
       if A[j] > A[j+1] then
         swap( A[j], A[j+1] )
            swapped = true
            newbound = j
       end if
     end for

     bound = newbound

     if swapped is false
        break
     end if

   end for
end procedure
```

Here, we are setting the bound after completion of each inner loop and making sure we are not iterating unnecessarily. Here is the actual PHP code using the preceding pseudocode:

```
function bubbleSort(array $arr): array {
    $len = count($arr);
    $count = 0;
    $bound = $len-1;

    for ($i = 0; $i < $len; $i++) {
     $swapped = FALSE;
     $newBound = 0;
       for ($j = 0; $j < $bound; $j++) {
            $count++;
            if ($arr[$j] > $arr[$j + 1]) {
                $tmp = $arr[$j + 1];
                $arr[$j + 1] = $arr[$j];
                $arr[$j] = $tmp;
```

```
            $swapped = TRUE;
            $newBound = $j;

        }
    }
    $bound = $newBound;

    if(! $swapped) break;
    }
    echo $count."\n";
    return $arr;
}
```

We have seen different variations of bubble sort implementations, but the output will always be the same: **10, 20, 33, 45, 52, 67, 88, 92, 93, 97**. If this is the case, then how can we be sure that our improvements have actually had some impact on the algorithm? Here are some statistics on the number of comparisons for all four implementations for our initial list 20, 45, 93, 67, 10, 97, 52, 88, 33, 92:

Solution	Comparison count
Regular bubble sort	90
After first improvement	63
After second improvement	42
After third improvement	38

As we can see, we have reduced the number of comparisons from **90** to **38** with our improvement. So, we can certainly boost up the algorithm with some improvements to reduce the number of comparisons required.

Understanding selection sort

Selection sort is another comparison-based sorting algorithm, which looks similar to bubble sort. The biggest difference is that it takes fewer swapping than bubble sort. In selection sort, we first find the minimum/maximum item of the array and place it in the first place. If we are sorting in descending order, then we will take the maximum value from the array. For ascending order, we will take the minimum value. In the second iteration, we will find the second-most maximum or minimum value of the array and place it in second place. This goes on until we place each number into a correctly sorted position. This is known as selection sort. The pseudocode for selection sort looks like this:

```
procedure selectionSort( A : list of sortable items )
   n = length(A)
   for i = 1 to n inclusive do
     min = i
     for j = i+1 to n inclusive do
       if A[j] < A[min] then
         min = j
       end if
     end for

     if min != i
         swap(a[i],a[min])
     end if

   end for
end procedure
```

If we look at the preceding algorithm, we can see that, after iteration one in the outer loop, the first minimum item is stored in position one. During the first iteration, we selected the first item and then found the minimum value from the remaining items (from 2 to n). We assumed that the first item is the minimum value. If we find another minimum value, we would mark its position until we have scanned the remaining list and found a new minimum value. If no minimum value is found, then our assumption is correct, and that is indeed the minimum value. Here is a picture illustrating our **20**, **45**, **93**, **67**, **10**, **97**, **52**, **88**, **33**, **92** arrays during the first two steps in selection sort:

As we can see in the preceding image, we started with the first item in the list, which is **20**. Then, we found the minimum value from the rest of the array, which is **10**. At the end of the first iteration, we just swapped the values from two places (marked by arrows). As a result, at the end of the first iteration, we have the minimum value from the array stored in the first place. Then, we pointed to the next item, which is **45**, and started finding the next smallest items compared to **45** from the right side of its position. We found **20** from the remaining items (as shown by two arrows). At the end of the second iteration, we are just swapping the second position number to the newly found smallest one from the remainder of the list. This continues until the last element, and, at the end of the process, we have a sorted list of arrays. Let's now convert the pseudocode into a PHP code.

Implementing selection sort

We will take the same approach as the bubble sort where our implementation will take an array as an argument and return a sorted array. Here is the implementation in PHP:

```php
function selectionSort(array $arr): array {
    $len = count($arr);
    for ($i = 0; $i < $len; $i++) {
      $min = $i;
      for ($j = $i+1; $j < $len; $j++) {
          if ($arr[$j] < $arr[$min]) {
            $min = $j;
          }
      }

      if ($min != $i) {
```

```
        $tmp = $arr[$i];
        $arr[$i] = $arr[$min];
        $arr[$min] = $tmp;
    }
  }
  return $arr;
}
```

As can be seen, this is the simplest way to sort an array in ascending order. If you want to do it in descending order, we just need to change the comparison `$arr[$j] < $arr[$min]` to `$arr[$j] > $arr[$min]` and replace `$min` with `$max`.

Complexity of selection sort

Selection sort also looks similar to bubble sort and has two `for` loops with 0 to *n*. The basic difference between bubble sort and selection sort is that, selection sort makes maximum *n-1* number of swapping, whereas bubble sort can have *n*n* number of swapping, in the worst case scenario. However, in the selection sort, the best case, worst case, and average case have similar complexity. Here is the complexity chart for selection sort:

Best time complexity	$\Omega(n^2)$
Worst time complexity	$O(n^2)$
Average time complexity	$\Theta(n^2)$
Space complexity (worst case)	$O(1)$

Understanding insertion Sort

So far, we have seen two comparison-based sorting algorithms. Now, we will explore another sorting algorithm that is somewhat efficient compared to the previous two. We are talking about the insertion sort. It has the simplest implementation compared to the other two sorting algorithms we have just seen. If the number of items is smaller, insertion sort works better than bubble sort and selection sort. If the data set is large, then it becomes inefficient, like bubble sort. Since the swapping is almost linear for insertion sort, it is recommended that you use insertion sort instead of bubble sort and selection sort.

As the name suggests, insertion sort works on the principle of inserting the number to its correct place on the left-hand side. It starts from the second item of the array and checks whether the items that are left to it are smaller than the current value or not. If so, it shifts the item and stores the smaller item in its correct position. Then, it moves to the next item, and the same principle continues until the full array is sorted. The pseudocode for insertion sort looks like this:

```
procedure insertionSort( A : list of sortable items )
   n = length(A)
   for i = 1 to n inclusive do
     key = A[i]
     j = i - 1
     while j >= 0 and A[j] > key    do
       A[j+1] = A[j]
       j--
     end while

     A[j+1] = key

   end for
end procedure
```

If we consider our previous list of numbers used for bubble sort and selection sort, then we will have the following scenario for which we must do insertion sort.
The elements of our array were: **20**, **45**, **93**, **67**, **10**, **97**, **52**, **88**, **33**, **92**.

Let's start with the second item, which is **45**. Now, we will start from the first item to the left of **45** and go to the beginning of the array to see whether there is a value greater than **45** on the left. As there is only **20**, no insertion is required as the item so far is sorted until the second element (**20,45**). Now, we will move our pointer to **93,** and it starts again, comparing left of the array starting from **45** and search if the value is bigger. Since **45** is not bigger than **93**, it stops there, as previously, we concluded that the first two items are already sorted. Now, we have the first three items (**20**, **45**, **93**) sorted. Next, we have **67**, and we start again by comparing from the left of the numbers. The first number to the left is **93**, which is bigger, so it has to move one place. We move **93** to the position that was held by **67**. Then, we move to the next item to the left of it, which is **45**. **45** is smaller than **67**, and no further comparison is required. Now, we will insert **67** at the position that was held by **93** and **93** will have to be moved to **67**'s position. This continues until the full array is sorted.

This image illustrates the full sorting process using insertion sort at each step:

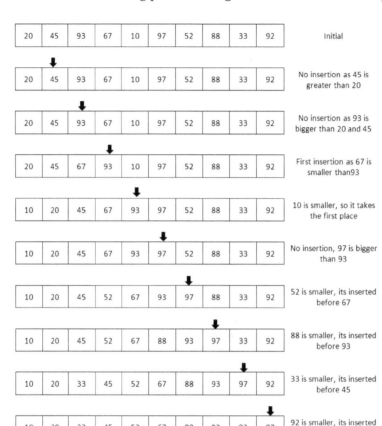

Implementing insertion sort

We will implement the insertion sort in a similar way to the other two sorts but with a subtle difference. This time, we will pass the array as a reference. By doing so, we will not require any return value from the function. We can also pass the argument by value and return the array at the end of the function if we want. Here is the code for this:

```
function insertionSort(array &$arr) {
    $len = count($arr);
    for ($i = 1; $i < $len; $i++) {
        $key = $arr[$i];
        $j = $i - 1;
```

```
    while($j >= 0 && $arr[$j] > $key) {
        $arr[$j+1] = $arr[$j];
        $j--;
    }
    $arr[$j+1] = $key;
    }
}
```

The parameter array is passed to the function by reference (`&$arr`). Thus, the original array, not a copy of it, will be modified directly. Now, we want to run the code and check the output. For this, we have to run the following code:

```
$arr = [20, 45, 93, 67, 10, 97, 52, 88, 33, 92];

insertionSort($arr);
echo implode(",", $arr);
```

This will produce the same output we had in the previous two cases. The only difference is that we are not expecting any return array from the function and not storing it into any new variable.

 If we pass the array by reference, then we do not have to return the array. The passed array will be modified inside the function. It is down to choice how we want to achieve the sorting.

Complexity of insertion sort

Insertion sort has a complexity similar to bubble sort. The basic difference with bubble sort is that the number of swapping is much lower than bubble sort. Here is the complexity for insertion sort:

Best time complexity	$\Omega(n)$
Worst time complexity	$O(n^2)$
Average time complexity	$\Theta(n^2)$
Space complexity (worst case)	$O(1)$

Understanding divide-and-conquer technique for sorting

So far, we have explored the sorting option with a full list of numbers. As a result, we had a big list of numbers to compare every time. This can be solved if we can somehow make the list smaller. The divide-and-conquer method can be very helpful for us. With this method, we will divide a problem into two or more subproblems or sets, and then solve the smaller problems before combining all those results from the subproblems to get the final result. This is what is known as divide-and-conquer.

The divide-and-conquer method can allow us to solve our sorting problems efficiently and reduce the complexity of our algorithm. Two of the most popular sorting algorithms are merge sort and quick sort, which apply the divide-and-conquer algorithm to sort a list of items, and hence, they are considered to be the best sorting algorithms. Now, we will explore these two algorithms in the next section.

Understanding merge sort

As we already know that merge sort applies the divide-and-conquer approach to solve the sorting problem, we need to find out two processes to address the issue. The first one is to divide the problem set into smaller enough problems to solve easily, and then combine those results. We will apply a recursive approach here for the divide-and-conquer part. The following image shows how to take the approach for divide-and-conquer. We will now consider a smaller list of numbers **20, 45, 93, 67, 97, 52, 88, 33** to explain the divide-and-conquer part:

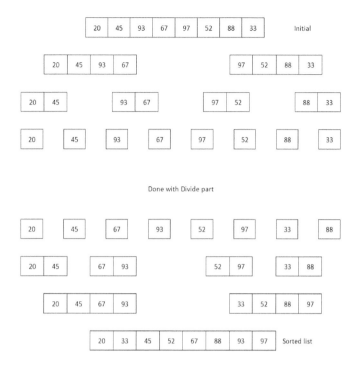

Based on the preceding image, we can now start preparing our pseudocode, which will have two parts - divide and conquer. Here is the pseudocode to achieve that

`func` mergesort (A : array of sortable items):

```
n = length(A)
if ( n == 1 ) return a

var l1 as array = a[0] ... a[n/2]
var l2 as array = a[n/2+1] ... a[n]

l1 = mergesort ( l1 )
l2 = mergesort ( l2 )

return merge ( l1, l2 )
end func

func merge( a: array, b : array )
c = array

while ( a and b have elements )
    if ( a[0] > b[0] )
```

```
                add b[0] to the end of c
                remove b[0] from b
        else
                add a[0] to the end of c
                remove a[0] from a
    end while

    while ( a has elements )
        add a[0] to the end of c
        remove a[0] from a
    end while

    while ( b has elements )
        add b[0] to the end of c
        remove b[0] from b
    return c
    end while
end func
```

Our first part of the pseudocode shows the divide process. We divided the array of items until it reaches the size of 1. Then, we started to merge the results using the merge function. In the merge function, we had an array to store the merged results. Because of this, merge sort actually has more space complexity than the other algorithms we have seen so far. Now, let's get into coding and implement this pseudocode using PHP.

Implementing merge sort

We will first write the divide part followed by the merge or conquer part. PHP has some built-in functions to split an array. We will use the array_slice function to do the splitting. Here is the code to do this:

```php
function mergeSort(array $arr): array {
    $len = count($arr);
    $mid = (int) $len / 2;
    if ($len == 1)
        return $arr;

    $left  = mergeSort(array_slice($arr, 0, $mid));
    $right = mergeSort(array_slice($arr, $mid));

    return merge($left, $right);
}
```

As we can see from the code, we split the array in a recursive way until the array size becomes 1. When array size is 1, we start to merge backward, just like the last image. Here is the code for the merge function, which will take two arrays, and merge them into one as per our pseudocode:

```
function merge(array $left, array $right): array {
    $combined = [];
    $countLeft = count($left);
    $countRight = count($right);
    $leftIndex = $rightIndex = 0;

    while ($leftIndex < $countLeft && $rightIndex < $countRight) {
      if ($left[$leftIndex] > $right[$rightIndex]) {
          $combined[] = $right[$rightIndex];
          $rightIndex++;
      } else {
          $combined[] = $left[$leftIndex];
          $leftIndex++;
      }
    }
    while ($leftIndex < $countLeft) {
      $combined[] = $left[$leftIndex];
      $leftIndex++;
    }
    while ($rightIndex < $countRight) {
      $combined[] = $right[$rightIndex];
      $rightIndex++;
    }
    return $combined;
}
```

The code is now complete as we have merged the two supplied arrays and returned the combined results to the mergeSort function. We have just solved the problem recursively. If you run the following code, you will have a list of items in ascending order:

```
$arr = [20, 45, 93, 67, 10, 97, 52, 88, 33, 92];

$arr = mergeSort($arr);
echo implode(",", $arr);
```

Now, let's explore the complexity for merge sort.

Complexity of merge sort

Since merge sort follows the divide-and-conquer method, we have to address both complexities here. For an n-sized array, we first need to divide the array into two halves and then merge them to get an n-sized array. This can be written in terms of `T(n)` as:

```
T(n)       = T(n/2) + T(n/2) + n    , for N>1 with T(1) = 0
           = 2 T(n/2)+n

T(n)/n     = 2 T(n/2)/n + 1               // divide both side by n
           = T(n/2)/(n/2)   + 1
           = T(n/4)/(n/4)   + 1+ 1        // telescoping
           = T(n/8)/(n/8)   + 1+ 1 + 1     // again telescoping
           = ......
           = T(n/n)/(n/n)   + 1 + 1 + 1 + ....... + 1
           = log (n)                      // since T(1) = 0

So T(n)  = n log (n)                      // multiply both side with n
```

So, the complexity for merge sort is `O(n log(n))`. Here is the complexity chart for merge sort:

Best time complexity	`Ω(nlog(n))`
Worst time complexity	`O(nlog(n))`
Average time complexity	`Θ(nlog(n))`
Space complexity (worst case)	`O(n)`

Understanding quick sort

Quick sort is another efficient sorting algorithm that applies the divide-and-conquer method. Although it does not divide into equal halves like merge sort, it creates dynamic partitions to sort the data. This is how quick sort works:

1. Pick a random value from the array, which we will call pivot.
2. Reorder the array so that the item that is smaller than the pivot goes to the left of it, and the items that are greater than, or equal to, the pivot go to the right of it. This is known as partitioning.
3. Recursively call *steps 1* and *2* to solve the two subarrays (left and right of pivot) until all items are sorted.

There are many ways to picking a pivot from the array. We can either choose the left-most item of the array or the right-most item of the array. In both cases, if the array is already sorted, it will take worst case complexity. Choosing a good pivot can improve the efficiency of the algorithm. There are some different ways of doing a partition. We will explain the *Hoare Partition*, which makes comparatively fewer swaps than other partition methods. Here is our pseudo algorithm for the quick sort. We will do in-place sorting so that no extra space is required:

```
procedure Quicksort(A : array,p :int ,r: int)
    if (p < r)
        q = Partition(A,p,r)
        Quicksort(A,p,q)
        Quicksort(A,q+1,r)
    end if
end procedure

procedure Partition(A : array,p :int ,r: int)
    pivot = A[p]
    i = p-1
    j = r+1
    while (true)
            do
             i := i + 1
            while A[i] < pivot
            do
             j := j - 1
            while A[j] > pivot

        if i < j then
            swap A[i] with A[j]
        else
            return j
        end if
    end while
end procedure
```

We used the first item as the pivot element. We can also choose the last item or take a median for choosing the pivot element. Let's now implement the algorithm using PHP.

Implementing quick sort

As shown in the pseudocode, we will have two functions to implement a quick sort: one function to do the quick sort itself, and the other for the partitioning. Here is the implementation to do the quick sort:

```
function quickSort(array &$arr, int $p, int $r) {
  if($p < $r) {
    $q = partition($arr, $p, $r);
    quickSort($arr, $p, $q);
    quickSort($arr, $q+1, $r);
  }
}
```

Here is the implementation to do the partitioning:

```
function partition(array &$arr, int $p, int $r){
  $pivot = $arr[$p];
  $i = $p-1;
  $j = $r+1;
  while(true)
  {
   do {
    $i++;
   } while($arr[$i] < $pivot && $arr[$i] != $pivot);
   do {
    $j--;
   } while($arr[$j] > $pivot && $arr[$j] != $pivot);

   if($i < $j) {
    $temp = $arr[$i];
    $arr[$i] = $arr[$j];
    $arr[$j] = $temp;
   } else {
    return $j;
      }
  }
}

 $arr = [20, 45, 93, 67, 10, 97, 52, 88, 33, 92];

quickSort($arr, 0, count($arr)-1);
echo implode(",", $arr);
```

If we visually illustrate the pivot and the sorting in the partitions, we can see the following image. For simplicity, we are only showing the steps where swapping took place:

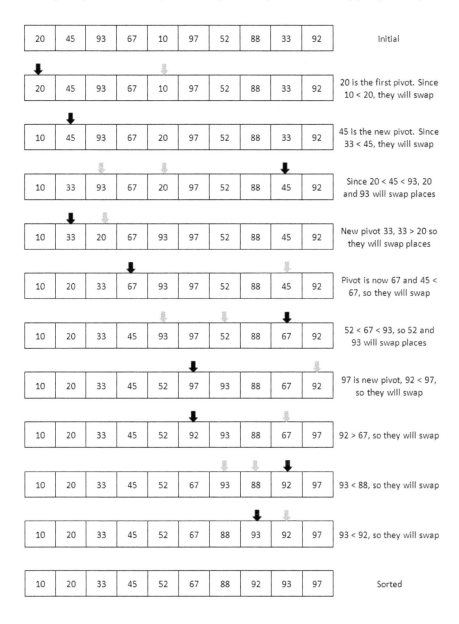

Complexity of quick sort

The worst case complexity of quick sort can be similar to bubble sort's complexity. The selection of the pivot actually causes this. Here is the complexity chart for a quick sort:

Best time complexity	$\Omega(n\log(n))$
Worst time complexity	$O(n^2)$
Average time complexity	$\Theta(n\log(n))$
Space complexity (worst case)	$O(\log(n))$

Understanding bucket sort

The bucket sort is also known as bin sort. Bucket sort is a distribution sorting system where array elements are placed in different buckets. Each bucket is then sorted individually by either another sorting algorithm, or by applying recursive bucket sorting. An implementation of bucket sort using PHP can look like this:

```php
function bucketSort(array &$data) {

    $n = count($data);
    if ($n <= 0)
        return;

    $min = min($data);
    $max = max($data);
    $bucket = [];
    $bLen = $max - $min + 1;

    $bucket = array_fill(0, $bLen, []);

    for ($i = 0; $i < $n; $i++) {
        array_push($bucket[$data[$i] - $min], $data[$i]);
    }

    $k = 0;
    for ($i = 0; $i < $bLen; $i++) {
        $bCount = count($bucket[$i]);

      for ($j = 0; $j < $bCount; $j++) {
            $data[$k] = $bucket[$i][$j];
```

```
            $k++;
        }
      }
    }
```

The time complexity of bucket sort is comparatively better than other comparison-based sorting algorithms. Here are the complexities for bucket sort:

Best time complexity	$\Omega(n+k)$
Worst time complexity	$O(n^2)$
Average time complexity	$\Theta(n+k)$
Space complexity (worst case)	$O(n)$

Using PHP's built-in sorting function

PHP has a rich library of predefined functions, and that also includes different sorting functions. It has different functions to sort a list of items in an array either by value or by key/index. We can also keep the association of the array's values with their respective keys while doing the sorting. Another important function of PHP is the built-in function for sorting a multi-dimensional array. Here is a summary of these functions:

Function name	Purpose
sort()	This sorts an array in ascending order. Value/key association is not preserved.
rsort()	Sort an array in reverse/descending order. Index/key association is not preserved.
asort()	Sort an array while maintaining index association.
arsort()	Sort an array in reverse order and maintain index association.
ksort()	Sort an array by key. It maintains key to data correlations. This is useful mainly for associative arrays.
krsort()	Sort an array by key in reverse order.
natsort()	Sort an array using a natural order algorithm, and Value/key association is maintained.
natcasesort()	Sort an array using a case insensitive "natural order" algorithm, and Value/key association is maintained.

usort()	Sort an array by values using a user-defined comparison function, and Value/Key association is not maintained. The second parameter is a callable function for comparison.
uksort()	Sort an array by keys using a user-defined comparison function, and Value/key association is maintained. The second parameter is a callable function for comparison.
uasort()	Sort an array by values using a user-defined comparison function, and Value/key association is maintained. The second parameter is a callable function for comparison.

For sort, rsort, ksort, krsort, asort, and arsort, the following sorting flags are available:

- **SORT_REGULAR**: compare items as they are (don't change types)
- **SORT_NUMERIC**: compare items numerically
- **SORT_STRING**: compare items as strings
- **SORT_LOCALE_STRING**: compare items as strings, based on the current locale
- **SORT_NATURAL**: compare items as strings using "natural ordering"

Summary

In this chapter, you learned about different sorting algorithms. Sorting is an integral part of our development process, and knowledge of different sorting algorithms and their complexity will help us decide the best choice for sorting algorithms based on our problem set. There are other algorithms for sorting, which can be found online for further study. We intentionally did not cover the heapsort in this chapter as we will discuss that in *Chapter 10*. In the next chapter, we will discuss another important topic concerning algorithms - searching.

8
Exploring Search Options

Along with sorting, searching is one of the most used algorithms in the programming world. Whether we are searching our phone book, e-mails, database, or files, we are actually performing some sort of search technique to locate the item we wish to find. It is imperative that searching and sorting are the two most important components of programming. In this chapter, you will learn about different searching techniques and how efficient they are. We will also learn about different ways of searching tree data structures.

Linear searching

One of the most common ways of performing a search is to compare each item with the one we are looking for. This is known as linear search or sequential search. It is the most basic way of performing a search. If we consider that we have n items in a list, in the worst case, we have to search n items to find a particular item. We can iterate through a list or array to find an item. Let's consider the following example:

```php
function search(array $numbers, int $needle): bool {
    $totalItems = count($numbers);

    for ($i = 0; $i < $totalItems; $i++) {
      if($numbers[$i] === $needle){
        return TRUE;
      }
     }
    return FALSE;
}
```

We have a function named `search`, which takes two arguments. One is the list of numbers, and the other is the number we are looking for in the list. We are running a for loop to iterate through each item in the list and compare them with our item. If a match is found, we return true and do not continue with the search. However, if the loop ends and nothing is found, we return false at the end of the function definition. Let's use the `search` function to find something using the following program:

```
$numbers = range(1, 200, 5);

if (search($numbers, 31)) {
    echo "Found";
} else {
    echo "Not found";
}
```

Here, we are generating a random array using PHP's built-in function range, with a range of 1 to 200 inclusive. Each item will have a gap of 5 like 1, 6, 11, 16, and so on; then we are searching 31, which is in the list as we have 6, 11, 16, 21, 26, 31, and so on. However, if we want to search for 32 or 33, then the item will not be found. So, for this case, our output will be `Found`.

One thing we need to remember here is that we are not worried about whether our list is in any particular order or organized in a certain way. If the item we are looking for is in the first position, that will be the best result. The worst result can be the last item or an item that is not in the list. In both cases, we have to iterate over all n items of the list. Here is the complexity for linear/sequential search:

Best time complexity	O(1)
Worst time complexity	O(n)
Average time complexity	O(n)
Space complexity (worst case)	O(1)

As we can see, the average or worst time complexity for a linear search is `O(n)`, and that does not change how we order the list of items. Now, if the items in the array are sorted in a particular order, then we might not have to do a linear search, and we can get a better result by doing a selective or calculative search. The most popular and well-known search algorithm is "binary search". Yes, it sounds like the binary search tree you learned in `Chapter 6`, *Understanding and Implementing Trees*, but we can use this algorithm without even constructing a binary search tree. So, let's explore this.

Binary search

Binary search is a very popular search algorithm in the programming world. In sequential search, we started from the beginning and scanned through each item to find the desired one. However, if the list is already sorted, then we do not need to search from the beginning or the end of the list. In a binary search algorithm, we start with the middle of the list, check whether the item in the middle is smaller or greater than the item we are looking for, and decide which way to go. This way, we divide the list by half and discard one half completely, just like the following image:

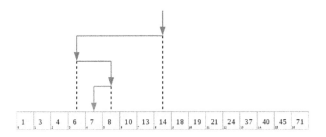

If we look at the preceding image, we have a sorted (ascending order) list of numbers in an array. We want to know whether item **7** is in the array or not. Since the array has 17 items (0 to 16 index), we will first go to the middle index, which is the eighth index for this example. Now, the eighth index has a value of **14**, which is greater than the value we are searching for, which is **7**. This means that if **7** is present in this array, it is to the left of **14**, since the numbers are already sorted. So, we are discarding the array from the eighth index to the sixteenth index as the number cannot be in that part of the array. Now, we repeat the same process and take the middle of the remaining part of the array, which is the third element of the remaining part. Now, the third element has a value of **6**, which is less than **7**. As a result, the item we are looking for is on the right-hand side of the third element, not on its left.

Now, we will check the fourth element to the seventh element of the array, with the middle element to now point at the fifth element. The fifth element value is **8**, which is more than **7**, the one we are looking for. So, we have to consider the left-hand side of the fifth element to find the item we are looking. This time, we have only two items remaining for the array to check, and the elements are fourth and fifth elements. As we are moving to the left, we will check the fourth element, and we see the value matches with **7**, which we are looking for. If the fourth index value was not **7**, the function will return false as there are no more elements left for checking. If we look at the arrow marks in the preceding image, we can see that within four steps, we have found the value we are looking for, whereas we had to take 17 steps to check all 17 numbers in a linear search function in a worst case situation. This is known as a binary search, or half-interval search, or logarithmic search.

As we have seen in our last image, we have to divide our initial list into halves and continue until we reach a point where we cannot make any further division to find our item. We can use an iterative way or recursive way to perform the division part. We will actually use both ways. So, let's first define the pseudocode of a binary search in the iterative way:

```
BinarySearch(A : list of sorted items, value) {
      low = 0
      high = N
      while (low <= high) {
// lowest int value, no fraction
          mid = (low + high) / 2
          if (A[mid] > value)
              high = mid - 1
          else if (A[mid] < value)
              low = mid + 1
          else
            return true
      }
      return false
  }
```

If we look at the pseudocode, we can see that we are adjusting our low and high based on our mid value. If the value we are looking for is greater than what we have in mid, we are adjusting the lower bound to be mid+1. If it's less than the mid value, then we are setting the higher value as mid-1. It continues until the lower value becomes bigger than the higher value or the item is found. If the item is not found, we return false at the end of the function. Now, let's implement the pseudocode using PHP:

```php
function binarySearch(array $numbers, int $needle): bool {
    $low = 0;
    $high = count($numbers) - 1;
    while ($low <= $high) {
      $mid = (int) (($low + $high) / 2);

      if ($numbers[$mid] > $needle) {
          $high = $mid - 1;
      } else if ($numbers[$mid] < $needle) {
          $low = $mid + 1;
      } else {
          return TRUE;
      }
    }
    return FALSE;
}
```

In our implementation, we have followed most of the pseudocode in the preceding page. Now, let's run the code with two searches, where we know one value is in the list and one is not in the list:

```
$numbers = range(1, 200, 5);

$number = 31;
if (binarySearch($numbers, $number) !== FALSE) {
    echo "$number Found \n";
} else {
    echo "$number Not found \n";
}

$number = 500;
if (binarySearch($numbers, $number) !== FALSE) {
    echo "$number Found \n";
} else {
    echo "$number Not found \n";
}
```

As we know from our previous linear search code, 31 is in the list, and it should show Found. However, 500 is not in the list, and it should show Not found. If we run the code, here is the output we will see in our console:

```
31 Found
500 Not found
```

We will now write the recursive algorithm for the binary search, which can also be handy for us. The pseudocode will require us to send extra arguments every time we call the function. We need to send the low and high with every recursive call, which we did not do for the iterative one:

```
BinarySearch(A : list of sorted items, value, low, high) {

    if (high < low)
          return false

      // lowest int value, no fraction
          mid = (low + high) / 2

          if (A[mid] > value)
              return BinarySearch(A, value, low, mid - 1)
          else if (A[mid] < value)
              return BinarySearch(A, value, mid + 1, high)
      else
        return TRUE;
}
```

We can see from the preceding pseudocode that we are now having low and high as parameters, and in each call, the new values are sent as arguments. We have the boundary condition where we are checking whether the low is bigger than the high. The code looks smaller and cleaner compared to the iterative one. Now, let's implement this using PHP 7:

```php
function binarySearch(array $numbers, int $needle,
int $low, int $high): bool {

    if ($high < $low) {
    return FALSE;
    }

    $mid = (int) (($low + $high) / 2);

    if ($numbers[$mid] > $needle) {
       return binarySearch($numbers, $needle, $low, $mid - 1);
    } else if ($numbers[$mid] < $needle) {
       return binarySearch($numbers, $needle, $mid + 1, $high);
    } else {
       return TRUE;
    }
}
```

Now, let's use the following code to run this search recursively:

```php
$numbers = range(1, 200, 5);

$number = 31;
if (binarySearch($numbers, $number, 0, count($numbers) - 1) !== FALSE) {
    echo "$number Found \n";
} else {
    echo "$number Not found \n";
}

$number = 500;
if (binarySearch($numbers, $number, 0, count($numbers) - 1) !== FALSE) {
    echo "$number Found \n";
} else {
    echo "$number Not found \n";
}
```

As we can see from the preceding code, we sent 0 and `count($numbers)` -1 in each call of recursive binary search for the first time. Then, this high and low is auto-adjusted on each recursive call based on the mid value. So, we have seen both the iterative and recursive implementation of binary search. Based on our needs, we can use any one of these in our program. Now, let's analyze the binary search algorithm and find out how it is better than our linear or sequential search algorithm.

Analysis of binary search algorithm

So far, we have seen that for each iteration, we are dividing the list by half and discarding one half completely for searching. This makes our list look like $n/2$, $n/4$, $n/8$, and so on after 1, 2, and 3 iterations, respectively. So, we can say that after Kth iteration, $n/2^k$ items will be left. We can easily say that, the last iteration occurs when $n/2^k = 1$, or we can say that, $2^k = n$. So, taking log from both side yields, $k = log(n)$, which is the worst case running time for binary search algorithm. Here is the complexity for binary search algorithm:

Best time complexity	`O(1)`
Worst time complexity	`O(log n)`
Average time complexity	`O(log n)`
Space complexity (worst case)	`O(1)`

If our array or list is already sorted, it is always preferred to apply binary search for better performance. Now, whether the list is sorted in the ascending order or descending order, it can have some impact on our calculation of low and high. The logic we have seen so far is for the ascending order. If an array is sorted in the descending order, the logic will be swapped where greater than will become less than, and vice versa. One thing to notice here is that the binary search algorithm provides us with the index we have found of the search item. However, there might be some cases where we not only need to know whether the number exists, but also to find the first appearance or last appearance in the list. If we use binary search algorithm, then it will return true or maximum index number, where the search algorithm found the number. However, it might not be the first appearance or last appearance. For that, we will modify the binary search algorithm a little, which we will call repetitive binary search tree algorithm.

Repetitive binary search tree algorithm

Consider the following image. We have an array with repetitive items. If we try to find the first appearance of **2** from the array, binary search algorithm from the last section will give us the fifth element. However, from the following image, we can see clearly it is not the fifth element; instead, it is the second element, which is the correct answer. So, a modification is required in our binary search algorithm. The modification will be a repetitive searching until we reach the first appearance:

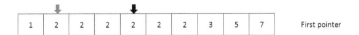

Here is the modified solution using iterative approach:

```
function repetitiveBinarySearch(array $numbers, int $needle): int {
    $low = 0;
    $high = count($numbers) - 1;
    $firstOccurrence = -1;

    while ($low <= $high) {
      $mid = (int) (($low + $high) / 2);

      if ($numbers[$mid] === $needle) {
          $firstOccurrence = $mid;
          $high = $mid - 1;
      } else if ($numbers[$mid] > $needle) {
          $high = $mid - 1;
      } else {
          $low = $mid + 1;
      }
    }
    return $firstOccurrence;
}
```

As we can see, first we are checking whether the mid has the value we are looking for. If it is true, then we are assigning the middle index as first occurrence, and we will search the left of the middle element to check for any occurrences of the number we are looking for. We then continue the iteration until we have searched each index ($low is greater than $high). If no further occurrence is found, then the variable first occurrence will have the value of the first index where we found the item. If not, we are returning -1 as usual. Let's run the following code to check whether our results are correct or not:

```
$numbers = [1, 2, 2, 2, 2, 2, 2, 2, 2, 3, 3, 3, 3, 3, 4, 4, 5, 5];

$number = 2;

$pos = repetitiveBinarySearch($numbers, $number);

if ($pos >= 0) {
    echo "$number Found at position $pos \n";
} else {
    echo "$number Not found \n";
}

$number = 5;
$pos = repetitiveBinarySearch($numbers, $number);

if ($pos >= 0) {
    echo "$number Found at position $pos \n";
```

```
} else {
    echo "$number Not found \n";
}
```

Now, we have an array with repetitive values of 2, 3, 4, and 5. We want to search the array and find the position or index where the value has appeared for the first time. For example, if we are searching 2 in a regular binary search function, it will return eighth as the position where it found the value 2. In our case, we are actually looking for the second index, which actually holds the first appearance of item 2. Our function `repetitiveBinarySearch` does exactly that, and we are storing the return position to a variable called `$pos`. We are showing the output if the number is found along with the position. Now, if we run the preceding code in our console, we will have the following output:

```
2 Found at position 1
5 Found at position 16
```

This matches our expected results. So, we can say we now have a repetitive binary search algorithm to find first and last occurrences of an item from a given sorted list. This might be a very handy function to solve many problems.

So far, from our examples and analysis, we can conclude that binary searching is definitely faster than linear searching. However, the major prerequisite is to have the list sorted before applying binary search. Applying binary search in an unsorted array will lead us to inaccurate results. There can be situations where we receive an array and we are not sure whether the array is sorted or not. Now, the question is, "Should we sort the array first and apply binary search algorithm in such cases? Or should we just run a linear search algorithm to find an item?" Let's discuss this a little, so that we know how to handle such situations.

Searching an unsorted array - should we sort first?

So now, we are in a situation where we have an array with *n* items and they are not sorted. Since we know binary search is faster, we have decided to sort it first and then search for the item using a binary search. If we do so, we have to remember that the best sorting algorithms have a worst time complexity of `O(nlog n)`, and for binary search, the worst case complexity is `O(log n)`. So, if we sort and then apply the binary search, the complexity will be `O(n log n)` as it is the biggest one compared to `O(log n)`. However, we also know that for any linear or sequential search (sorted or unsorted), the worst time complexity is `O(n)`, which is much better than `O(n log n)`.

Based on the complexity comparison of `O(n)` and `O(n log n)`, we can clearly say that performing a linear search is a better option if the array is not sorted.

Let's consider another situation where we need to search a given array a multiple number of times. Let's denote *k* as the number of times we want to search the array. If *k* is 1, then we can easily apply our linear approach discussed in the last paragraph. It will be fine if the value of *k* is smaller compared to the size of the array, which is denoted by *n*. However, if the value of *k* is closer or bigger than *n*, then we have some problems applying the linear approach here.

Let's assume that *k = n*, then for *n* time, linear search will have a complexity of $O(n^2)$. Now, if we go for the sort and then search option then even if *k* is bigger, the onetime sorting will take `O(n log n)` time complexity. Then, each search will take `O(log n)`, and *n* times searching will have a worst case of `O(n log n)` complexity. If we take the worst running case here, we will have `O(n log n)` for sorting and searching *k* items, which is better than sequential searching.

So, we can come to the conclusion that if a number of search operations is smaller compared to the size of the array, it is better not to sort the array and perform the sequential search. However, if the number of search operation is bigger compared to the size of array, it is better to sort the array first and then apply the binary search.

Over the years, the binary search algorithm evolved and came up with different variations. Instead of choosing the middle index every time, we can make calculative decisions to choose which index we should use next. That is what makes these variations work efficiently. We will now talk about two such variations of binary search algorithm: interpolation search and exponential search.

Interpolation search

In binary search algorithm, we always start with the middle of the array to start the searching process. If an array is uniformly distributed and we are looking for an item, which, may be close to the end of array, then searching from the middle might not sound like a good choice to us. Interpolation search can be very helpful in such cases. Interpolation search is an improvement over binary search algorithm. Interpolation search may go to different location based on the value of the searched key. For example, if we are searching a key that is close to the beginning of the array, it will go to the first part of the array instead of starting from the middle. The position is calculated using a probe position calculator equation, which looks like this:

```
pos = low + [ (key-arr[low])*(high-low) / (arr[high]-arr[low]) ]
```

As we can see, we are going from our generic `mid = (low+high)/2` equation to a more complex looking equation. This formula will return a higher value if the searched key is closer to `arr[high]` and a much lower value if the key is closer to `arr[low]`. Now, let's implement this search method with the help of our binary search code:

```
function interpolationSearch(array $arr, int $key): int {
    $low = 0;
    $high = count($arr) - 1;

    while ($arr[$high] != $arr[$low] && $key >= $arr[$low] &&
      $key <= $arr[$high]) {

    $mid = intval($low + (($key - $arr[$low]) * ($high - $low)
    / ($arr[$high] - $arr[$low])));

      if ($arr[$mid] < $key)
          $low = $mid + 1;
      else if ($key < $arr[$mid])
          $high = $mid - 1;
      else
          return $mid;
    }

    if ($key == $arr[$low])
      return $low;
    else
      return -1;
}
```

Here, we are calculating in a different way. Though it is taking more computational steps, the good part is that if the list is uniformly distributed, then the average complexity of this algorithm is `O(log (log n))`, which is much better compared to binary search's complexity of `O(log n)`. Also, we have to be careful if the distributions of the keys are not uniform. In this case, the performance of the interpolation search could degrade.

Now, we will explore another variation of binary search known as exponential search, which can improve the algorithm.

Exponential search

In binary search, we are searching the whole list for a given key. Exponential search improves binary search by deciding the lower and upper bound of the search so that we do not end up searching the whole list. It improves the number of comparisons we need to find an element. The search is done in the following two steps:

1. We determine the bound size by looking for the first exponent k where the value of 2^k is greater than the search item. Now, 2^k and 2^{k-1} become the upper bound and lower bound, respectively.
2. Apply binary search algorithm for the bound 2^k and 2^{k-1}.

Let's now implement the exponential search using our recursive `binarySearch` function:

```
function exponentialSearch(array $arr, int $key): int {
    $size = count($arr);

    if ($size == 0)
        return -1;

    $bound = 1;
    while ($bound < $size && $arr[$bound] < $key) {
        $bound *= 2;
    }
    return binarySearch($arr, $key, intval($bound / 2),
min($bound, $size));
}
```

Here, in step one, we are taking i steps to determine the boundary. So, the algorithm takes `O(log i)` complexity. We have to remember that here, i is much smaller than n. Then, we are doing a binary search with a bound of 2^j to 2^{j-1} where $j = log\ i$. We know binary search takes `O(log n)` complexity where n is the size of the list. However, since we are doing a smaller bound search, we are actually searching $2^{log\ i} \backslash - 2^{log\ i} - 1 = 2^{log\ i - 1}$ size. So, the complexity of this bound will be $log\ (2^{log\ i - 1}) = log\ (i) - 1 = O(log\ i)$.

So, the complexity of the exponential search is as follows:

Best time complexity	`O(1)`
Worst time complexity	`O(log i)`
Average time complexity	`O(log i)`
Space complexity (worst case)	`O(1)`

Search using hash table

Hash table can be a very efficient data structure when it comes to search operations. Since hash tables store data in an associative manner, if we know where to look for the data, we can easily get the data quickly. In the hash table, each data has a unique index associated with it. If we know which index to look at, we can find the key very easily. Usually, in other programming languages, we have to use a separate hash function to calculate the hash index to store the value. The hash function is designed to generate the same index for the same key and also avoid collision. However, one of the great features of PHP is that PHP array itself is a hash table, in its underlying C implementation. Since an array is dynamic, we do not have to worry about the size of array or overflow array with many values. We need to store the values in an associative array so that we can associate the value with a key. The key can be the value itself if it is a string or an integer. Let's run an example to understand searching with a hash table:

```
$arr = [];
$count = rand(10, 30);

for($i = 0; $i<$count;$i++) {
    $val = rand(1,500);
    $arr[$val] = $val;
}

$number = 100;
if(isset($arr[$number])) {
    echo "$number found ";
} else {
    echo "$number not found";
}
```

We have just built a simple random associative array where value and key are the same. Since we are using PHP array, though value can have a range of 1 to 500, the actual array size is anything from 10 to 30. If it were in any other language, we would have constructed an array with a size of 501 to accommodate this value to be a key. That is why the hash function is used to calculate the index. If we want, we can also use the PHP's built-in function for hashing:

```
string hash(string $algo ,string $data [,bool $raw_output = false ])
```

The first parameter takes the type of algorithm we want to use for hashing. We can choose from md5, sha1, sha256, crc32, and so on. Each of the algorithms produces a fixed length hash output, which we can use as key for our hash table.

If we look at our searching part, we can see that we are actually checking the associated index directly. This makes our searching in complexity `O(1)`. In PHP, it might be beneficial to use the hash table for quick searching even without using the hash function. However, we can always use the hash function if we want.

So far, we have covered searching based on arrays and linear structures. We will now shift our focus to hierarchical data structure searching such as searching trees and graphs. Though we have not discussed graphs yet (we will discuss them in the next chapter), we will keep our focus on tree searching, which can also be applied in graph searching.

Tree searching

One of the best ways to search hierarchical data is to create a search tree. In `Chapter 6`, *Understanding and Implementing Trees*, we saw how to construct a binary search tree and increase the efficiency in searching. We have also discovered different ways to traverse a tree. Now, we will explore the two most popular ways of searching a tree structure commonly known as breadth first search (BFS) and depth first search (DFS).

Breadth first search

In a tree structure, a root is connected to its child node, and each child node can be represented as a tree. We have already seen this in `Chapter 6`, *Understanding and Implementing Trees*. In a breadth first search, popularly known as BFS, we start from a node (mostly root node) and first visit all adjacent or neighbor nodes before visiting the other neighbor nodes. In other words, we have to move level by level while we are applying BFS. As we search level by level, this technique is known as breadth first search. In the following tree structure, we can use BFS:

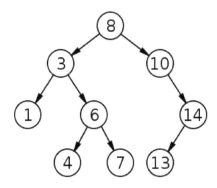

For this tree, the BFS will follow the nodes like this: $8 \rightarrow 3 \rightarrow 10 \rightarrow 1 \rightarrow 6 \rightarrow 14 \rightarrow 4 \rightarrow 7 \rightarrow 13$

The pseudocode of BFS will look like this:

```
procedure BFS(Node root)
  Q := empty queue
  Q.enqueue(root);

  while(Q != empty)
     u := Q.dequeue()

     for each node w that is childnode of u
        Q.enqueue(w)
     end for each
  end while
end procedure
```

We can see that we have kept one queue for tracking which nodes we need to visit. We can keep another queue to hold the sequence of visits and return it to show the visit sequence. Now, we will implement the BFS using PHP 7.

Implementing breadth first search

Since we have not covered the graph in detail so far, we will keep our implementation for BFS and DFS strictly for tree structure. Also, we will use the generic tree structure we have seen in Chapter 6, *Understanding and Implementing Trees*, (not even binary tree). We will use the same TreeNode class to define our nodes and relationship with children. So, let's now define the Tree class with BFS functionality:

```
class TreeNode {

    public $data = NULL;
    public $children = [];

    public function __construct(string $data = NULL) {
      $this->data = $data;
    }

    public function addChildren(TreeNode $node) {
      $this->children[] = $node;
    }
}

class Tree {

    public $root = NULL;
```

```
public function __construct(TreeNode $node) {
  $this->root = $node;
}

public function BFS(TreeNode $node): SplQueue {

  $queue = new SplQueue;
  $visited = new SplQueue;

  $queue->enqueue($node);

  while (!$queue->isEmpty()) {
      $current = $queue->dequeue();
      $visited->enqueue($current);

      foreach ($current->children as $child) {
        $queue->enqueue($child);
      }
  }
  return $visited;
  }
}
```

We have implemented the BFS method inside the tree class. We are taking the root node as the starting point for the breadth first search. Here, we have two queues: one for keeping the nodes that we need to visit, and one for nodes which we have visited. We are also returning the visited queue at the end of the method. Let's now imitate the tree we have seen at the beginning of the section. We want to put the data just like the tree shown in the image and also check whether the BFS actually returns our expected pattern of;
$8 \rightarrow 3 \rightarrow 10 \rightarrow 1 \rightarrow 6 \rightarrow 14 \rightarrow 4 \rightarrow 7 \rightarrow 13$:

```
$root = new TreeNode("8");

$tree = new Tree($root);

$node1 = new TreeNode("3");
$node2 = new TreeNode("10");
$root->addChildren($node1);
$root->addChildren($node2);

$node3 = new TreeNode("1");
$node4 = new TreeNode("6");
$node5 = new TreeNode("14");
$node1->addChildren($node3);
$node1->addChildren($node4);
$node2->addChildren($node5);
```

```
$node6 = new TreeNode("4");
$node7 = new TreeNode("7");
$node8 = new TreeNode("13");
$node4->addChildren($node6);
$node4->addChildren($node7);
$node5->addChildren($node8);


$visited = $tree->BFS($tree->root);

while (!$visited->isEmpty()) {
  echo $visited->dequeue()->data . "\n";
}
```

We are building the whole tree structure here by creating nodes and attaching them to root and other nodes. Once the tree is done, we are calling the BFS method to find the full sequence of traversal. The while loop at the end is printing sequences of our visited nodes. Here is the output of the preceding code:

```
8
3
10
1
6
14
4
7
13
```

We have received our expected result. Now, if we want to search to find whether a node is there or not, we can add a simple condition check for our $current node value. If it matches, then we can return the visited queue.

The BFS has a worst complexity of **O** ($|V| + |E|$), where *V* is the number of vertices or nodes and *E* is the number of edges or connections between the nodes. For space complexity, worst case is **O** ($|V|$).

> The graph BFS is similar, but with a minor difference. Since the graph can be cyclic (can create a loop), we need to make sure we are not visiting the same node again and again to create an infinite loop. In order to avoid revisiting graph nodes, we have to keep track of the node we have visited. For marking a visited node, we can either use a queue, or use a graph coloring algorithm. We will explore this in the next chapter.

Depth first search

Depth first search, or DFS, is a search technique where we start searching from a node and go as deep as possible to the node from the target node through the branches. DFS is different from BFS, and we try to dig deeper instead of spreading out first. DFS grows vertically and backtracks when it reaches the end of the branch and moves the next available adjacent nodes until the search is over. We can take the same tree image from the last section, which is shown as follows:

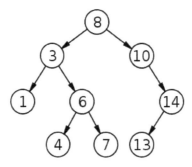

If we apply DFS here, the traversal will be $8 \rightarrow 3 \rightarrow 1 \rightarrow 6 \rightarrow 4 \rightarrow 7 \rightarrow 10 \rightarrow 14 \rightarrow 13$.
We start from the root and then visit the first child, which is **3**. However, instead of going to **10** like the BFS, we will explore the child nodes of **3** and do this repeatedly until we reach the bottom of the branch. In BFS, we had taken the iterative approach. For DFS, we will take the recursive approach. Let's now write the pseudocode for DFS:

```
procedure DFS(Node current)
    for each node v that is childnode of current
        DFS(v)
    end for each
end procedure
```

Implementing depth first search

The pseudocode for DFS looks straightforward. In order to track the sequence of node visits, we need to use a queue, which will track the nodes inside our `Tree` class. Here is our implementation of `Tree` class with recursive DFS:

```
class TreeNode {

    public $data = NULL;
    public $children = [];
```

```
    public function __construct(string $data = NULL) {
      $this->data = $data;
    }

    public function addChildren(TreeNode $node) {
      $this->children[] = $node;
    }
}

class Tree {

    public $root = NULL;
    public $visited;


    public function __construct(TreeNode $node) {
      $this->root = $node;
      $this->visited = new SplQueue;
    }

    public function DFS(TreeNode $node) {

      $this->visited->enqueue($node);

      if($node->children){
          foreach ($node->children as $child) {
        $this->DFS($child);
          }
      }

    }
}
```

As we can see, we have added one extra property in the tree class $visited to keep track of the visited nodes. When we are calling the DFS method, we are adding the node to the queue. Now, if we use the same tree structure from the previous section, and just add the DFS call and fetch the visited part, it will look like this:

```
try {

    $root = new TreeNode("8");

    $tree = new Tree($root);

    $node1 = new TreeNode("3");
    $node2 = new TreeNode("10");
    $root->addChildren($node1);
    $root->addChildren($node2);
```

```
$node3 = new TreeNode("1");
$node4 = new TreeNode("6");
$node5 = new TreeNode("14");
$node1->addChildren($node3);
$node1->addChildren($node4);
$node2->addChildren($node5);

$node6 = new TreeNode("4");
$node7 = new TreeNode("7");
$node8 = new TreeNode("13");
$node4->addChildren($node6);
$node4->addChildren($node7);
$node5->addChildren($node8);


$tree->DFS($tree->root);

$visited = $tree->visited;
while (!$visited->isEmpty()) {
  echo $visited->dequeue()->data . "\n";
}
} catch (Exception $e) {
  echo $e->getMessage();
}
```

Since DFS does not return anything, we are using the class property `visited` to get the queue so that we can show the sequence of visited nodes. If we run this program in console, we will have the following output:

```
8
3
1
6
4
7
10
14
13
```

The results correspond to what was expected. If we need an iterative solution for DFS, we have to remember that we need to use stack instead of queue to track the next node to visit. However, as stack follows the LIFO principle, for our mentioned graph image, the output will be different from our initial thought. Here is the implementation using the iterative approach:

```
class TreeNode {
    public $data = NULL;
```

```php
    public $children = [];

    public function __construct(string $data = NULL) {
      $this->data = $data;
    }

    public function addChildren(TreeNode $node) {
      $this->children[] = $node;
    }

}

class Tree {
    public $root = NULL;

    public function __construct(TreeNode $node) {
      $this->root = $node;
    }

    public function DFS(TreeNode $node): SplQueue {

      $stack = new SplStack;
      $visited = new SplQueue;

      $stack->push($node);

      while (!$stack->isEmpty()) {
          $current = $stack->pop();
          $visited->enqueue($current);
          foreach ($current->children as $child) {
            $stack->push($child);
          }
      }
      return $visited;
    }
}

try {

    $root = new TreeNode("8");
    $tree = new Tree($root);

    $node1 = new TreeNode("3");
    $node2 = new TreeNode("10");
    $root->addChildren($node1);
    $root->addChildren($node2);

    $node3 = new TreeNode("1");
```

```
$node4 = new TreeNode("6");
$node5 = new TreeNode("14");
$node1->addChildren($node3);
$node1->addChildren($node4);
$node2->addChildren($node5);

$node6 = new TreeNode("4");
$node7 = new TreeNode("7");
$node8 = new TreeNode("13");
$node4->addChildren($node6);
$node4->addChildren($node7);
$node5->addChildren($node8);

$visited = $tree->DFS($tree->root);

while (!$visited->isEmpty()) {
    echo $visited->dequeue()->data . "\n";
}
} catch (Exception $e) {
    echo $e->getMessage();
}
```

It looks very similar to our iterative BFS algorithm. The main difference is the use of stack data structure instead of queue data structure to store the visited nodes. It will also have an impact on the output. The preceding code will produce the output 8 → 10 → 14 → 13 → 3 → 6 → 7 → 4 → 1. This is different from our previous output shown in the last section. As we are using stack, the output is actually correct. We are using stack to push the child nodes of a particular node. For our root node, which has value **8**, we have the first child node with value of **3**. It is pushed to the stack, and then, the second child node of root has the value of **10** and is also pushed to the stack. Since value **10** was pushed last, it will come first, following the LIFO principle of stack. So, the ordering is always going to be starting from the last branch to the first branch if we are using stack. However, if we want to keep the node ordering from left to right, then we need to make a small adjustment in our DFS code. Here is the code block with the change:

```
public function DFS(TreeNode $node): SplQueue {

    $stack = new SplStack;
    $visited = new SplQueue;

    $stack->push($node);

    while (!$stack->isEmpty()) {
        $current = $stack->pop();
        $visited->enqueue($current);
        $current->children = array_reverse($current->children);
```

```
      foreach ($current->children as $child) {
        $stack->push($child);
      }
    }
    return $visited;
  }
```

The only difference from the previous code block is that we are adding the following line before visiting the child nodes from a particular node:

```
$current->children = array_reverse($current->children);
```

Since stack does the Last-In, First-Out (LIFO), by reversing, we are making sure the first node is visited first, as we reversed the order. In fact, it will simply work as a queue. This will produce the desired sequence as shown in the DFS section. If we have a binary tree, then we do it easily without requiring any reversal as we can choose to push the right child first, followed by the left child node to pop the left child first.

DFS has a worst complexity of **O** ($|V| + |E|$), where V is the number of vertices or nodes and E is the number of edges or connections between the nodes. For space complexity, the worst case is **O** ($|V|$), which is similar to BFS.

Summary

In this chapter, we discussed different searching algorithms and their complexities. You learned how to improve searching with a hash table to get a constant time result. We also explored BFS and DFS, two of the most important methods for hierarchical data searching. We will use similar concepts for graph data structure, which we are about to explore in the next chapter. Graph algorithms are crucial for solving many problems and are used heavily in the programming world. Let's get going with another interesting topic - the graph.

9
Putting Graphs into Action

The graph is one of the most interesting data structures that is used to solve various real-life problems. Whether we are talking about showing directions on maps, finding the shortest route, planning for complex network flow, finding a connection between profiles in social media, or recommendations, we are dealing with graph data structures and their associated algorithms. Graphs give us so many ways to solve problems that they have been used frequently to solve complex problems. As a result, it is very important for us to understand graphs and how we can use them in our solutions.

Understanding graph properties

A graph is a collection of vertices or nodes that are connected to each other through edges. These edges can be ordered or unordered, which means that the edge can have a direction associated with it or it can be non-directed, which is also known as bidirectional edge. We represent a graph using a set G in relationship with vertices V and edges E as follows:

$G = (V, E)$

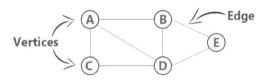

In the preceding diagram, we have five vertices and six edges:

$V = \{A, B, C, D, E\}$

$E = \{AB, AC, AD, BD, BE, CD, DE\}$

If we consider the previous diagram, the connectivity between **A** and **B** can be represented as **AB** or **BA** as we have not defined the direction for the connectivity. One of the significant differences between the graph and the tree data structures is that the graph can form a cycle or loop, but a tree data structure cannot. Unlike a tree data structure, we can start from any vertices in a graph data structure. Also, we can have a direct edge between any two vertices, whereas in a tree, two nodes can only be connected if the child node is the immediate descendant of the parent node.

There are different properties and keywords related to graphs. We will now explore those terms before moving on to further discussions on graphs and their applications.

Vertex

Each node in a graph is called a vertex. Usually, a vertex is represented as a circle. In our diagram, the nodes **A**, **B**, **C**, **D**, and **E** are vertices.

Edge

An edge is a connection between two vertices. Usually, it is represented by a line drawn between two vertices. In the previous diagram, we had edges between **A** and **B**, **A** and **C**, **A** and **D**, **B** and **D**, **C** and **D**, **B** and **E**, and **D** and **E**. We can represent the edge as **AB** or (**A**, **B**). Edges can be of three types:

- **Directed edge**: If an edge is marked with an arrow, then it indicates a directed edge. A directed edge is unidirectional. The head of the arrow is the end vertex and the tail of the arrow is the start vertex:

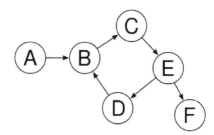

In the preceding diagram, we can see that **A** has a directed edge to **B**, which means **A**, **B** is an edge, but not vice versa (**B**, **A**). So, this is an example of a unidirectional edge, or directed edge.

- **Undirected edge**: An undirected edge is a connection between two vertices without any direction. This means that the edge satisfies a bidirectional relationship. The following diagram is an example of an undirected graph, where **A** is connected to **B** in such a way that both edges (**A**, **B**) and (**B**, **A**) are the same:

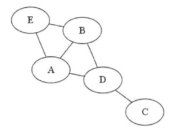

- **Weighted edge**: When an edge carries additional information, such as cost, distance, or other information, we call that edge a weighted edge. This is used for many graph algorithms. In the following diagram, the weight for edge (**A**, **B**) is **5**. This can be distance, or cost, or anything, as per the definition of the graph:

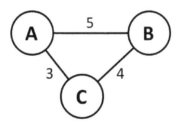

Adjacent

Two vertices are adjacent if they have an edge in between them. Two vertices A and B are said to be adjacent if they have a direct edge between them. In the following diagram, we can see that vertex **1** and vertex **2** are connected with the edge **e1**, and as a result, they are called adjacent. Since vertex **2** has no edge between vertex 3 and 4, vertex **2** is not adjacent to vertex **3** and vertex **4**.

Incident

An edge is incident on a vertex if the vertex is one of the end points of the edge. Also, two edges are incident if both of them share a vertex. If we consider the following diagram, we can see the incident edges (**e1**, **e2**), (**e2**, **e3**), and (**e1**, **e3**) sharing vertex **1** among themselves. We also have incident edges (**e3**, **e4**) that share vertex **4** among themselves and edges (**e2**, **e4**) that share vertex **3** among themselves. Similarly, we can say that vertex **1** is incident on edges **e1**, **e2**, and **e3**, vertex **2** is incident on edge **e1**, vertex **3** is incident on edges **e2**, and **e4**, and vertex **4** is incident on edges **e3**, and **e4**:

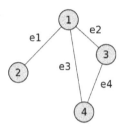

Indegree and outdegree

The total count of incoming edges to a particular vertex is known as the indegree of that vertex, and the total number of outgoing edges from a particular vertex is known as the outdegree of that vertex. If we consider the directed edges of the following diagram, we can say that vertex **A** has an indegree of 0 and an outdegree of 1, vertex **B** has an indegree of 2 and an outdegree 1, vertex **C** has an indegree 1 and an outdegree of 1, vertex **D** has an indegree of 1 and an outdegree of 1, vertex **E** has an indegree of 1 and an outdegree of 2, and lastly, vertex **F** has an indegree of 1 and an outdegree of 0.

Path

A path is a sequence of vertices and edges that starts from a starting vertex and ends in another vertex that we are trying to reach. In the following diagram, the path from **A** to **F** is represented by (**A**, **B**), (**B**, **C**), (**C**, **E**), and (**E**, **F**):

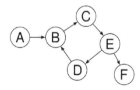

Types of graphs

There are different types of graphs available based on how they are drawn or represented. Each type of graph has a different behavior and usage. We will focus on four main types of graph.

Directed graphs

If a graph contains only directed edges, then the graph is known as a directed graph. A directed graph is also known as a digraph or a directed network. The following diagram represents a directed graph. Here, the (**A**, **B**), (**B**, **C**), (**C**, **E**), (**E**, **D**), (**E**, **F**), and (**D**, **B**) edges are directed edges. Since the edges are directed, edge **AB** is not the same as edge **BA**:

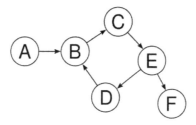

Undirected graphs

If a graph contains only undirected edges, then the graph is an undirected graph. In other words, the edges in an undirected graph are bidirectional. Sometimes, the undirected graph is also known as an undirected network. In an undirected graph, if vertex A is connected to vertex B, then it is assumed that both (A, B) and (B, A) represent the same edge. The following diagram shows an example of an undirected graph where all the edges do not have arrows to indicate direction:

Weighted graphs

If all the edges of a graph are weighted edges, then the graph is known as a weighted graph. We will talk a lot about weighted graphs in the upcoming sections. Weighted graphs can be directed or undirected graphs. Each edge must have a value associated with it. The weight of an edge is always referred to as the cost of the edge. The following diagram represents an undirected weighted graph with five vertices and seven edges. Here, the weight of the edge between vertex **1** and **2** is **2**, the edge between vertex **1** and **4** is **5**, and the edge between vertex **4** and **5** is **58**:

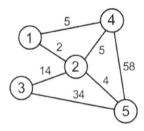

Directed acyclic graphs (DAG)

An acyclic graph is a graph without a cycle or loop. If we want to visit other nodes from a particular node, we will not visit any of the nodes twice. A directed acyclic graph, popularly known as a DAG, is a directed graph that is acyclic. A directed acyclic graph has many usages in graph algorithms. A directed acyclic graph has a topological ordering, where the ordering of the vertices is such that the starting endpoint of every edge occurs earlier in the ordering than the ending endpoints of the edges. The following diagram represents a DAG:

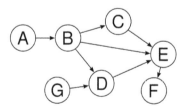

From the first look, it seems that **B**, **C**, **E**, and **D** form a cycle, but close observation shows that they do not form a cycle, whereas, the example we have used in the directed graph section is a perfect example of a cyclic graph.

Representing graphs in PHP

Since graphs are represented with vertices and edges, we have to consider both in representing the graph. There are several ways to represent a graph, but the most popular ones are as follows:

- Adjacency list
- Adjacency matrix

Adjacency lists

We can represent a graph using a linked list where one array will be used for vertices and each vertex will have a linked list, which will represent the edges between adjacent vertices. An example graph looks like this when represented in an adjacency list:

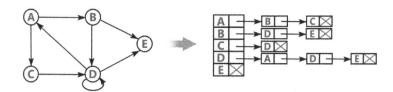

Adjacency matrix

In an adjacency matrix, we represent the graph in a two-dimensional array, where each node represents the array index horizontally and vertically. If the edge from A to B is directional, then we mark that array index [A][B] to 1 to mark the connection; otherwise, it's 0. If the edge is not directional, then both [A][B] and [B][A] are set to 1. If the graph is a weighted graph, then [A][B] or [B][A] will store the weight instead of 1. The following diagram shows the undirected graph representation using a matrix:

$$
\begin{array}{c c c c c c}
 & A & B & C & D & E \\
A & 0 & 1 & 1 & 1 & 0 \\
B & 1 & 0 & 0 & 1 & 1 \\
C & 1 & 0 & 0 & 1 & 0 \\
D & 1 & 1 & 1 & 1 & 1 \\
E & 0 & 1 & 0 & 1 & 0
\end{array}
$$

This one shows the directed graph representation of the matrix:

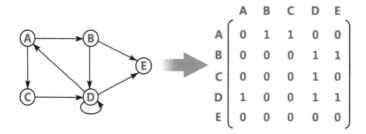

Though our graph representation shows an alphabetic representation of array indexes in both an adjacency list and matrix, we can use a numeric index to represent vertices as well.

Revisiting BFS and DFS for graphs

We have already seen how we can implement a **breadth first search** (**BFS**) and a **depth first search** (**DFS**) in a tree structure. We will revisit our BFS and DFS for graphs. The difference between a tree implementation and a graph implementation is that in a graph implementation, we can start from any vertex, whereas we start from the root of the tree in a tree data structure. Another important thing to consider is that our graphs can have cycles, which were absent in the tree, so, we cannot revisit a node or vertex as it will end up in an infinite loop. We will use a concept called graph coloring where we keep the status of different node visits with a color or a value to keep it simple. Let's now write some code to implement the BFS and DFS in the graph.

Breadth first search

We are now going to implement a BFS for a graph. Considering the following undirected graph, first, we need to represent the graph in a matrix or list. For the sake of simplicity, we will use the adjacency matrix for the graph representation:

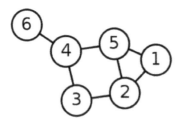

The preceding adjacency graph has six vertices, and the vertices are labeled from **1** to **6** (no 0). Since our vertices are numbered, we can use those as array indexes for faster access. We will can construct the graph like this:

```
$graph = [];
$visited = [];
$vertexCount = 6;

for($i = 1;$i<=$vertexCount;$i++) {
    $graph[$i] = array_fill(1, $vertexCount, 0);
    $visited[$i] = 0;
}
```

Here, we have two arrays, one for representing the actual graph and the other one for keeping track of the visited nodes. We want to make sure that we do not visit a node multiple times as it might end up in an infinite loop. Since our graph has six vertices, we kept $vertexCount as 6. We then initialize the graph array as a two-dimensional array with an initial value of 0. We will start the index from 1 for the array. We also set each vertex as not visited by assigning each vertex to 0 in the $visited array. Now, we will add the edges in our graph representation. Since the graph is undirected, we need to set two properties for each edge. In other words, we need to set bidirectional edge values for edges between the vertex labeled 1 and 2 since both share an edge between them. Here is the code for the full representation of the earlier graph:

```
$graph[1][2] = $graph[2][1] = 1;
$graph[1][5] = $graph[5][1] = 1;
$graph[5][2] = $graph[2][5] = 1;
$graph[5][4] = $graph[4][5] = 1;
$graph[4][3] = $graph[3][4] = 1;
$graph[3][2] = $graph[2][3] = 1;
$graph[6][4] = $graph[4][6] = 1;
```

So, we have represented the graph using an adjacency matrix. Now, let's define the BFS algorithm for the matrix:

```
function BFS(array &$graph, int $start, array $visited): SplQueue {
    $queue = new SplQueue;
    $path = new SplQueue;

    $queue->enqueue($start);
    $visited[$start] = 1;

    while (!$queue->isEmpty()) {
        $node = $queue->dequeue();
        $path->enqueue($node);
        foreach ($graph[$node] as $key => $vertex) {
```

```
            if (!$visited[$key] && $vertex == 1) {
            $visited[$key] = 1;
            $queue->enqueue($key);
            }
        }
    }

    return $path;
}
```

Our implemented BFS function takes three arguments: the actual graph, the starting vertex, and the empty visited array. We could have avoided the third argument and written the initialization inside the BFS function. At the end of the day, we can choose either of the ways to accomplish this. Inside our function implementation, we have two queues: one to keep the nodes that we need to visit and another one for the order of the visited nodes, or the path of the search. At the end of the function, we return the path queue.

Inside the function, we first add the starting node to the queue. Then, we start from that node to visit its adjacent nodes. If the node is not visited and has a connection to the current node, we add it to our queue for visiting. We also mark the current node as visited and add it to our path. Now, we will call our BFS function with our constructed graph matrix and a visiting node. Here is the program to execute the BFS functionality:

```
$path = BFS($graph, 1, $visited);

while (!$path->isEmpty()) {
    echo $path->dequeue()."\t";
}
```

As we can see from the preceding code snippet, we start the search from node 1. The output will look like this:

1	2	5	3	4	6

If we had 5 as the starting node by changing the second argument of the BFS function call from 1 to 5, then the output would have been the following:

5	1	2	4	3	6

Depth first search

As we have seen for the BFS, we can define any starting vertex for the DFS as well. The difference is that for a list of visited nodes, we will use a stack instead of a queue. Other parts of the code will be similar to our BFS code. We will also use the same graph we used for the BFS implementation. The DFS implementation we will implement is an iterative one. Here is the code for it:

```
function DFS(array &$graph, int $start, array $visited): SplQueue {
    $stack = new SplStack;
    $path = new SplQueue;

    $stack->push($start);
    $visited[$start] = 1;

    while (!$stack->isEmpty()) {
      $node = $stack->pop();
      $path->enqueue($node);
      foreach ($graph[$node] as $key => $vertex) {
          if (!$visited[$key] && $vertex == 1) {
          $visited[$key] = 1;
          $stack->push($key);
          }
      }
    }

    return $path;
}
```

As mentioned earlier, for a DFS, we have to use a stack instead of a queue as we need the last vertex from the stack instead of the first one (if we have used a queue). For the path part, we use a queue so that we can show the path sequentially during the display. Here is the code to call for our graph $graph:

```
$path = DFS($graph, 1, $visited);
while (!$path->isEmpty()) {
    echo $path->dequeue()."\t";
}
```

The code will produce the following output:

1	5	4	6	3	2

For the preceding example, we start from vertex 1, and we will visit vertex 5 first out of the two adjacent vertices with the labels 5 and 2 of vertex 1. Now, vertex 5 has two vertices with labels 4 and 2. Vertex 4 will be visited first as it appears as the first edge from vertex 5 (bearing in mind our left to right direction of visiting nodes). Next, we will visit vertex 6 from vertex 4. Since, we cannot go any further from vertex 6, it will return to vertex 4 and visit the unvisited adjacent vertex with the label 3. When we are at vertex 3, there are two adjacent vertices available from 3. They are labeled as vertex 4 and vertex 2. We already visited vertex 4 earlier, so we cannot revisit it, and we have to visit vertex 2 from vertex 3. Since vertex 2 has three vertices, vertex 3, 5, and 1, and all of them are already visited, we are actually done with our DFS implementation here.

 We can pass an extra parameter if we are looking for a specific end vertex from a starting vertex. In the earlier example, we were just getting the adjacent vertex and visiting all of them. For a specific end vertex, we had to match the target vertex with each of our visiting vertex during the iteration of the DFS algorithm.

Topological sorting using Kahn's algorithm

Let's assume that we have some tasks to do, and each of the tasks has some dependencies that mean that the dependent tasks should be done first before doing the actual task. The problem arises when we have an interrelationship between tasks and dependencies. Now, we need to come up with a proper order for completing the tasks. We need a special type of sorting so that we can sort these connected tasks without violating our rules for finishing the tasks. Topological sorting will be the right choice for solving such problems. In topological sorting, a directed edge AB from vertex A to B is sorted in such a way that A will always come before B in the ordering. This will be applicable for all the vertices and edges. Another important factor for applying a topological sort is that the graph must be a DAG. Any DAG has at least one topological sorting. Most of the time, there are multiple topological sortings that are possible for a given graph. There are two popular algorithms available for topological sorting: Kahn's algorithm and the DFS approach. We will talk about Kahn's algorithm here as we have already discussed DFS a few times in this book.

Kahn's algorithm has the following steps to find the topological ordering from a DAG:

1. Calculate the indegree (incoming edges) for each of the vertex and put all vertices in a queue where the indegree is 0. Also, initialize the count for the visited node to 0.

2. Remove a vertex from the queue and perform the following operations on it:

    1. Increment the visited node count by 1.

    2. Reduce the indegree for all adjacent vertices by 1.

    3. If the indegree of the adjacent vertex becomes 0, add it to the queue.

3. Repeat *step 2* until the queue is empty.
4. If the count of the visited node is not the same as the count of the nodes, then topological sorting is not possible for the given DAG.

Let's consider the following graph. It is a perfect example of DAG. Now, we want to sort it using topological sorting and Kahn's algorithm:

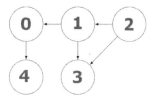

Now let us represent this graph using an adjacency matrix as we did previously for the other graphs. The matrix will look as follows:

```
$graph = [
    [0, 0, 0, 0, 1],
    [1, 0, 0, 1, 0],
    [0, 1, 0, 1, 0],
    [0, 0, 0, 0, 0],
    [0, 0, 0, 0, 0],
];
```

Now, we will implement Kahn's algorithm as per our defined steps. Here is the implementation for it:

```
function topologicalSort(array $matrix): SplQueue {
    $order = new SplQueue;
    $queue = new SplQueue;
    $size = count($matrix);
    $incoming = array_fill(0, $size, 0);


    for ($i = 0; $i < $size; $i++) {
      for ($j = 0; $j < $size; $j++) {
            if ($matrix[$j][$i]) {
```

```
            $incoming[$i] ++;
        }
    }
    if ($incoming[$i] == 0) {
        $queue->enqueue($i);
    }
}

while (!$queue->isEmpty()) {
    $node = $queue->dequeue();

    for ($i = 0; $i < $size; $i++) {
        if ($matrix[$node][$i] == 1) {
            $matrix[$node][$i] = 0;
            $incoming[$i] --;
            if ($incoming[$i] == 0) {
                $queue->enqueue($i);
            }
        }
    }
    $order->enqueue($node);
}

if ($order->count() != $size) // cycle detected
    return new SplQueue;

return $order;
}
```

As we can see from the preceding implementation, we have actually considered every step we mentioned for Kahn's algorithm. We started by finding the indegree for vertices and also putting the 0 indegree vertices in a queue. Then, we checked each node of the queue and reduced the indegree of the neighbor vertices and again added any neighbor with 0 indegrees to the queue. At the end, we returned the sorted queue, or an empty queue if the count of ordered vertices and actual vertices count does not match. We can now call the function to return the sorted list of vertices as a queue. Here is the code to do this:

```
$sorted = topologicalSort($graph);

while (!$sorted->isEmpty()) {
    echo $sorted->dequeue() . "\t";
}
```

Now, this will go through each of the queue elements and print them. The output will look like this:

```
    2       1       0       3       4
```

The output corresponds to our expectations. As we can see from the earlier diagram, vertex **2** has a direct edge to vertex **1** and vertex **3**, and vertex **1** has a direct edge to vertex **0** and vertex **3**. Since vertex **2** has no incoming edges, we will start from vertex **2** for the topological sorting. Vertex **1** has one incoming edge and vertex **3** has two, so, after vertex **2**, we will visit vertex **1** as per the algorithm. The same principle will take us to vertex **0** followed by vertex **3** and at the end to vertex **4**. We have to also remember that there can be multiple topological orderings possible for a given graph. The complexity of Kahn's algorithm is **O** ($V+E$), where **V** is the number of vertices and **E** is the number of edges.

Shortest path using the Floyd-Warshall algorithm

A common scenario for a pizza-delivery company is to deliver the pizza as quickly as possible. Graph algorithms can help us in such situations. The Floyd-Warshall algorithm is a very common algorithm that is used to find the shortest path from u to v using all pairs of vertices (u, v). The shortest path indicates the shortest possible distance between two nodes that are interconnected. The graph for calculating the shortest path has to be a weighted graph. In some cases, the weight can be negative as well. The algorithm is very simple and one of the easiest to implement. It is shown here:

```
for i:= 1 to n do
   for j:= 1 to n do
      dis[i][j] = w[i][j]

for k:= 1 to n do
   for i:= 1 to n do
      for j:= 1 to n do
         sum := dis[i][k] + dis[k][j]
         if (sum < dis[i][j])
               dis[i][j] := sum
```

First, we copied each of our weights to a cost or distance matrix. Then, we ran through each vertex and figured out the cost or distance of visiting from vertex i to vertex j through vertex k. If the distance or cost is less than a direct path between vertex i and vertex j, we choose the path i to k to j instead of the direct path of i to j.

Let's consider the following diagram:

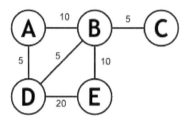

Here, we can see an undirected graph with weights on each edge. Now, if we look for the shortest path from **A** to **E**, then we have the following options:

- **A** to **E** via **B** has a distance of **20**
- **A** to **E** via **D** has a distance of **25**
- **A** to **E** via **D** and **B** has a distance of **20**
- **A** to **E** via **B** and **D** has a distance of **35**

So, we can see that the lowest distance is **20**. Now, let's implement this programmatically with numeric representations of the vertices. We will use 0, 1, 2, 3, and 4 instead of A, B, C, D, and E, respectively. Now, let's represent the earlier graph in an adjacency matrix format:

```
$totalVertices = 5;
$graph = [];
for ($i = 0; $i < $totalVertices; $i++) {
    for ($j = 0; $j < $totalVertices; $j++) {
        $graph[$i][$j] = $i == $j ? 0 : PHP_INT_MAX;
    }
}
```

Here, we took a difference approach and initialized all the edges to the maximum value of the PHP integer. The reason for doing this is to ensure that a value of 0 for non-edges does not impact the algorithm logic, as we are searching for the minimum value. Now, we need to add the weights to the graph as shown in the earlier diagram:

```
$graph[0][1] = $graph[1][0] = 10;
$graph[2][1] = $graph[1][2] = 5;
$graph[0][3] = $graph[3][0] = 5;
$graph[3][1] = $graph[1][3] = 5;
$graph[4][1] = $graph[1][4] = 10;
$graph[3][4] = $graph[4][3] = 20;
```

Since this is an undirected graph, we assign both edges the same value. If it were a directed graph, we could have made only one entry for each weight. Now, it is time to implement the Floyd-Warshall algorithm to find the shortest paths for any given pair of nodes. Here is our implementation of this function:

```
function floydWarshall(array $graph): array {
    $dist = [];
    $dist = $graph;
    $size = count($dist);

    for ($k = 0; $k < $size; $k++)
      for ($i = 0; $i < $size; $i++)
          for ($j = 0; $j < $size; $j++)
        $dist[$i][$j] = min($dist[$i][$j],
    $dist[$i][$k] + $dist[$k][$j]);

    return $dist;
}
```

As we mentioned earlier, the implementation is really simple. We have three inner loops to calculate the minimum distance, and we also return the distance array at the end of the function. Now, let's call this function and check whether our expected results match:

```
$distance = floydWarshall($graph);

echo "Shortest distance between A to E is:" . $distance[0][4] . "\n";
echo "Shortest distance between D to C is:" . $distance[3][2] . "\n";
```

Here is the output of the code:

```
Shortest distance between A to E is:20
Shortest distance between D to C is:10
```

If we check our previous graph, we can see that the shortest distance between **D** and **C** is actually **10**, and the path is D ◉ B ◉ C (5+5), which is the shortest distance out of all the possible routes (D ◉ A ◉ B ◉ C (20), or D ◉ E ◉ B ◉ C (35)).

The complexity for the Floyd-Warshall algorithm is **O** (*V3*), where **V** is the number of vertices in the graph. Now we will explore another algorithm that is famous for finding the single source shortest path.

Single source shortest path using Dijkstra's algorithm

We can easily find the shortest path using the Floyd-Warshall algorithm, but we do not get the actual path to go from node X to Y. This is because the Floyd-Warshall algorithm does the calculation for the distance or cost and does not store the actual path for the minimum cost. For example, using Google Maps, we can always find a route to our destination from any given location. Google Maps can show us the best route as regards the distance, time of travel, or other factors. This is a perfect example of single source shortest path algorithm usage. There are many algorithms to find the solution for a single source shortest path problem; however, Dijkstra's shortest path algorithm is the most popular one. There are many ways to implement Dijkstra's algorithm, such as using Fibonacci heaps, min-heaps, priority queues, and so on. Each implementation has its own advantage regarding the performance and improvement of Dijkstra's solution. Let's go through the pseudocode for the algorithm:

```
function Dijkstra(Graph, source):

    create vertex set Q
    for each vertex v in Graph:
        dist[v] := INFINITY
        prev[v] := UNDEFINED
        add v to Q

    dist[source] := 0

    while Q is not empty:
        u := vertex in Q with min dist[u]
        remove u from Q

        for each neighbor v of u:
            alt := dist[u] + length(u, v)
            if alt < dist[v]:
                dist[v] := alt
                prev[v] := u

    return dist[], prev[]
```

Now, we will implement the algorithm using a priority queue. First, let's choose a graph to implement the algorithm. We can select the following undirected weighted graph. It has six nodes with many connections between the nodes and vertices. First, we need to represent the following graph in an adjacency matrix:

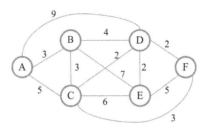

As we can see from the preceding diagram, our vertices are labeled with the letters **A** to **F**, so we will use the vertex name as the key in a PHP associative array:

```
$graph = [
    'A' => ['B' => 3, 'C' => 5, 'D' => 9],
    'B' => ['A' => 3, 'C' => 3, 'D' => 4, 'E' => 7],
    'C' => ['A' => 5, 'B' => 3, 'D' => 2, 'E' => 6, 'F' => 3],
    'D' => ['A' => 9, 'B' => 4, 'C' => 2, 'E' => 2, 'F' => 2],
    'E' => ['B' => 7, 'C' => 6, 'D' => 2, 'F' => 5],
    'F' => ['C' => 3, 'D' => 2, 'E' => 5],
];
```

Now, we will implement Dijkstra's algorithm using a priority queue. We will find a path from the source vertex to the target vertex using the adjacency matrix we created for the last diagram. Our Dijkstra's algorithm will return an array with the minimum distance between two nodes and the followed path. We will return the path as a stack so that we can get the actual path in the reverse order. Here is the implementation:

```
function Dijkstra(array $graph, string $source, string $target):array{
    $dist = [];
    $pred = [];
    $Queue = new SplPriorityQueue();

    foreach ($graph as $v => $adj) {
        $dist[$v] = PHP_INT_MAX;
        $pred[$v] = null;
        $Queue->insert($v, min($adj));
    }

    $dist[$source] = 0;
```

```
        while (!$Queue->isEmpty()) {
          $u = $Queue->extract();
          if (!empty($graph[$u])) {
              foreach ($graph[$u] as $v => $cost) {
                if ($dist[$u] + $cost < $dist[$v]) {
                  $dist[$v] = $dist[$u] + $cost;
                  $pred[$v] = $u;
            }
              }
          }
        }

        $S = new SplStack();
        $u = $target;
        $distance = 0;

        while (isset($pred[$u]) && $pred[$u]) {
          $S->push($u);
          $distance += $graph[$u][$pred[$u]];
          $u = $pred[$u];
        }

        if ($S->isEmpty()) {
          return ["distance" => 0, "path" => $S];
        } else {
          $S->push($source);
          return ["distance" => $distance, "path" => $S];
        }
    }
```

As we can see from the preceding implementation, first, we created two arrays to store the distance and predecessors, along with the priority queue. Then, we set each vertex as the maximum integer (PHP_INT_MAX) value of PHP (INFINITY in the pseudocode) and the predecessor as NULL. We also took the minimum value of all adjacent nodes and stored them in the queue. After the loop, we set the source node distance as 0. Then we checked each node in the queue and checked the nearest neighbors to find a minimum path. If a path is found using if ($dist[$u] + $cost < $dist[$v]), we assign it to the vertex.

We then created a stack named $s to store the path. We started from our target vertex and visited adjacent vertices to reach our source vertex. As we moved through the adjacent vertices, we also calculated the distance we covered by visiting those vertices. Since our function is returning both the distance and the path, we constructed an array to return both the distance and path for the given graph, source, and target. If no path exists, we return 0 as the distance and an empty stack for the output. Now, we will write a few lines of code to use the graph $graph and the function Dijkstra to check our implementation:

```
$source = "A";
$target = "F";

$result = Dijkstra($graph, $source, $target);
extract($result);

echo "Distance from $source to $target is $distance \n";
echo "Path to follow : ";

while (!$path->isEmpty()) {
    echo $path->pop() . "\t";
}
```

If we run this code, it will have the following output in our command line:

```
Distance from A to F is 8
Path to follow : A       C       F
```

The output looks exactly right, as we can see from the graph that the shortest path from **A** to **F** is through **C** and the shortest distance is *5 + 3 = 8*.

Dijkstra's algorithm has a running complexity of **O** (*V2*). Since we are using the minimum priority queue, the runtime complexity is **O** (*E + V log V*).

Finding the shortest path using the Bellman-Ford algorithm

Though Dijkstra's algorithm is the most popular and efficient one that is used to find the single source shortest path, there is one problem that it does not address. If the graph has a negative cycle, Dijkstra's algorithm cannot detect the negative cycle, and, thus, it does not work. A negative cycle is a cycle where the sum of all the edges in the cycle is negative. If a graph contains a negative cycle, then finding the shortest path will not be possible, so it is important that we address the issue while finding the shortest path. That is why we use the Bellman-Ford algorithm, even though it is slower compared to Dijkstra's algorithm.

Here is the algorithm pseudocode for the Bellman-Ford algorithm for the shortest path:

```
function BellmanFord(list vertices, list edges, vertex source)
  // This implementation takes a vertex source
  // and fills distance array with shortest-path information

  // Step 1: initialize graph
  for each vertex v in vertices:
    if v is source
      distance[v] := 0
    else
      distance[v] := infinity

  // Step 2: relax edges repeatedly
  for i from 1 to size(vertices)-1:
    for each edge (u, v) with weight w in edges:
      if distance[u] + w < distance[v]:
        distance[v] := distance[u] + w

  // Step 3: check for negative-weight cycles
    for each edge (u, v) with weight w in edges:
      if distance[u] + w < distance[v]:
      error "Graph contains a negative-weight cycle"
```

We can see that the Bellman-Ford algorithm also considers the edge sand vertices in finding the shortest path between nodes. This is known as the relaxation process, which is also used in Dijkstra's algorithm. The relaxation process in graph algorithms refers to the updating of the cost of all vertices connected to a vertex V if those costs would be improved by including the path via V. In simple words, the relaxation process is trying to lower the cost of getting to a vertex using another vertex. Now, we will implement this algorithm for the same graph we used in Dijkstra's algorithm. The only difference is that here we will use numeric labels for our nodes and vertex here:

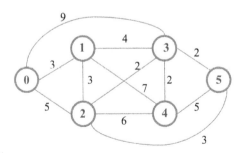

Now it is time to represent the graph in an adjacency matrix format. Here is the matrix in PHP:

```
$graph = [
    0 => [0, 3, 5, 9, 0, 0],
    1 => [3, 0, 3, 4, 7, 0],
    2 => [5, 3, 0, 2, 6, 3],
    3 => [9, 4, 2, 0, 2, 2],
    4 => [0, 7, 6, 2, 0, 5],
    5 => [0, 0, 3, 2, 5, 0]
];
```

Previously, we used a value of 0 to indicate that there was no edge between two vertices. If we do the same here, then taking a minimum between two edges where one represents 0 will always yield a 0 during the relaxation process, which actually means that there is no connection between two vertices. As a result, we have to choose a larger number to represent the non-existent edges. We can use the MAX_INT_VALUE constant of PHP to represent those edges so that those non-existent edges are not considered. This can be our new graph representation:

```
define("I", PHP_INT_MAX);

$graph = [
    0 => [I, 3, 5, 9, I, I],
    1 => [3, I, 3, 4, 7, I],
    2 => [5, 3, I, 2, 6, 3],
    3 => [9, 4, 2, I, 2, 2],
    4 => [I, 7, 6, 2, I, 5],
    5 => [I, I, 3, 2, 5, I]
];
```

Now, let's write the implementation for the Bellman-Ford algorithm. We will use the same approach we defined in the pseudocode:

```
function bellmanFord(array $graph, int $source): array {
    $dist = [];
    $len = count($graph);

    foreach ($graph as $v => $adj) {
        $dist[$v] = PHP_INT_MAX;
    }

    $dist[$source] = 0;

    for ($k = 0; $k < $len - 1; $k++) {
        for ($i = 0; $i < $len; $i++) {
            for ($j = 0; $j < $len; $j++) {
```

```
                if ($dist[$i] > $dist[$j] + $graph[$j][$i]) {
                $dist[$i] = $dist[$j] + $graph[$j][$i];
            }
          }
        }
    }

    for ($i = 0; $i < $len; $i++) {
       for ($j = 0; $j < $len; $j++) {
          if ($dist[$i] > $dist[$j] + $graph[$j][$i]) {
            echo 'The graph contains a negative-weight cycle!';
            return [];
          }
       }
     }
    return $dist;
  }
```

Unlike Dijkstra's algorithm, we are not tracking the predecessors. We are considering the distance during the relaxation process. Since we are using the maximum value for an integer in PHP, it automatically cancels outs the possibility of choosing a nonexistent edge with a value of 0 as the minimum path. The last part of the implementation detects any negative cycle in the given graph and returns an empty array in that case:

```
$source = 0;
$distances = bellmanFord($graph, $source);

foreach($distances as $target => $distance) {
    echo "distance from $source to $target is $distance \n";
}
```

This will have the following output, which shows the shortest path distance from our source node to other nodes:

```
distance from 0 to 0 is 0
distance from 0 to 1 is 3
distance from 0 to 2 is 5
distance from 0 to 3 is 7
distance from 0 to 4 is 9
distance from 0 to 5 is 8
```

The Bellman-Ford algorithm has the run-time complexity of **O** (*V, E*).

Understanding the minimum spanning tree (MST)

Suppose we are designing our new office campus with multiple buildings interconnected to each other. If we approach the problem by considering the interconnectivity between each building, it will take a huge number of cables. However, if we could somehow connect all the buildings through a common connectivity where each building is connected to every other building with only one connection, then this solution will reduce the redundancy and cost. If we think of our buildings as vertices and the connectivity between buildings as the edges, we can construct a graph using this approach. The problem we are trying to solve is also known as the **minimum spanning tree,** or **MST**. Consider the following graph. We have 10 vertices and 21 edges. However, we can connect all 10 vertices with only nine edges (the dark line). This will keep our cost or distance to a minimal level:

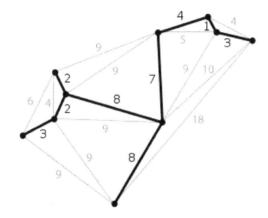

There are several algorithms that we can use to find an MST from a given graph. The two most popular are Prim's algorithm and Kruskal's algorithm. We will explore these two algorithms in the upcoming sections.

Implementing Prim's spanning tree algorithm

Prim's algorithm for finding the minimum spanning tree relies on a greedy approach. A greedy approach is defined as an algorithm paradigm where we try to find the global optimal solution by considering the local optimal solution at each stage. We will explore greedy algorithms in Chapter 11, *Solve Problems with Advanced Techniques*. In a greedy approach, the algorithm creates subsets of edges and finds out the least costly one from the subset of edges. This subset of edges will include all vertices. It starts from an arbitrary position and grows the tree one vertex at a time by choosing the cheapest possible connection between the vertices. Let's consider the following graph:

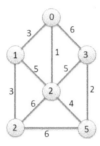

Now, we will apply a very basic version of Prim's algorithm to get the minimum spanning tree as well as the minimum cost or weight of the edges. The graph will look like this as an adjacency matrix:

```
$G = [
    [0, 3, 1, 6, 0, 0],
    [3, 0, 5, 0, 3, 0],
    [1, 5, 0, 5, 6, 4],
    [6, 0, 5, 0, 0, 2],
    [0, 3, 6, 0, 0, 6],
    [0, 0, 4, 2, 6, 0]
];
```

Now, we will implement the algorithm for Prim's minimum spanning tree. We are assuming that we are going to start from vertex 0 to find out the whole spanning tree, so we will just pass the graph adjacency matrix in the function, and it will display the connecting edges for the spanning tree along with the minimum cost:

```php
function primMST(array $graph) {
    $parent = [];    // Array to store the MST
    $key = [];       // used to pick minimum weight edge
    $visited = [];    // set of vertices not yet included in MST
    $len = count($graph);

    // Initialize all keys as MAX
    for ($i = 0; $i < $len; $i++) {
      $key[$i] = PHP_INT_MAX;
      $visited[$i] = false;
    }

    $key[0] = 0;
    $parent[0] = -1;

    // The MST will have V vertices
    for ($count = 0; $count < $len - 1; $count++) {
// Pick the minimum key vertex
$minValue = PHP_INT_MAX;
$minIndex = -1;

foreach (array_keys($graph) as $v) {
    if ($visited[$v] == false && $key[$v] < $minValue) {
      $minValue = $key[$v];
      $minIndex = $v;
    }
}

$u = $minIndex;

// Add the picked vertex to the MST Set
$visited[$u] = true;

for ($v = 0; $v < $len; $v++) {
    if ($graph[$u][$v] != 0 && $visited[$v] == false &&
      $graph[$u][$v] < $key[$v]) {
        $parent[$v] = $u;
        $key[$v] = $graph[$u][$v];
    }
}
    }

    // Print MST
```

```
echo "Edge\tWeight\n";
$minimumCost = 0;
for ($i = 1; $i < $len; $i++) {
  echo $parent[$i] . " - " . $i . "\t" . $graph[$i][$parent[$i]]
    "\n";
  $minimumCost += $graph[$i][$parent[$i]];
}
echo "Minimum cost: $minimumCost \n";
}
```

Now, if we call the function `primMST` with our graph `$G`, the following will be the output and the MST constructed by the algorithm:

```
Edge    Weight
0 - 1   3
0 - 2   1
5 - 3   2
1 - 4   3
2 - 5   4
Minimum cost: 13
```

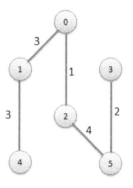

There are other ways to implement Prim's algorithm with the help of a Fibonacci heap, a priority queue, and so on. It is quite similar to Dijkstra's algorithm to find the shortest path. Our implementation has a time complexity of **O** (V^2). Using the binary heap and the Fibonacci heap, we can reduce the complexity significantly.

Kruskal's algorithm for spanning tree

Another popular algorithm for finding a minimum spanning tree is Kruskal's algorithm. It is similar to Prim's algorithm and uses a greedy approach to find the solution. Here are the steps we need to implement Kruskal's algorithm:

1. Create a forest **T** (a set of trees), where each vertex in the graph is a separate tree.
2. Create a set **S** containing all the edges in the graph.
3. While **S** is non-empty and **T** is not yet spanning:

    1. Remove an edge with the minimum weight from **S**.

    2. If that edge connects two different trees, then add it to the forest, combining two trees into a single tree; otherwise, discard that edge.

We will use the same graph that we used for Prim's algorithm. Here is the implementation of Kruskal's algorithm:

```
function Kruskal(array $graph): array {
    $len = count($graph);
    $tree = [];

    $set = [];
    foreach ($graph as $k => $adj) {
    $set[$k] = [$k];
    }

    $edges = [];
    for ($i = 0; $i < $len; $i++) {
      for ($j = 0; $j < $i; $j++) {
        if ($graph[$i][$j]) {
          $edges[$i . ',' . $j] = $graph[$i][$j];
        }
      }
    }

    asort($edges);

    foreach ($edges as $k => $w) {
    list($i, $j) = explode(',', $k);

    $iSet = findSet($set, $i);
    $jSet = findSet($set, $j);
    if ($iSet != $jSet) {
        $tree[] = ["from" => $i, "to" => $j,
    "cost" => $graph[$i][$j]];
```

```
        unionSet($set, $iSet, $jSet);
    }
    }

    return $tree;
}

function findSet(array &$set, int $index) {
    foreach ($set as $k => $v) {
      if (in_array($index, $v)) {
        return $k;
      }
    }

    return false;
}

function unionSet(array &$set, int $i, int $j) {
    $a = $set[$i];
    $b = $set[$j];
    unset($set[$i], $set[$j]);
    $set[] = array_merge($a, $b);
}
```

As we can see, we have two separate functions—unionSet and findSet—to perform the union operations of two disjointed sets, as well as find out whether a number exists in a set or not. Now, let's run the program with our constructed graph like this:

```
$graph = [
    [0, 3, 1, 6, 0, 0],
    [3, 0, 5, 0, 3, 0],
    [1, 5, 0, 5, 6, 4],
    [6, 0, 5, 0, 0, 2],
    [0, 3, 6, 0, 0, 6],
    [0, 0, 4, 2, 6, 0]
];

$mst = Kruskal($graph);

$minimumCost = 0;

foreach($mst as $v) {
    echo "From {$v['from']} to {$v['to']} cost is {$v['cost']} \n";
    $minimumCost += $v['cost'];
}

echo "Minimum cost: $minimumCost \n";
```

This will produce the following output, which is similar to our output from Prim's algorithm:

```
From 2 to 0 cost is 1
From 5 to 3 cost is 2
From 1 to 0 cost is 3
From 4 to 1 cost is 3
From 5 to 2 cost is 4
Minimum cost: 13
```

The complexity of Kruskal's algorithm is **O** (*E log V*), which is better than the generic implementation of Prim's algorithm.

Summary

In this chapter, we discussed different graph algorithms and their operations. Graphs are very handy in solving a wide range of problems. We have seen that for the same graph, we can apply different algorithms and get different performances. We have to choose carefully which algorithms we want to apply based on the nature of the problem. There are many other graph topics that we left out of this book due to some constraints. There are topics such as graph coloring, bipartite matching, and flow problems, which should be studied and applied where applicable. In the next chapter, we will shift our focus to our last data structure topic for this book, called heap, and learn the different usages of the heap data structure.

10
Understanding and Using Heaps

A heap is a specialized data structure that is based on the tree abstract data type and used in many algorithms and data structures. A common data structure that can be built using a heap is the Priority Queue. Also, one of the most popular and efficient sorting algorithms that heap sort is based on is heap data structure. In this chapter, we are going to discuss a heap's properties, different variants of heaps, and heap operations. We will also discover the heap sort and will be implementing heap using SPL as we progress through the chapter. We are now going to explore the heap and its definition in the next section.

What is a heap?

By definition, a heap is a specialized tree data structure that supports a heap property. A heap property is defined in such a way that the root of a heap structure will be either smaller or larger than its child nodes. If the parent node is greater than the child nodes, then it is known as max-heap and if the parent node is smaller than the child nodes then it is known as min-heap.

The following figure shows an example of max-heap:

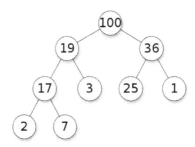

If we look at the root node, the value **100** is greater than the two child nodes **19** and **36**. Similarly for **19**, the value is greater than **17** and **3**. It applies the same rule for **36** and **17**. As we can see from the tree structure, the tree is not completely sorted or ordered. But the important fact is we can always find the maximum or minimum at the root of the tree, which can be very efficient for many use cases.

There are many variations of heap structure, such as binary heap, b-heap, Fibonacci heap, ternary heap, treap, weak heap, and so on. A Binary heap is one of the most popular for heap implementations. A binary heap is a complete binary tree where all inner levels of the tree are fully filled. The last level can be fully filled or partially filled. Since we are considering a binary heap, we can perform most of our operations in logarithmic time. In this book, we are going to focus on binary heap implementation and operations.

Heap operations

As we have mentioned a few times that heap is a specialized tree data structure, we have to make sure that we first construct a heap from a given list of items. As heap has a strict heap property, we have to satisfy the heap property on each step. Here are some of the core operations for heap:

- Create heap
- Insert a new value
- Extract minimum or maximum from heap
- Remove a value
- Swapping

Creating a heap from a given list of items or numbers requires us to ensure that both heap property and binary tree property are satisfied. Which means the parent node must be greater or less than the child nodes and that will be true for all nodes in the tree. Also the tree must be a complete binary tree all the time. While creating a heap, we start with one node and insert a new node to the heap.

The insert node operation has a defined set of steps. We cannot start from an arbitrary node. The steps for insert operation are as follows:

1. Insert the new node at the bottom of the heap.
2. Check the new node with parent value if they are in the right order. If they are in the right order, stop there.
3. If they are not in the right order, swap them and move to the previous step to check the newly swapped node with its parent node. This step along with the previous one is known as sift up or up-heap, or bubble-up, or heapify-up, and so on.

The extract operation (minimum or maximum) takes out the root node from the heap. After this we have to do the following operations to ensure heap properties for the remaining heap:

1. Move the last node from the heap as the new root.
2. Compare the new root node with the child nodes, if they are in the correct order, stop.
3. If not, swap the root node with the child node (minimum child for `MinHeap`, maximum child for `MaxHeap`) and continue with the previous step. This step along with the previous one is known as sift down or down-heap, or bubble-down or heapify-down, and so on.

In heap, one of the important operations is swapping. In many cases, we have to swap two values from two nodes without impacting the tree's properties. Now we are going to implement a binary heap using PHP 7.

Implementing a binary heap in PHP

One of the most popular ways to implement a binary heap is using an array. Since heaps are complete binary trees, they can be easily implemented using an array. If we consider the root item to be at index 1, then the child items will be at index 2 and 3. We can represent this as *i* for the root and *2*i* for the left child and *2*i +1* for the right child. Also, we are going to implement the mean heap as our example. So, let us get started with the class structure for the min-heap implementation.

First, we are going to start by creating a class for `MinHeap`, which will have two properties, one for storing the heap array and another count for the number of elements in the heap at any given moment. Here is the code for the class:

```
class MinHeap {

    public $heap;
    public $count;

    public function __construct(int $size) {
        $this->heap = array_fill(0, $size + 1, 0);
        $this->count = 0;
    }
}
```

If we look at the preceding code, we can see that we have initialized the heap array to have all 0 values from 0 index to `$size + 1`. Since we are considering putting the root at index 1, we are going to require an array with one extra space. Now we need a way to build a heap from a given array. As we have to satisfy heap property, we have to add one item to the heap and check if the heap property satisfies or not by using the C steps. Here is the code block for creating a heap by inserting one item at a time and also the `siftUp` process:

```
public function create(array $arr = []) {
    if ($arr) {
        foreach ($arr as $val) {
            $this->insert($val);
        }
    }
}

public function insert(int $i) {
    if ($this->count == 0) {
        $this->heap[1] = $i;
        $this->count = 2;
    }
    else {
        $this->heap[$this->count++] = $i;
```

```
            $this->siftUp();
    }
}

public function siftUp() {
    $tmpPos = $this->count - 1;
    $tmp = intval($tmpPos / 2);

    while ($tmpPos > 0 &&
    $this->heap[$tmp] > $this->heap[$tmpPos]) {
        $this->swap($tmpPos, $tmp);
        $tmpPos = intval($tmpPos / 2);
        $tmp = intval($tmpPos / 2);
    }
}
```

First we use the `create` method to build a heap from an array. For each element in the array, we insert it to the heap using an `insert` method. In the `insert` method, we check if the current size of the heap is 0 or not. If the current size is 0, we add the first item to index 1 and setting the next counter at 2. If the heap already has an item, we will store the new item in the last position and increment the counter. We also call the `siftUp()` method to make sure the newly inserted value satisfies the heap property.

Inside the `siftUp` method, we consider the last position and its parent position to compare. If the child value is less than the parent one, we swap them. We continue this until we reach the root node at the top. This method ensures that if the inserted value at the end is smallest, it will be sifted up in the tree. But if it is not, the tree will remain as it is. Though we have talked about swapping, we have not seen the implementation yet. Here is the implementation:

```
public function swap(int $a, int $b) {
    $tmp = $this->heap[$a];
    $this->heap[$a] = $this->heap[$b];
    $this->heap[$b] = $tmp;
}
```

Since the root element has the minimum value in the heap (we are implementing min-heap). The `extract` method will return the minimum value of the current heap all the time:

```
public function extractMin() {
    $min = $this->heap[1];
    $this->heap[1] = $this->heap[$this->count - 1];
    $this->heap[--$this->count] = 0;
    $this->siftDown(1);
    return $min;
}
```

The `extractMin` method returns the first index of the array and replaces it with the last item of the array. After that, it performs the siftDown check for the newly placed root so that it ensures the heap property. Since we are extracting the root value, we are replacing the last index value with 0, which we have used for initializing the heap array. Now we are going to write the `siftDown` method, which we are calling the `extract` method:

```
public function siftDown(int $k) {
    $smallest = $k;
    $left = 2 * $k;
    $right = 2 * $k + 1;

    if ($left < $this->count &&
    $this->heap[$smallest] > $this->heap[$left]) {
        $smallest = $left;
    }

    if ($right < $this->count && $this->heap[$smallest] > $this-
      >heap[$right]) {
        $smallest = $right;
    }

    if ($smallest != $k) {
        $this->swap($k, $smallest);
        $this->siftDown($smallest);
    }
}
```

We consider that the item at index `$k` is the smallest value. Then we compare the smallest value with the left and right child. If there is smaller value available, we swap the smallest value with the root node and it continues until the tree satisfies the heap property. This function calls itself recursively every time swapping is required. Now we need one more method to display the current heap as a string. For that we can write a small method as follows:

```
public function display() {
    echo implode("\t", array_slice($this->heap, 1)) . "\n";
}
```

If we pull all the pieces together now, we have a solid implementation for min-heap. Let us now run a test to see if our implementation satisfies the min-heap properties. Here is the code we can run to build the heap and also extract the minimum from the heap multiple times:

```
$numbers = [37, 44, 34, 65, 26, 86, 129, 83, 9];
echo "Initial array \n" . implode("\t", $numbers) . "\n";
$heap = new MinHeap(count($numbers));
```

```
$heap->create($numbers);
echo "Constructed Heap\n";
$heap->display();
echo "Min Extract: " . $heap->extractMin() . "\n";
$heap->display();
echo "Min Extract: " . $heap->extractMin() . "\n";
$heap->display();
echo "Min Extract: " . $heap->extractMin() . "\n";
$heap->display();
echo "Min Extract: " . $heap->extractMin() . "\n";
$heap->display();
echo "Min Extract: " . $heap->extractMin() . "\n";
$heap->display();
echo "Min Extract: " . $heap->extractMin() . "\n";
$heap->display();
```

If we run this code, the following output will be shown in the terminal:

```
Initial array
37       44       34       65       26       86       129      83       9
Constructed Heap
9        26       37       34       44       86       129      83       65
Min Extract: 9
26       34       37       65       44       86       129      83       0
Min Extract: 26
34       44       37       65       83       86       129      0        0
Min Extract: 34
37       44       86       65       83       129      0        0        0
Min Extract: 37
44       65       86       129      83       0        0        0        0
Min Extract: 44
65       83       86       129      0        0        0        0        0
Min Extract: 65
83       129      86       0        0        0        0        0        0
```

As we can see from the preceding output, when we constructed the min-heap, the lowest value of 9 is in the root. Then we extracted the minimum value, we took 9 from the heap. The root was then taken by the next minimum value of 26 and then followed by 34, 37, 44, and 65. Every time we take the minimum out, the heap is reconstructed again for the minimum value. Since we have seen all applicable operations for a heap data structure, we are now going to analyze the complexity for different heap operations.

Analyzing the complexity of heap operations

Since there are different variations for heap implementation, the complexity also varies in the different implementation. One of the key facts for the heap is the extract operation that will always take O(1) time to get the maximum or minimum from the heap. Since we have focused on binary heap implementation, we are going to see the analysis of binary heap operations:

Operation	Complexity - average	Complexity - Worst
Search	O(n)	O(n)
Insert	O(1)	O(log n)
Delete	O(log n)	O(log n)
Extract	O(1)	O(1)
Space	O(n)	O(n)

Since the heap is not fully sorted, the search operation will take more than a regular binary search tree.

Using heaps as a priority queue

One of the main ways to use the heap data structure is to create a priority queue. As we have seen in Chapter 4, *Constructing Stacks and Queues*, priority queues are special queues where the FIFO behavior depends on the priority of the element rather than the way items are added to the queue. We have already seen the implementation using Linked list and SPL. Now we are going to explore the priority queue implementation using heap and especially max-heap.

Now we are going to implement the priority queue using MaxHeap. Here, the maximum priority item is removed from the queue first. Our implementation will be similar to our last implementation of MinHeap with a little difference. Instead of starting the root at 1, we want to start it from 0. So, the calculation of the left and right child changes as well. This will help us to understand both approaches of constructing a heap using an array. Here is the implementation for the MaxHeap class:

```
class MaxHeap {
```

```php
    public $heap;
    public $count;

    public function __construct(int $size) {
        $this->heap = array_fill(0, $size, 0);
        $this->count = 0;
    }

    public function create(array $arr = []) {
        if ($arr) {
            foreach ($arr as $val) {
                $this->insert($val);
            }
        }
    }

    public function display() {
        echo implode("\t", array_slice($this->heap, 0)) . "\n";
    }

    public function insert(int $i) {
    if ($this->count == 0) {
        $this->heap[0] = $i;
        $this->count = 1;
    } else {
        $this->heap[$this->count++] = $i;
        $this->siftUp();
    }
    }

public function siftUp() {
    $tmpPos = $this->count - 1;
    $tmp = intval($tmpPos / 2);

    while ($tmpPos > 0 && $this->heap[$tmp] < $this->heap[$tmpPos]) {
        $this->swap($tmpPos, $tmp);

        $tmpPos = intval($tmpPos / 2);
        $tmp = intval($tmpPos / 2);
    }
}

public function extractMax() {
    $min = $this->heap[0];
    $this->heap[0] = $this->heap[$this->count - 1];
    $this->heap[$this->count - 1] = 0;
    $this->count--;
    $this->siftDown(0);
```

```
        return $min;
    }

public function siftDown(int $k) {
    $largest= $k;
    $left = 2 * $k + 1;
    $right = 2 * $k + 2;

    if ($left < $this->count
      && $this->heap[$largest] < $this->heap[$left]) {
        $largest = $left;
    }

    if ($right < $this->count
      && $this->heap[$largest] < $this->heap[$right]) {
        $largest = $right;
    }

    if ($largest!= $k) {
        $this->swap($k, $largest);
        $this->siftDown($largest);
    }
}

    public function swap(int $a, int $b) {
      $temp = $this->heap[$a];
      $this->heap[$a] = $this->heap[$b];
      $this->heap[$b] = $temp;
    }
}
```

Let's go through our implementation of the MaxHeap class. There are some minor differences in our MaxHeap implementation from our MinHeap implementation in the last section. The first difference is that we have an array of size *n* for MaxHeap, whereas we had an array of size *n+1* for MinHeap. That makes our insert operation for MaxHeap start inserting from index 0, whereas in MinHeap, we started from index 1. The siftUp functionality only sifts a value to the top if the value of the newly inserted item is greater than the immediate parent value. Also, the extractMax method returns the first value of the array at index 0, which is the maximum from the heap. Once we extract the maximum value, we need to get the maximum value from the remaining items and store it at index 0. The siftDown function also operates to check if the left or right child value is bigger than the parent node value and we swap the values to store the maximum value at parent node. We continue to do this recursively to ensure the maximum value is stored in the root at the end of function calls. This MaxHeap implementation can be used as standalone heap implementation if we want.

Since we are planning to implement the priority queue using a heap, we are going to add another class to extend the `MaxHeap` class to show the characteristics of a Priority Queue. Let us explore the following code:

```
class PriorityQ extends MaxHeap {

    public function __construct(int $size) {
        parent::__construct($size);
    }

    public function enqueue(int $val) {
        parent::insert($val);
    }

    public function dequeue() {
        return parent::extractMax();
    }

}
```

Here we are just extending the `MaxHeap` class and adding a wrapper for `enqueue` and `dequeue` operations using the `insert` and `extractMax` at stealth mode. Let us now run the `PriorityQ` code with the same numbers we did for `MinHeap`:

```
$numbers = [37, 44, 34, 65, 26, 86, 129, 83, 9];

$pq = new PriorityQ(count($numbers));

foreach ($numbers as $number) {
    $pq->enqueue($number);
}
echo "Constructed Heap\n";
$pq->display();
echo "DeQueued: " . $pq->dequeue() . "\n";
$pq->display();
echo "DeQueued: " . $pq->dequeue() . "\n";
$pq->display();
echo "DeQueued: " . $pq->dequeue() . "\n";
$pq->display();
echo "DeQueued: " . $pq->dequeue() . "\n";
$pq->display();
echo "DeQueued: " . $pq->dequeue() . "\n";
$pq->display();
echo "DeQueued: " . $pq->dequeue() . "\n";
$pq->display();
```

As we can see from the preceding code, we are not constructing the heap directly from the array. We are using the priority queue class to enqueue each number in the queue. Also, the dequeue operation will get the top priority item from the queue. If we run this code from the command line, we will have the following output:

```
Constructed Heap
129      86      44      83      26      34      37      65      9
DeQueued: 129
86       83      44      65      26      34      37      9       0
DeQueued: 86
83       65      44      9       26      34      37      0       0
DeQueued: 83
65       37      44      9       26      34      0       0       0
DeQueued: 65
44       37      34      9       26      0       0       0       0
DeQueued: 44
37       26      34      9       0       0       0       0       0
DeQueued: 37
34       26      9       0       0       0       0       0       0
```

As we can see from the output, the `MaxHeap` implementation is helping us to get the maximum value item on each dequeue operation. This is one of the ways of implementing the priority queue. If we want, we can also sort the whole heap at one go and then use the sorted array as the priority queue. For that, we can implement a sorting function that is known as heap sort. It is one of the most efficient and used sorting mechanisms in computer programming. We are now going to explore that in the next section.

Using heap sort

Heap sort requires us to build a heap from a given list of elements and then continuously checks the heap property so that the whole heap remains sorted all the time. Unlike a regular heap where we stop checking the heap property once the newly inserted value satisfies the conditions, we continue to do so for the next elements during the heap sort implementation. The pseudocode of the heap sort looks like this:

```
Heapsort(A as array)
    BuildHeap(A)
    for i = n-1 to 0
        swap(A[0], A[i])
        n = n - 1
        Heapify(A, 0)

BuildHeap(A as array)
    n = elements_in(A)
```

```
        for i = floor(n/2) to 0
            Heapify(A,i)

Heapify(A as array, i as int)
    left = 2i+1
    right = 2i+2
    max = i

    if (left <= n) and (A[left] > A[i])
        max = left

    if (right<=n) and (A[right] > A[max])
        max = right

    if (max != i)
        swap(A[i], A[max])
        Heapify(A, max)
```

The pseudocode shows that whenever we are trying to sort a list of elements, the start process depends on building the heap. Each time we add an item to the heap, we check if that satisfies heap properties through the `heapify` function. Once the heap is built, we check the heap properties of all elements. Let us now implement the heap sort based on the preceding pseudocode:

```
function heapSort(array &$a) {
    $length = count($a);
    buildHeap($a);
    $heapSize = $length - 1;
    for ($i = $heapSize; $i >= 0; $i--) {
      $tmp = $a[0];
      $a[0] = $a[$heapSize];
      $a[$heapSize] = $tmp;
      $heapSize--;
      heapify($a, 0, $heapSize);
    }
}

function buildHeap(array &$a) {
    $length = count($a);
    $heapSize = $length - 1;
    for ($i = ($length / 2); $i >= 0; $i--) {
        heapify($a, $i, $heapSize);
    }
}

function heapify(array &$a, int $i, int $heapSize) {
    $largest = $i;
```

```
$l = 2 * $i + 1;
$r = 2 * $i + 2;
if ($l <= $heapSize && $a[$l] > $a[$i]) {
    $largest = $l;
}

if ($r <= $heapSize && $a[$r] > $a[$largest]) {
    $largest = $r;
}

if ($largest != $i) {
    $tmp = $a[$i];
    $a[$i] = $a[$largest];
    $a[$largest] = $tmp;
    heapify($a, $largest, $heapSize);
}
}
```

Let us now use the heapSort function to sort an array. Since we are passing the argument as by reference, we are not returning anything from the function. The actual array will be sorted at the end of the operation:

```
$numbers = [37, 44, 34, 65, 26, 86, 143, 129, 9];
heapSort($numbers);
echo implode("\t", $numbers);
```

If we run this code, it will have the following output in the command line:

| 9 | 26 | 34 | 37 | 44 | 65 | 86 | 129 | 143 |

If we want to change the sorting to descending order, we just need to change the comparison in the heapify function. If we consider time and space complexity for the heapSort algorithm, we will see that heap sort has the best complexity for a sorting algorithm:

Best time complexity	Ω(nlog(n))
Worst time complexity	O (nlog(n))
Average time complexity	Θ(nlog(n))
Space Complexity (Worst case)	O(1)

Compared to merge sort, heap sort has better space complexity. As a result, many developers prefer heap sort for sorting lists of items.

Using SplHeap, SplMaxHeap, and SplMinHeap

If we do not want to implement our own Heap implementations, we can use the built-in heap classes from the Standard PHP Library - SPL. SPL has three different implementations for the heap. One for generic Heap, which is `SplHeap`, for `MaxHeap` we have `SplMaxHeap`, and for `MinHeap` we have `SplMinHeap`. It is important to know that SPL classes are not considered as very performant while running on PHP 7. So we are not going to explore in details about them here. We will just focus on a sample example here so that if we are using any other version than PHP 7, we can use those built-in classes. Let us try an example using `SplMaxHeap`:

```
$numbers = [37, 44, 34, 65, 26, 86, 143, 129, 9];

$heap = new SplMaxHeap;

foreach ($numbers as $number) {
    $heap->insert($number);
}

while (!$heap->isEmpty()) {
    echo $heap->extract() . "\t";
}
```

Since we have used max-heap, we are expecting the output to be in descending order. Here is the output from the command line:

```
143     129     86      65      44      37      34      26      9
```

If we want to sort it the other way around, we can use `SplMinHeap` for that.

Summary

In this chapter, we have learned about another efficient data structure, named heap. When we implement priority queues using a heap, they are considered maximally efficient implementations. We have also learned about another efficient sorting method named heap sort, which can be achieved through a heap data structure. Here, we are going to conclude our discussion regarding data structures for this book. In the remaining chapters, we are going to focus on advanced algorithms, built-in functions for algorithms, and data structures, along with functional data structures at the end. First, we are going to explore the world of dynamic programming in the next chapter.

11
Solving Problems with Advanced Techniques

We have explored different data structures and algorithms so far in this book. We are yet to explore some of the most exciting areas of algorithms. There are many efficient ways of doing things in computer programming. We will focus on some of the key advanced techniques and concepts in this chapter. These topics are so important that a separate book could be written about them. However, we will keep our focus on the very basic understanding of these advanced topics. When we say advanced topics, we are referring to memoization, dynamic programming, greedy algorithm, backtracking, puzzle solving, machine learning, and so on. Let's learn some new and exciting topics in the following sections.

Memoization

Memoization is an optimization technique where we the store results of previous expensive operations and use them without repeating the operation. It helps us speed up the solution significantly. When we have problems where we can have repetitive sub problems, we can easily apply this technique to store those results and use them later on without repeating the steps. Since PHP has a great support for associative arrays and dynamic array properties, we can cache the results without any problems. One thing we have to remember is that though we are saving time by caching the results, we will require more memory to store these results in the cache. So, we have to make the trade-off between space and memory.

Now, let's revisit `Chapter 5`, *Applying Recursive Algorithms - Recursion*, for our recursive example of generating Fibonacci numbers. We will just modify that function with a counter to know how many times the function is called and the running time of the function to get the thirtieth Fibonacci number. Here is the code for this:

```
$start Time = microtime();
$count = 0;

function fibonacci(int $n): int {
    global $count;
    $count++;
    if ($n == 0) {
        return 1;
    } else if ($n == 1) {
        return 1;
    } else {
        return fibonacci($n - 1) + fibonacci($n - 2);
    }
}

echo fibonacci(30) . "\n";
echo "Function called: " . $count . "\n";
$endTime = microtime();
echo "time =" . ($endTime - $startTime) . "\n";
```

This will have the following output in the command line. Note that timing and results may vary from one system to the other or from one version of PHP to the other. It completely depends on the where the program is running:

```
1346269
Function called: 2692537
time =0.531349
```

The first number 1346269 is the thirtieth Fibonacci number, and the next line shows that the `fibonacci` function was called 2692537 times during the generation of the thirtieth number. The whole process took 0.5 seconds (we are using the `microtime` function of PHP). If we were generating the fiftieth Fibonacci number, the function call count would be more than 40 billion times. That is one big number. However, we know from our Fibonacci formula that when we are calculating n. We are doing it through $n-1$ and $n-2$; those are already calculated in the previous steps. So, we are repeating the steps, and hence, it is costing us time and efficiency. Now, let's store the Fibonacci results in an indexed array, and we will check whether the Fibonacci number we are looking for is already calculated or not. If it is calculated, we will use it; otherwise, we will calculate that and store the result.

Here is the modified code for generating Fibonacci numbers using the same recursive process, but with help of memorization:

```
$startTime = microtime();
$fibCache = [];
$count = 0;

function fibonacciMemoized(int $n): int {
    global $fibCache;
    global $count;
    $count++;
    if ($n == 0 || $n == 1) {
        return 1;
    } else {

        if (isset($fibCache[$n - 1])) {
            $tmp = $fibCache[$n - 1];
        } else {
            $tmp = fibonacciMemoized($n - 1);
            $fibCache[$n - 1] = $tmp;
        }

        if (isset($fibCache[$n - 2])) {
            $tmp1 = $fibCache[$n - 2];
        } else {
            $tmp1 = fibonacciMemoized($n - 2);
            $fibCache[$n - 2] = $tmp1;
        }

    return $tmp + $tmp1;
    }
}

echo fibonacciMemoized(30) . "\n";
echo "Function called: " . $count . "\n";

$endTime = microtime();
echo "time =" . ($endTime - $startTime) . "\n";
```

As we can see from the preceding code, we have introduced a new global variable called $fibCache, which will store the calculated Fibonacci numbers. We also check whether the number we are looking for is already in the array or not. We do not calculate the Fibonacci if the number is already stored in our cache array. If we run this code now, we will see the following output:

```
1346269
Function called: 31
time =5.299999999997E-5
```

Now, let's examine the result. The thirtieth Fibonacci number is the same as we had the last time. However, look at the function call count. It is just 31 instead of 2.7 million calls. Now, let's look at the time. We have taken only 0.00005299 seconds, which is 10,000 times faster than the non-memoized version.

With a simple example, we can see that we can optimize our solutions by utilizing memoization where it is applicable. One thing we have to remember is that memoization will work better where we have repeating sub problems or where we have to consider the previous calculation to compute the current or future calculation. Although memoization will take extra space to store the partially computed data, utilization of memoization can increase performance by a big margin

Pattern matching algorithms

Pattern matching is one of the most common tasks we perform on a day-to-day basis. PHP has built-in support for regular expression, and mostly, we rely on the regular expression and built-in string functions to solve our regular needs for such problems. PHP has a readymade function named strops, which returns the position of the first occurrence of the string in a text. Since it only returns the position of the first occurrence, we can try to write a function that will return all possible positions. We will explore the brute-force approach first, where we will check each of the character for the actual string with each one of the pattern string. Here is the function that will do the job for us:

```
function strFindAll(string $pattern, string $txt): array {
    $M = strlen($pattern);
    $N = strlen($txt);
    $positions = [];

    for ($i = 0; $i <= $N - $M; $i++) {
        for ($j = 0; $j < $M; $j++)
            if ($txt[$i + $j] != $pattern[$j])
            break;
```

```
        if ($j == $M)
            $positions[] = $i;
    }

    return $positions;
}
```

The approach is very straightforward. We start from position 0 of the actual string and keep on going until the $N-$M position, where $M is the length of the pattern we are looking for. We do not need to search the full string even at the worst case where there is no match for the pattern. Now, let's call the function with some arguments:

```
$txt = "AABAACAADAABABBBAABAA";
$pattern = "AABA";
$matches = strFindAll($pattern, $txt);

if ($matches) {
    foreach ($matches as $pos) {
        echo "Pattern found at index : " . $pos . "\n";
    }
}
```

This will produce following output:

```
Pattern found at index : 0
Pattern found at index : 9
Pattern found at index : 16
```

If we look at our $txt string, we can find that there are tree occurrences of our pattern AABA. The first one is at the beginning, second one is at the center, and third one is close to the end of the string. The algorithm we have written will take $O((N - M) * M)$ complexity, where N is the length of the text and M is the length of the pattern we are searching for. If we want, we can improve the efficiency of such matching using a popular algorithm known as **Knuth-Morris-Pratt** (**KMP**) string-matching algorithm.

Implementing Knuth-Morris-Pratt algorithm

Knuth-Morris-Pratt (KMP) string-matching algorithm is very similar to the naive algorithm we just implemented. The basic difference is that the KMP algorithm uses information from the partial matches and takes a decision to stop matching on any mismatch. It can also precompute the locations where the pattern can exist so that we can reduce the number of repeating comparison or false checks. The KMP algorithm pre-computes a table that helps during the search operation and increases efficiency. While implementing KMP algorithm, we need to computer the **Longest Proper Prefix Suffix** (**LPS**).

Let's check the function to generate the LPS part:

```
function ComputeLPS(string $pattern, array &$lps) {
    $len = 0;
    $i = 1;
    $M = strlen($pattern);

    $lps[0] = 0;

    while ($i < $M) {
    if ($pattern[$i] == $pattern[$len]) {
        $len++;
        $lps[$i] = $len;
        $i++;
    } else {
        if ($len != 0) {
            $len = $lps[$len - 1];
        } else {
            $lps[$i] = 0;
            $i++;
        }
    }
    }
}
```

For our pattern from the previous example AABA, the LPS will be [0, 1, 0, 1]; now, let's write the KMP implementation for our string/pattern search problem:

```
function KMPStringMatching(string $str, string $pattern): array {
    $matches = [];
    $M = strlen($pattern);
    $N = strlen($str);
    $i = $j = 0;
    $lps = [];

    ComputeLPS($pattern, $lps);

    while ($i < $N) {
    if ($pattern[$j] == $str[$i]) {
        $j++;
        $i++;
    }

    if ($j == $M) {
        array_push($matches, $i - $j);
        $j = $lps[$j - 1];
    } else if ($i < $N && $pattern[$j] != $str[$i]) {
        if ($j != 0)
```

```
        $j = $lps[$j - 1];
        else
        $i = $i + 1;
    }
    }
    return $matches;
}
```

The preceding code is the implementation of the KMP algorithm. Now, let's run the following example with our implemented algorithm:

```
$txt = "AABAACAADAABABBBAABAA";
$pattern = "AABA";
$matches = KMPStringMatching($txt, $pattern);

if ($matches) {
    foreach ($matches as $pos) {
        echo "Pattern found at index : " . $pos . "\n";
    }
}
```

This will produce the following output:

```
Pattern found at index : 0
Pattern found at index : 9
Pattern found at index : 16
```

The complexity of the KMP algorithm is $O(N + M)$, which is much better than regular pattern matching. Here, $O(M)$ is for computing LPS and $O(N)$ for KMP algorithm itself.

 There are many detailed descriptions of the KMP algorithm that can be found online.

Greedy algorithms

Though the name is greedy algorithms, actually, it is a programming technique that focuses on finding out the best possible solution at the given moment. This means that greedy algorithm makes a locally optimal choice in the hope that it will lead to the globally optimal solution. One thing we have to remember is that not all greedy approaches will take us to globally optimal solutions. However, still, greedy algorithm is applied in many problem-solving areas. One of the most popular uses of greedy algorithm is in Huffman encoding, which is used to encode a big text and compress the string by converting them into different codes. We will explore the concept and implementation of Huffman coding in the next section.

Implementing Huffman coding algorithm

Huffman coding is a compression technique used to reduce the number of bits required to send or store a message or string. It is based on the idea that frequently appearing characters will have shorter bit representation, and less frequent characters will have longer bit representation. If we consider the Huffman coding as a tree structure, the less frequent characters or items will be at the top part of the tree and more frequent items will be at the bottom of the tree or in the leaf. Huffman encoding relies a lot on the priority queue. Huffman encoding can be computed by first creating a tree of nodes.

Process to create a tree of nodes:

1. We have to create a leaf node for each symbol and add it to the priority queue.
2. While there is more than one node in the queue, do the following:

    1. Remove the node of highest priority (lowest probability/frequency) twice to get two nodes.

    2. Create a new internal node with these two nodes as children and with probability/frequency equal to the sum of the two nodes' probabilities/frequencies.

    3. Add the new node to the queue.

3. The remaining node is the root node, and the tree is complete.

Then, we have to traverse the constructed binary tree from root to leaves assigning and accumulating a "0" for one branch and a "1" for the other at each node. The accumulated zeros and ones at each leaf constitute a Huffman encoding for those symbols and weights. Here is an implementation of Huffman encoding algorithm using the SPL priority queue:

```
function huffmanEncode(array $symbols): array {
    $heap = new SplPriorityQueue;
    $heap->setExtractFlags(SplPriorityQueue::EXTR_BOTH);
    foreach ($symbols as $symbol => $weight) {
        $heap->insert(array($symbol => ''), -$weight);
    }

    while ($heap->count() > 1) {
    $low = $heap->extract();
    $high = $heap->extract();
    foreach ($low['data'] as &$x)
        $x = '0' . $x;
    foreach ($high['data'] as &$x)
        $x = '1' . $x;
    $heap->insert($low['data'] + $high['data'],
            $low['priority'] + $high['priority']);
    }
    $result = $heap->extract();
    return $result['data'];
}
```

Here, we are building a min heap for each of the symbols and using their weight to set the priority. Once the heap is constructed, we extract two nodes one after another and combining their data and priority to add them back to the heap. This continues unless only one node exists, which is the root node. Now, let's run the following code to generate the Huffman code:

```
$txt = 'PHP 7 Data structures and Algorithms';
$symbols = array_count_values(str_split($txt));
$codes = huffmanEncode($symbols);

echo "Symbol\t\tWeight\t\tHuffman Code\n";
foreach ($codes as $sym => $code) {
    echo "$sym\t\t$symbols[$sym]\t\t$code\n";
}
```

Here, we are using `str_split` to break the string into an array and then using array count values to convert it into an associative array where the character will be the key and its number of appearance in the string will be the value. The preceding code will produce the following output:

```
Symbol          Weight          Huffman Code
i               1               00000
D               1               00001
d               1               00010
A               1               00011
t               4               001
H               1               01000
m               1               01001
P               2               0101
g               1               01100
o               1               01101
e               1               01110
n               1               01111
7               1               10000
1               1               10001
u               2               1001
                5               101
h               1               11000
c               1               11001
a               3               1101
r               3               1110
s               3               1111
```

There are many other practical usages of greedy algorithms. We will solve a job-scheduling problem with greedy algorithms. Let's consider an example of a team of agile software developers who are working in a two-week iteration or sprint. They have some user stories to complete with some deadlines (by date) for the tasks and velocity (size of the story) attached to the story. The target for the team is to gain maximum velocity for the sprint within the given deadline. Let's consider the following tasks with deadline and velocity:

Index	1	2	3	4	5	6
Story	S1	S2	S3	S4	S5	S6
Deadline	2	1	2	1	3	4
Velocity	95	32	47	42	28	64

As we can see from the preceding table, we have six user stories, and they have four different deadlines from **1** to **4**. We have to finish the user story **S2** or **S4** for slot 1 since the deadline for the task is 1. The same goes for story **S1** and **S3,** and they have to be finished on or before slot **2**. However, since we have **S3** and the velocity of **S3** is bigger than **S2** and **S4, S3** will be chosen for slot 1 by the greedy approach. Let's write the greedy code for our velocity calculation:

```
function velocityMagnifier(array $jobs) {

    $n = count($jobs);

    usort($jobs, function($opt1, $opt2) {
        return $opt1['velocity'] < $opt2['velocity'];
    });

    $dMax = max(array_column($jobs, "deadline"));

    $slot = array_fill(1, $dMax, -1);
    $filledTimeSlot = 0;

    for ($i = 0; $i < $n; $i++) {
    $k = min($dMax, $jobs[$i]['deadline']);
    while ($k >= 1) {
        if ($slot[$k] == -1) {
          $slot[$k] = $i;
          $filledTimeSlot++;
          break;
        }
        $k--;
    }

      if ($filledTimeSlot == $dMax) {
         break;
      }
    }

    echo("Stories to Complete: ");
    for ($i = 1; $i <= $dMax; $i++) {
        echo $jobs[$slot[$i]]['id'];

        if ($i < $dMax) {
            echo "\t";
        }
    }

    $maxVelocity = 0;
    for ($i = 1; $i <= $dMax; $i++) {
```

```
            $maxVelocity += $jobs[$slot[$i]]['velocity'];
    }
    echo "\nMax Velocity: " . $maxVelocity;
}
```

Here, we are getting the list of jobs (user story ID, deadline, and velocity) that we will use to find the maximum velocity and their respective user story ID. First, we sort the jobs array with custom user sort function `usort` and sort the array in the descending order based on their velocity. After that, we calculate the maximum number of slots available from the deadline column. We are then initializing the slot array to -1 to keep a flag of used slots. The next code block is to traverse through each of the user stories and find a proper slot for the user story. If the available timeslots are filled, we don't continue further. Now, let's run this code using the following code block:

```
$jobs = [
    ["id" => "S1", "deadline" => 2, "velocity" => 95],
    ["id" => "S2", "deadline" => 1, "velocity" => 32],
    ["id" => "S3", "deadline" => 2, "velocity" => 47],
    ["id" => "S4", "deadline" => 1, "velocity" => 42],
    ["id" => "S5", "deadline" => 3, "velocity" => 28],
    ["id" => "S6", "deadline" => 4, "velocity" => 64]
];

velocityMagnifier($jobs);
```

This will produce the following output in command line:

```
Stories to Complete: S3    S1    S5    S6
Max Velocity: 234
```

Greedy algorithms can be helpful in solving locally optimized problems such as job scheduling, network traffic control, graph algorithm, among other things. However, to get a globally optimized solution, we need to focus on another aspect of algorithms, which is known as dynamic programming.

Understanding dynamic programming

Dynamic programming is a way of solving complex problems by dividing them into smaller sub problems and finding solution for those sub problems. We accumulate the solutions of sub problems to find the global solution. The good part of dynamic programming is that we reduce the recalculation of sub problems by storing their results. Dynamic programming is a very well-known method for optimization. The use of dynamic algorithm can be found everywhere in the programming world.

Dynamic programming can solve problems such as coin changing, finding the longest common subsequence, finding the longest increasing sequences, sequencing DNA strings, and so on. The core difference between the greedy algorithm and dynamic programming is that dynamic programming will always prefer a globally optimized solution.

We can solve a problem with dynamic programming if the problem has either optimal substructure or overlapping sub problems. Optimal substructure means that the optimization for the actual problem can be solved using a combination of optimal solution of its sub problems. In other words, if a problem is optimized for n, it will be optimized for any size less than n or more than n. The overlapping sub problems indicates that smaller sub problems will be solved over and over again as they are overlapping with each other. Fibonacci series is a great example for overlapping sub problems. So, having basic recursion here will not help at all. Dynamic programming solves each subproblem exactly once and does not attempt to resolve any further. It is achieved either via a top-down approach or a bottom-up approach.

In a top-down approach, we start with a bigger problem and recursively solve the smaller sub problems. However, we have to use the memoization technique to store the subproblem results so that we do not have to recalculate that subproblem in future. In the bottom-up approach, we solve the smallest subproblem first and then move to the other smaller sub problems. Usually, subproblem results are stored in a tabular format using a multidimensional array for bottom-up approach.

Now, we will explore some examples from the dynamic programming world. Some might sound very familiar from our day-to-day programming problems. We will get started with the famous knapsack problem.

0 - 1 knapsack

A knapsack is a bag with straps, usually carried by soldiers to help them take their necessary items or valuables during their journey. Each item has a value and definite weight attached to it. So, the soldier has to pick the most valuable items within their maximum weight limit as they cannot put everything in their bag. The word 0/1 means that either we can take it or leave it. We cannot take an item partially. This is known as the famous 0-1 knapsack problem. We will take the bottom-up approach for solving the 0-1 knapsack problem. Here is the pseudocode for the solution:

```
Procedure knapsack(n, W, w1,...,wN, v1,...,vN)
for w = 0 to W
    M[0, w] = 0

for i = 1 to n
```

```
    for w = 0 to W

    if wi > w :
        M[i, w] = M[i-1, w]
    else :
        M[i, w] = max (M[i-1, w], vi + M[i-1, w-wi ])
return M[n, W]

end procedure
```

For example, if we have five items, [1,2,3,4,5], and they have the weight of 10,20,30,40,50, respectively, a maximum allowed weight of 10 will produce the following table using the bottom-up approach:

	Weights										
	0	1	2	3	4	5	6	7	8	9	10
Items	0	0	0	0	0	0	0	0	0	0	0
1	0	10	10	10	10	10	10	10	10	10	10
1,2	0	10	20	30	30	30	30	30	30	30	30
1,2,3	0	10	20	30	40	50	60	60	60	60	60
1,2,3,4	0	10	20	30	40	50	60	70	80	90	100
1,2,3,4,5	0	10	20	30	40	50	60	70	80	90	100

As we can see, we build the up the table bottom up where we start with one item and one weight and increase it to our desired weight and maximize the value count by choosing the best possible items. At the end, the last cell in the bottom-right corner is the one with the expected result for the 0-1 knapsack problem. Here is the implementation and code to run the function:

```
function knapSack(int $maxWeight, array $weights, array $values, int $n) {
    $DP = [];
    for ($i = 0; $i <= $n; $i++) {
      for ($w = 0; $w <= $maxWeight; $w++) {
          if ($i == 0 || $w == 0)
          $DP[$i][$w] = 0;
          else if ($weights[$i - 1] <= $w)
          $DP[$i][$w] =
            max($values[$i-1]+$DP[$i - 1][$w - $weights[$i-1]]
            , $DP[$i - 1][$w]);
          else
          $DP[$i][$w] = $DP[$i - 1][$w];
      }
    }
```

```
        return $DP[$n][$maxWeight];
    }

    $values = [10, 20, 30, 40, 50];
    $weights = [1, 2, 3, 4, 5];
    $maxWeight = 10;
    $n = count($values);
    echo knapSack($maxWeight, $weights, $values, $n);
```

This will show 100 on the command line, which actually matches our expected result from the preceding table. The complexity of this algorithm is O ($n*W$), where n is the number of items and W is the target weight.

Finding the longest common subsequence-LCS

Another very popular algorithm to solve using dynamic programming is finding the longest common subsequence, or LCS, between two strings. The process is very similar to the knapsack solution where we had a two-dimensional table and we started with one weight to move to our target weight. Here, we will start with the first character of the first string and move across the whole string for the second string to match the characters. We will continue this until all the characters of the first string are matched with individual characters of the second string. So, when we find a match, we consider the top-left corner cell or diagonally left cell of the matched cell. Let's consider the following two tables to understand how the matching occurs:

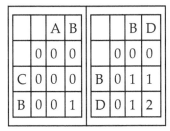

On the left table, we have two strings AB and CB. When B matches B in the table, the value of the matched cell will be the value of its diagonal cell plus one. That is why the dark background cell of the first table has a value of 1 since the diagonally left cell has a value of 0. For the same reason, the table on the right has right lowest cell of value 2 as the diagonal cell has a value of 1. Here is the pseudocode for finding the LCS length:

```
function LCSLength(X[1..m], Y[1..n])
    C = array[m][n]
    for i := 0..m
        C[i,0] = 0
    for j := 0..n
        C[0,j] = 0
    for i := 1..m
        for j := 1..n
            if(i = 0 or j = 0)
                C[i,j] := 0
            else if X[i] = Y[j]
                C[i,j] := C[i-1,j-1] + 1
            else
                C[i,j] := max(C[i,j-1], C[i-1,j])
    return C[m,n]
```

Here is the implementation of our pseudocode to find the LCS length:

```
function LCS(string $X, string $Y): int {
    $M = strlen($X);
    $N = strlen($Y);
    $L = [];

    for ($i = 0; $i <= $M; $i++)
        $L[$i][0] = 0;
    for ($j = 0; $j <= $N; $j++)
        $L[0][$j] = 0;

    for ($i = 0; $i <= $M; $i++) {
        for ($j = 0; $j <= $N; $j++) {
            if($i == 0 || $j == 0)
            $L[$i][$j] = 0;
            else if ($X[$i - 1] == $Y[$j - 1])
            $L[$i][$j] = $L[$i - 1][$j - 1] + 1;
            else
            $L[$i][$j] = max($L[$i - 1][$j], $L[$i][$j - 1]);
        }
    }
    return $L[$M][$N];
}
```

Now, let's run the LCS function with two strings to see whether we can find the longest common subsequence:

```
$X = "AGGTAB";
$Y = "GGTXAYB";
echo "LCS Length:".LCS( $X, $Y );
```

This will produce the output LCS Length:5 in the command line. This seems to be correct as both the strings have GGTAB as the common subsequence.

DNA sequencing using dynamic programming

We have just seen how to find the longest common subsequence. Using the same principle, we can implement DNA or protein sequencing, which can be very helpful for us in solving bioinformatic problems. For alignment purpose, we will use the most popular algorithm known as the Needleman-Wunsch algorithm. It is similar to our LCS algorithm, but the scoring system is different. Here, we score a match, mismatch, and gap in a different scoring system. There are two parts of the algorithm: one to calculate the matrix with possible sequence and the second part is tracking back the actual sequence with the best possible one. The Needleman-Wunsch algorithm provides the best global alignment solution for any given sequence. Since the algorithm itself is little bigger along with the scoring system explanation, which we can find in many websites or books, we want to keep our focus on the implementation part of the algorithm. We will divide the problem into two parts. First, we will generate the computational table using dynamic programming, and then, we will track it backwards to generate the actual sequence alignment. For our implementation, we will use 1 for matching, and -1 for gap penalty and mismatch score. Here is the first part of our implementation:

```
define("GC", "-");
define("SP", 1);
define("GP", -1);
define("MS", -1);

function NWSquencing(string $s1, string $s2) {
    $grid = [];
    $M = strlen($s1);
    $N = strlen($s2);

    for ($i = 0; $i <= $N; $i++) {
    $grid[$i] = [];
      for ($j = 0; $j <= $M; $j++) {
```

```
            $grid[$i][$j] = null;
        }
    }
    $grid[0][0] = 0;

    for ($i = 1; $i <= $M; $i++) {
        $grid[0][$i] = -1 * $i;
    }

    for ($i = 1; $i <= $N; $i++) {
        $grid[$i][0] = -1 * $i;
    }

    for ($i = 1; $i <= $N; $i++) {
      for ($j = 1; $j <= $M; $j++) {
          $grid[$i][$j] = max(
            $grid[$i - 1][$j - 1] + ($s2[$i - 1] === $s1[$j - 1] ? SP :
              MS), $grid[$i - 1][$j] + GP, $grid[$i][$j - 1] + GP
          );
      }
    }

    printSequence($grid, $s1, $s2, $M, $N);
}
```

Here, we have created a two-dimensional array of size M,N, where M is the size of string #1 and N is the size of string #2. We initialized the first row and column of the grid to a negative value in the decreasing order. We multiplied the index with a gap penalty to achieve this behavior. Here, our constant SP indicates the matching score point, MS for mismatch score, GP for gap penalty, and GC indicates the Gap Character, which we will use during sequence printing. At the end of dynamic programming, the matrix will be generated. Let's consider the following two strings:

```
$X = "GAATTCAGTTA";
$Y = "GGATCGA";
```

Then, our table will look like this after running the Needleman algorithm:

		G	A	A	T	T	C	A	G	T	T	Λ
	0	-1	-2	-3	-4	-5	-6	-7	-8	-9	-10	-11
G	-1	1	0	-1	-2	-3	-4	-5	-6	-7	-8	-9
G	-2	0	0	-1	-2	-3	-4	-5	-4	-5	-6	-7
A	-3	-1	1	1	0	-1	-2	-3	-4	-5	-6	-5

T	-4	-2	0	0	2	1	0	-1	-2	-3	-4	-5
C	-5	-3	-1	-1	1	1	2	1	0	-1	-2	-3
G	-6	-4	-2	-2	0	0	1	1	2	1	0	-1
A	-7	-5	-3	-1	-1	-1	0	2	1	1	0	1

Now, using this scoring table, we can find out the actual sequence. Here, we will start from the bottom-right cell in the table and consider the top cell, left cell, and the diagonal cell values. If the max value among the three cells is the top one, then the top string requires an insertion of gap character (-). If the maximum value is the diagonal one, then there is a better chance of matching. So, we can compare the two characters of the two strings, and if they match, then we can put a bar or pipe character to show the alignment. Here is what the sequencing function will look like:

```
function printSequence($grid, $s1, $s2, $j, $i) {
    $sq1 = [];
    $sq2 = [];
    $sq3 = [];

    do {
    $t = $grid[$i - 1][$j];
    $d = $grid[$i - 1][$j - 1];
    $l = $grid[$i][$j - 1];
    $max = max($t, $d, $l);

    switch ($max) {
        case $d:
        $j--;
        $i--;
          array_push($sq1, $s1[$j]);
          array_push($sq2, $s2[$i]);
          if ($s1[$j] == $s2[$i])
              array_push($sq3, "|");
          else
              array_push($sq3, " ");
        break;

        case $t:
        $i--;
          array_push($sq1, GC);
          array_push($sq2, $s2[$i]);
          array_push($sq3, " ");
        break;

        case $l:
          $j--;
```

```
            array_push($sq1, $s1[$j]);
            array_push($sq2, GC);
            array_push($sq3, " ");
        break;
    }
    } while ($i > 0 && $j > 0);

    echo implode("", array_reverse($sq1)) . "\n";
    echo implode("", array_reverse($sq3)) . "\n";
    echo implode("", array_reverse($sq2)) . "\n";
}
```

Since we are starting from back and slowly moving to the front, we are using array push to keep the alignment in order. Then, we are printing the array by reversing it. The complexity of the algorithm is O (M * N). Here is the output if we call NWSquencing for our two strings $X and $Y:

```
G-AATTCAGTTA
| | | | | |
GGA-T-C-G--A
```

Backtracking to solve puzzle problem

Backtracking is a recursive algorithm strategy where we backtrack when a result is not found and continue search for solution in other possible ways. Backtracking is a popular way to solve many famous problems, especially chess, Sudoku, crosswords, and so on. Since recursion is the key component of backtracking, we need to ensure that our problem can be divided into sub problems, and we apply recursion into those sub problems. In this section, we will solve one of the most popular games, Sudoku, using backtracking.

In Sudoku, we have a partially filled box with nice boxes of size 3X3. The rule of the game is to place a number 1 to 9 in each cell, where the same number cannot exist in the same row or column. So, in the 9X9 cell, each number 1 to 9 will be present only once for each row and each column:

	7	3	8	
	2	5		
4	9	6		1
4	3		2	1
1				5

	5	8				6	7	
5			1		8			9
			5		3			
		2		9		5		

For example, in the preceding Sudoku board, the first column has 4, 1, 5 and the first row have 7, 3, 8. As a result, we cannot use any of these six numbers in the first empty cell on the top left. So, the possible numbers can be 2, 6, and 9. We do not know which one of these numbers will satisfy the solution. We can pick two and put in the first cell and then start looking for values for the remaining empty cells. This will continue until all the cells are filled up or still there is a way to place a number in the empty cell without violating the game principle. If no solution is possible, we will backtrack and come back to 2 again, replace it with the next possible option 6, and run the same recursive way of finding numbers for other empty cells. This continues until the board is solved. Let's write some recursive code to solve the Sudoku:

```
define("N", 9);
define("UNASSIGNED", 0);

function FindUnassignedLocation(array &$grid, int &$row,
int &$col): bool {
    for ($row = 0; $row < N; $row++)
      for ($col = 0; $col < N; $col++)
          if ($grid[$row][$col] == UNASSIGNED)
          return true;
      return false;
}

function UsedInRow(array &$grid, int $row, int $num): bool {
    return in_array($num, $grid[$row]);
}

function UsedInColumn(array &$grid, int $col, int $num): bool {
    return in_array($num, array_column($grid, $col));
}

function UsedInBox(array &$grid, int $boxStartRow,
int $boxStartCol, int $num): bool {
    for ($row = 0; $row < 3; $row++)
    for ($col = 0; $col < 3; $col++)
if ($grid[$row + $boxStartRow][$col + $boxStartCol] == $num)
        return true;
    return false;
}
```

```
function isSafe(array $grid, int $row, int $col, int $num): bool {
    return !UsedInRow($grid, $row, $num) &&
        !UsedInColumn($grid, $col, $num) &&
        !UsedInBox($grid, $row - $row % 3, $col - $col % 3, $num);
}
```

Here, we can see all the auxiliary functions required to implement the Sudoku function. First, we defined the max size of the grid along with the unassigned cell indicator, which is 0 in this case. The first function we have is to find any unassigned location in the 9 X 9 grid, starting from the top-left corner cell, and search the empty cell row wise. Then, we have three functions to check whether a number is used in a particular row or column or a 3 X 3 box. If the number is not used in the row, column, or in the box, we can use it for a possible value in the cell, and that is why, we are returning true in the isSafe function check. If it is used in any one of these places, the function will return false. Now, we are ready to implement the recursive function for solving the Sudoku:

```
function SolveSudoku(array &$grid): bool {
    $row = $col = 0;

    if (!FindUnassignedLocation($grid, $row, $col))
        return true; // success! no empty space

    for ($num = 1; $num <= N; $num++) {
      if (isSafe($grid, $row, $col, $num)) {
          $grid[$row][$col] = $num; // make assignment

          if (SolveSudoku($grid))
          return true;  // return, if success

          $grid[$row][$col] = UNASSIGNED;  // failure
      }
    }
    return false; // triggers backtracking
}

function printGrid(array $grid) {
    foreach ($grid as $row) {
        echo implode("", $row) . "\n";
    }
}
```

The `SolveSudoku` function is self-explanatory. Here, we visited one cell, and if the cell is empty, put a temporary number, any number from 1 to 9, in the cell. Then, we checked whether the number is redundant in the row or in the column or in the 3 X 3 matrix. If it does not conflict, we keep the number in the cell and move to the next empty cell. We do this via recursion so that if required, we can track back and change the value in the case of a conflict. This continues until a solution is found. We also have added a `printGrid` function to print a given grid in the command line. Let's now run the code with the sample Sudoku matrix we have used in this example:

```
$grid = [
    [0, 0, 7, 0, 3, 0, 8, 0, 0],
    [0, 0, 0, 2, 0, 5, 0, 0, 0],
    [4, 0, 0, 9, 0, 6, 0, 0, 1],
    [0, 4, 3, 0, 0, 0, 2, 1, 0],
    [1, 0, 0, 0, 0, 0, 0, 0, 5],
    [0, 5, 8, 0, 0, 0, 6, 7, 0],
    [5, 0, 0, 1, 0, 8, 0, 0, 9],
    [0, 0, 0, 5, 0, 3, 0, 0, 0],
    [0, 0, 2, 0, 9, 0, 5, 0, 0]
];

if (SolveSudoku($grid) == true)
    printGrid($grid);
else
    echo "No solution exists";
```

We have used a two-dimensional array to represent our Sudoku matrix. If we run the code, it will produce following output in the command line:

```
297431856
361285497
485976321
743659218
126847935
958312674
534128769
879563142
612794583
```

Alternatively, if we present that in a nice Sudoku matrix, it will look like this:

2	9	7	4	3	1	8	5	6
3	6	1	2	8	5	4	9	7
4	8	5	9	7	6	3	2	1
7	4	3	6	5	9	2	1	8
1	2	6	8	4	7	9	3	5
9	5	8	3	1	2	6	7	4
5	3	4	1	2	8	7	6	9
8	7	9	5	6	3	1	4	2
6	1	2	7	9	4	5	8	3

Backtracking can be very useful to find solutions to find path or solve game problems. There are many references available online for backtracking, which can be very useful to us.

Collaborative filtering recommendation system

Recommendation systems are used everywhere in the Internet today. From e-commerce sites to restaurants, hotels, tickets, events, and so on. are recommended to us everywhere. Have we ever asked ourselves how do they know what will be the best for us? How do they come up with this calculation of showing the items we might like? The answer is most sites use collaborative filtering (CF) to recommend something. Collaborative filtering is a process of making automatic prediction (filtering) about the interests of a user by analyzing other user's choices or preferences (collaborative). We will build a simple recommendation system using the Pearson correlation method where a similarity score between two people is calculated on the range of -1 to +1. If the similarity score is +1, then it means two people are a perfect match. If the similarity score is 0, then it means no there is no similarity between them, and if the score is -1, then they are negatively similar. Usually, the scores are mostly fractional.

The Pearson correlation is calculated using the following formula:

$$Pearson(x, y) = \frac{\sum xy - \frac{\sum x \sum y}{N}}{\sqrt{(\sum x^2 - \frac{(\sum x)^2}{N})(\sum y^2 - \frac{(\sum y)^2}{N})}}$$

Here, x denotes preferences from person one, y represents preferences from person two, and N represents the number of items in the preferences, which are common between x and y. Let's now implement a sample review system for restaurants in Dhaka. There are reviewers who have reviewed some restaurants. Some of them are common, some are not. Our job will be to find a recommendation for person X based on the reviews of others. Our reviews look like this:

```
$reviews = [];
$reviews['Adiyan'] = ["McDonalds" => 5, "KFC" => 5, "Pizza Hut" => 4.5,
"Burger King" => 4.7, "American Burger" => 3.5, "Pizza Roma" => 2.5];
$reviews['Mikhael'] = ["McDonalds" => 3, "KFC" => 4, "Pizza Hut" => 3.5,
"Burger King" => 4, "American Burger" => 4, "Jafran" => 4];
$reviews['Zayeed'] = ["McDonalds" => 5, "KFC" => 4, "Pizza Hut" => 2.5,
"Burger King" => 4.5, "American Burger" => 3.5, "Sbarro" => 2];
$reviews['Arush'] = ["KFC" => 4.5, "Pizza Hut" => 3, "Burger King" => 4,
"American Burger" => 3, "Jafran" => 2.5, "FFC" => 3.5];
$reviews['Tajwar'] = ["Burger King" => 3, "American Burger" => 2, "KFC" =>
2.5, "Pizza Hut" => 3, "Pizza Roma" => 2.5, "FFC" => 3];
$reviews['Aayan'] = [ "KFC" => 5, "Pizza Hut" => 4, "Pizza Roma" => 4.5,
"FFC" => 4];
```

Now, based on the structure, we can write our Pearson correlation calculation between two reviewers. Here is the implementation:

```
function pearsonScore(array $reviews, string $person1, string $person2):
float {

$commonItems = array();

foreach ($reviews[$person1] as $restaurant1 => $rating) {
    foreach ($reviews[$person2] as $restaurant2 => $rating) {
        if ($restaurant1 == $restaurant2) {
            $commonItems[$restaurant1] = 1;
        }
    }
}

$n = count($commonItems);
```

```
if ($n == 0)
    return 0.0;

    $sum1 = 0;
    $sum2 = 0;
    $sqrSum1 = 0;
    $sqrSum2 = 0;
    $pSum = 0;
    foreach ($commonItems as $restaurant => $common) {
      $sum1 += $reviews[$person1][$restaurant];
      $sum2 += $reviews[$person2][$restaurant];
      $sqrSum1 += $reviews[$person1][$restaurant] ** 2;
      $sqrSum2 += $reviews[$person2][$restaurant] ** 2;
      $pSum += $reviews[$person1][$restaurant] *
      $reviews[$person2][$restaurant];
    }

    $num = $pSum - (($sum1 * $sum2) / $n);
    $den = sqrt(($sqrSum1 - (($sum1 ** 2) / $n))
      * ($sqrSum2 - (($sum2 ** 2) / $n)));

    if ($den == 0) {
      $pearsonCorrelation = 0;
    } else {
      $pearsonCorrelation = $num / $den;
    }

  return (float) $pearsonCorrelation;
}
```

Here, we have just implemented the equation we have shown for the Pearson correlation calculator. Now, we will write the recommendation function based on Pearson scoring:

```
function getRecommendations(array $reviews, string $person): array {
    $calculation = [];
    foreach ($reviews as $reviewer => $restaurants) {
    $similarityScore = pearsonScore($reviews, $person, $reviewer);
        if ($person == $reviewer || $similarityScore <= 0) {
            continue;
        }

        foreach ($restaurants as $restaurant => $rating) {
            if (!array_key_exists($restaurant, $reviews[$person])) {
                if (!array_key_exists($restaurant, $calculation)) {
                    $calculation[$restaurant] = [];
                    $calculation[$restaurant]['Total'] = 0;
                    $calculation[$restaurant]['SimilarityTotal'] = 0;
                }
```

```
            $calculation[$restaurant]['Total'] += $similarityScore *
              $rating;
            $calculation[$restaurant]['SimilarityTotal'] +=
              $similarityScore;
          }
      }
  }

  $recommendations = [];
  foreach ($calculation as $restaurant => $values) {
    $recommendations[$restaurant] = $calculation[$restaurant]['Total']
      / $calculation[$restaurant]['SimilarityTotal'];
  }

  arsort($recommendations);
  return $recommendations;
}
```

In the preceding function, we calculated the similarity score between each reviewer and weighted their reviews with each other. Based on the top score, we showed the recommendation for the reviewer. Let's run the following code to get some recommendations:

```
$person = 'Arush';
echo 'Restaurant recommendations for ' . $person . "\n";
$recommendations = getRecommendations($reviews, $person);
foreach ($recommendations as $restaurant => $score) {
    echo $restaurant . " \n";
}
```

This will produce the following output:

```
Restaurant recommendations for Arush
McDonalds
Pizza Roma
Sbarro
```

We can use the Pearson correlation scoring system to recommend items or show users who to follow to get better reviews. There are many other ways to get the collaborative filtering to work, but that is beyond the scope of this book.

Using bloom filters and sparse matrix

Sparse matrix can be used as highly efficient data structure. A sparse matrix has more 0 values compared to actual values. For example, a 100 X 100 matrix may have 10,000 cells. Now, out of this 10,000 cells, only 100 have values; rest are 0. Other than the 100 values, remaining cells are occupied with the default value of 0, and they are taking same byte size to store the value 0 to indicate the empty cell. It is a huge waste of space, and we can reduce it using the sparse matrix. We can use different techniques to store the values to the sparse matrix in a separate matrix that will be very lean and will not take any unnecessary spaces. We can also use a linked list to represent the sparse matrix. Here is an example of the sparse matrix:

0	0	0	0	0	1	0	0	0	0		Row	Col	Value
1	0	0	0	0	0	0	0	0	0		0	5	1
0	0	0	0	2	0	0	0	0	0		1	0	1
0	0	2	0	0	0	0	0	0	0		2	4	2
0	0	0	0	0	0	1	0	0	0		3	2	2
0	0	0	0	0	0	0	2	0	0		4	6	1
0	0	0	0	0	0	1	0	0	0		5	7	2
1	0	0	0	0	0	0	0	0	0		6	6	1
											7	1	1

Since PHP array is dynamic in nature, the best approach for sparse matrix in PHP will be using only the indexes that have values; others are not used at all. When we are using the cell, we can do a check to see whether the cell has any value; else, the default value of 0 is used, just as shown in the following example:

```php
$sparseArray = [];
$sparseArray[0][5] = 1;
$sparseArray[1][0] = 1;
$sparseArray[2][4] = 2;
$sparseArray[3][2] = 2;
$sparseArray[4][6] = 1;
$sparseArray[5][7] = 2;
$sparseArray[6][6] = 1;
$sparseArray[7][1] = 1;

function getSparseValue(array $array, int $i, int $j): int {
```

```
    if (isset($array[$i][$j]))
        return $array[$i][$j];
    else
        return 0;
}

echo getSparseValue($sparseArray, 0, 2) . "\n";
echo getSparseValue($sparseArray, 7, 1) . "\n";
echo getSparseValue($sparseArray, 8, 8) . "\n";
```

This will produce the following output in the command line:

```
0
1
0
```

When we have a large dataset, doing lookup in the dataset can be very time consuming and costly. Let's assume we have a dataset of 10 million phone numbers and we want to search for a particular phone number. This can be easily done using a database query. However, what if it is 1 billion phone numbers? Will it still be faster to find from a database? Such a big database can create slow-performing lookups. In order to solve this problem, an efficient approach can be using bloom filters.

A bloom filter is a space-efficient, probabilistic data structure that determines whether a particular item is part of a set or not. It returns two values: "possibly in set" and "definitely not in set". If an item does not belong to a set, bloom filter returns false. However, if it returns true, the item may or may not be in the set. The reason for this is described here.

In general, a bloom filter is a bit array of size m, where all initial values are 0. There is k different hash function, which converts an item to a hashed integer value, which is mapped in the bit array. This hash value can be between 0 to m, as m is the max size of our bit array. The hash functions are similar to md5, sha1, crc32, and so on, but they are very fast and efficient. Usually, in bloom filter fnv, murmur, Siphash, and so on, hash functions are used. Let's take an example of 16 (16+1 cells) bit bloom filter with the initial value of 0:

| 0 | 0 | 0 | 0 | 0 | 0 | 0 | 0 | 0 | 0 | 0 | 0 | 0 | 0 | 0 | 0 | 0 |

Let's assume that we have two hash functions, k1 and k2, to convert our items to integer values between 0 to 16. Let our first item to store in the bloom filter be "PHP". Then, our hash function will return following:

```
k1("PHP") = 5
k2("PHP") = 9
```

Two `hash` functions have returned two different values. We can now put 1 in the bit array to mark that. The bit array will now look like this:

0	0	0	0	0	1	0	0	0	1	0	0	0	0	0	0	0

Let's now add another item in the list, for example, "algorithm". Suppose our `hash` functions will return the following values:

```
k1("algorithm") = 2
k2("algorithm") = 5
```

Since we can see that 5 is already marked by another item, we do not have to mark it again. Now, the bit array will look like this:

0	0	1	0	0	1	0	0	0	1	0	0	0	0	0	0	0

For example, now, we want to check an item called "error", which is hashed to the following values:

```
k1("error") = 2
k2("error") = 9
```

As we can see that our `hash` functions `k1` and `k2` returned a hashed value for string "error," which is not present in the array. So, this is definitely an error, and we expect to have such errors if our `hash` functions are only few in number. The more `hash` functions we have, lesser the errors we will have, as different `hash` functions will return different values. There is a relationship between error rate, number of `hash` functions, and the size of bloom filter. For example, a bloom filter for 5000 items and 0.0001 error rate will require roughly 14 `hash` functions and approximately 96000 bits. We can get such numbers from online bloomfilter calculators such as `https://krisives.github.io/bloom-calculator/`.

Summary

We have seen many advanced algorithms and techniques that can be used to solve different types of problems in this chapter. There are many good resources available to study these topics. Dynamic programming is such an important topic and can be covered in several chapters or have a separate book for itself. We tried to explain few of the topics, but there are more to explore. You also learned about sparse matrix and bloom filter, which can be used for efficient data storage for big data blocks. We can use these data structure concepts whenever we need them. Now, as we are reaching the end of the book, we will wrap up our discussion with some available libraries, functions, and references for data structure and algorithm in PHP 7.

12
PHP Built-In Support for Data Structures and Algorithms

PHP is a language with an enriched library of predefined functions, along with super support from the community. Whether it is an algorithm or data structure, PHP already has solid built-in support for developers. In this chapter, we will explore some of the built-in functions and features that we can use in our data structure and algorithm implementations. Let's now explore those features in PHP.

Built-in PHP features for data structure

PHP has a rich collection of built-in data structures in Standard PHP Library SPL. After the release of PHP 7, it is believed that SPL data structure implementation is not very "performant" as compared to the old PHP version. So, we will discuss a new PECL extension just designed for data structures. We also have a very strong support for PHP array, which can be used as a set, vector, map, hash table, stack, queue, collection, dictionary, and so on. SPL is fairly new compared to the array and still managed to capture the limelight with the diverse implementation of core data structures as a built-in feature. Since PHP 5.0, SPL is shipped with core PHP so that no extra extension or build is required. We have already explored the dynamic nature of PHP array in Chapter 2, *Understanding PHP Arrays*. In this chapter, we will name few of the other useful functions available to PHP to operate on data structures.

Using PHP array

PHP array has a wider set of predefined functions that make PHP array one of the most used features of PHP. We will not discuss all the available PHP array functions. We will discuss few of the functions that can be very useful for us in our data structure operations. Here are the PHP array functions:

- **array_pop**: This pops the last element of the array similar to stack pop operation. The array is passed as reference to the function. It only takes one argument, that is, the name of the array.
- **array_push**: This pushes one or more elements at the end of the array, just like a stack push operation. We have seen that we can push one element at a time using push. In PHP array, we can push multiple values at the end of the current array. The array is passed as a reference in the function as shown:

    ```
    $countries = [];
    array_push($countries, 'Bangladesh', 'Bhutan');
    ```

- **current**: Each array has an internal pointer to identify where it is at the moment. Initially, it starts from the first element of the array. The current function returns the current pointer of the array and returns the value of the element in the current position. If we consider the array to be a list, these internal pointer functionalities will be required.
- **prev**: The prev function moves the internal pointer one step backward. The PHP array can work as a doubly linked list, and prev is used to go the previous pointer.
- **next**: The next function moves the internal pointer to the next element.
- **end**: The end function moves the internal array pointer to the end of the array.
- **reset**: The reset function moves the internal array to the beginning of the array.
- **array_search**: This is a very useful function for searching an element in the array. If the element is found in the array, it returns the corresponding index where it was found. If nothing is found, it will return false. If multiple elements are there with the same search key, it will return the first occurrence index. We have to be careful as this function might also return 0 if the element is found in the first index. So, we have to check the boolean false with strict type checking during comparison. The array_search function takes two mandatory arguments, needle, and haystack. Needle is the element we are looking for, and haystack is the array where we are looking for the element. For example, if we are looking for a word in a dictionary, then we can consider the search word such as "needle" and "dictionary" as the haystack.

- There is an optional third parameter that enables strict type checking for the element. So, if it is set true, it searches the element not only by value, but also by type:

```
$countries = ["Bangladesh", "Nepal", "Bhutan"];

$key = array_search("Bangladesh", $countries);
if ($key !== FALSE)
    echo "Found in: " . $key;
else
    echo "Not found";
```

This will produce the following output:

Found in: 0

If we had != inside the if condition check, then it would have shown Not found in the result.

- **array_sum**: This is another handy PHP built-in function to get the sum of a given array. It will return a single numeric value, which is the sum of all elements in the array. It can be an integer or float.

- **array_map**: This is a very useful function if we want to change the elements of the array with a certain type of properties. For example, we want to make all text of the array to be in upper case or lower case. Instead of running a loop, we can use this function to do that. The array_map function takes two arguments. The first one is the callable function, and the second one is the array itself. The function returns the modified array, as shown here:

```
$countries = ["bangladesh", "nepal", "bhutan"];
$newCountries = array_map(function($country) {
    return strtoupper($country);
}, $countries);

foreach ($newCountries as $country)
    echo $country . "\n";
```

Alternatively, we can write it simply like this:

```
$countries = ["bangladesh", "nepal", "bhutan"];
$newCountries = array_map('strtoupper', $countries);

foreach ($newCountries as $country)
    echo $country . "\n";
```

The preceding code applies an `array_map` function to capitalize each word in a given array. Both codes will produce the following output:

```
BANGLADESH
NEPAL
BHUTAN
```

- **array_rand**: If we need to pick one or more items randomly from a given array, this function can be very useful. The default value is 1 for the number of items to return, but we can always increase it.
- **array_shift**: This function shifts an element from the beginning of the array, which is very much similar to our dequeue operation in a queue data structure. The removed element is returned from the function:

```
$countries = ["bangladesh", "nepal", "bhutan"];
$top = array_shift($countries);
echo $top;
```

This will show the output `bangladesh` in the command line. The `$countries` array will have only `nepal` and `bhutan` in it.

- **array_unshift**: This function adds one or more items at the beginning of the array and unshift existing items.
- **shuffle**: If we need to shuffle an array for any reason, we can use this function. This function can be very handy to randomize the whole array.
- **array_intersect**: This function takes two or more arrays as arguments and returns the common items from the first array and finds out the existence in other arrays. This function also preserves the keys.
- **array_diff**: This function calculates the difference between an array and other given arrays. Like the `array_intersect` function, this function also takes multiple arrays as arguments, where the first argument is the base array and, others are compared for differentiating with it.

There are many useful array functions in PHP, and they are solving many existing data structure and algorithm problems. We can find a list of built-in array functions in PHP documentation. For the purpose of this book, we will explore a few more array functions for sorting in the upcoming sections. For other functions, PHP .NET is recommended for further reading.

SPL classes

Undoubtedly, SPL tries to solve common data structure implementation issues for PHP programmers. Many of us are either afraid or reluctant to implement proper data structure while programming. SPL comes with implementation of all basic data structure and, hence, makes life easier for developers by using built-in classes and methods. Since SPL comes as a bundle with PHP, we do not need to install it separately or enable any extension for it. In this section, we will discuss some of the common SPL classes in brief:

- **SplDoublyLinkedList**: This class gives us the option to implement a doubly linked list without writing a big chunk of code. Though it says doubly linked list, we can utilize this class to implement stack and queue as well, by setting the iteration mode in the `setIteratorMode` method.

- **SplStack**: `SplStack` class is an extended version of the `SplDoublyLinkedList` class where the standard stack functions are available, which are actually from the doubly linked list class.

- **SplQueue**: `SplQueue` class is an extended version of the `SplDoublyLinkedList` class where the standard queue functions such as `enqueue`, `dequeue` are available. However, these functions are actually from the doubly linked list class.

- **SplHeap**: This is a generic heap implementation for PHP. `SplMaxHeap` and `SplMinHeap` are two implementations from the generic heap class.

- **SplPriorityQueue**: `SplPriorityQueue` is implemented using `SplMaxHeap` and provides basic functionalities of a priority queue.

- **SplFixedArray**: As we have seen in `Chapter 2`, *Understanding PHP Arrays*, `SplFixedArray` can be very handy to resolve memory and performance issues. `SplFixedArray` takes integer as index, and hence, it has faster read and write operations compared to generic PHP array.

- **SplObjectStorage**: Usually, we store anything in array either using integer or string key. This SPL class provides us with a way to store a value against an object. In object storage, we can use the object directly as a key for mapping. Also, we can use this class to store object collection.

Built-in PHP algorithms

Now, we will check some of the built-in functionalities of PHP that solves lots of our algorithmic implementation required for day-to-day operations. We can categorize these functions into mathematics, string, cryptography and hashing, sorting, searching, and so on. We will explore the base conversion algorithms now:

- **base_convert**: This function is used for base conversion of a number. The base range is restricted from 2 to 36. Since the base number can be in any base and contains characters, the first parameter for the function is string. Here is an example of the function:

```
$baseNumber = "123456754";
$newNumber = base_convert($baseNumber, 8, 16);
echo $newNumber;
```

This will produce the following output:

14e5dec

- **bin2hex**: This converts a binary string to a hexadecimal string. It takes only the binary string as the parameter.
- **bindec**: This converts a binary string to a decimal number. It takes only the binary string as the parameter.
- **decbin**: This converts a decimal number to a binary string. It takes only the decimal value as the parameter.
- **dechex**: This converts a decimal number to a hexadecimal string. It takes only a decimal value as the parameter.
- **decoct**: This converts a decimal number to an octal string. It takes only a decimal value as the parameter.
- **hex2bin**: This converts a hexadecimal string into a binary string. It takes only the hexadecimal string as the parameter.
- **hexdec**: This converts a hexadecimal string to a decimal number. It takes only the hexadecimal string as the parameter.
- **octdec**: This converts an octal string to decimal number. It takes only an octal string as the parameter.

There are many other built-in functions for different purposes. One of the most important things to do is to encode and decode text strings while sending e-mail or transportation layers. Since we need to encode and have the option to decode, we do not use one-way encryption function. Also, there are many useful functions that can be used for different string operations. We will now explore such functions:

- **base64_encode**: This function encodes data with base 64 mime types. Usually, the encoded string is larger than the actual string and takes 33 percent more space than the actual string. Sometimes, the generated strings have one or two equal symbols at the end, which indicates the output padding for the string.
- **base64_decode**: This function takes a base 64 encoded string and generates the actual string out of it. It is just opposite of the previous function we discussed.
- **levenshtein**: One of the most common problems we face is to find similarity between two texts, for example, a user-typed name of a product that we do not have in the list. However, a quick inspection shows that there was a typo in the text. In order to show which is the closest matching string or the correct string based on minimal number of characters to add, edit, or delete them. We will call this edit distance. The `levenshtein` function or levenshtein distance is defined as the minimal number of characters we have to replace, insert, or delete to transform the first string to the second string. The complexity of the function is `O(m*n)`, and the limitation is each string has to be less than 255 characters. Here is an example:

```
$inputStr = 'Bingo';
$fruites = ['Apple', 'Orange', 'Grapes', 'Banana', 'Water
melon', 'Mango'];

$matchScore = -1;
$matchedStr = '';

foreach ($fruites as $fruit) {
    $tmpScore = levenshtein($inputStr, $fruit);

    if ($tmpScore == 0 || ($matchScore < 0 || $matchScore >
      $tmpScore)) {
      $matchScore = $tmpScore;
      $matchedStr = $fruit;
    }
}

echo $matchScore == 0 ? 'Exact match found : ' . $matchedStr :
'Did you mean: ' . $matchedStr . '?\n';
```

This will have the following output:

```
Did you mean: Mango?
```

Another variant of the function takes extra three parameters through which we can provide the cost of the insert, replace, and delete operations. This way, we can get the best possible result based on the cost function.

- **similar_text**: This function calculates the similarity between two strings. It has an option to return the similarity in a percentile manner. The function is case sensitive and returns the similarity score based on the matched characters. Here is one example:

```
$str1 = "Mango";
$str2 = "Tango";

echo "Match length: " . similar_text($str1, $str2) . "\n";
similar_text($str1, $str2, $percent);
echo "Percentile match: " . $percent . "%";
```

The preceding code will produce the percentile match between Mango and Tango. The output is as follows:

```
Match length: 4
Percentile match: 80%
```

- **soundex**: This is an interesting function using which we can find the soundex key of a given string. This soundex key can be used to find similar sounding words from the collection or find whether two words sound similar or not. The soundex key is four characters in length, where the first character is a letter and the remaining three are digits. Here are some soundex keys for familiar words:

```
$word1 = "Pray";
$word2 = "Prey";
echo $word1 . " = " . soundex($word1) . "\n";
echo $word2 . " = " . soundex($word2) . "\n";

$word3 = "There";
$word4 = "Their";
echo $word3 . " = " . soundex($word3) . "\n";
echo $word4 . " = " . soundex($word4) . "\n";
```

The preceding code will have following output:

```
Pray = P600
Prey = P600
There = T600
Their = T600
```

As we can see from the preceding output, both `pray` and `prey` are different words, but they have similar soundex keys. Soundex can be very useful to find out similar sounding words from the database in different use cases.

- **metaphone**: Metaphone is another function similar to soundex, which can help us find similar sounding words. The basic difference between the two is that, the metaphone is more accurate as it considers the basic english rules for pronunciation. The function generates metaphone keys, which are variable in length. We can also pass second arguments to limit the key generation length. Here is a similar example from soundex:

```
$word1 = "Pray";
$word2 = "Prey";
echo $word1 . " = " . metaphone($word1) . "\n";
echo $word2 . " = " . metaphone($word2) . "\n";

$word3 = "There";
$word4 = "Their";
echo $word3 . " = " . metaphone($word3) . "\n";
echo $word4 . " = " . metaphone($word4) . "\n";
```

Here is the output for the following code:

```
Pray = PR
Prey = PR
There = 0R
Their = 0R
```

Hashing

Hashing is one of the most important aspects of modern-day programming. In terms of data security and privacy, hashing plays a key role in computer cryptography. We do not feel comfortable to keep our data unsafe and open for all. PHP has several built-in hashing functions. Let's quickly go through them:

- **md5**: This calculates the md5 hash of a given string. It will generate 32 characters unique hash for each of the provided string. Hashing is one way, which means, there is no function to decrypt the hashed string to actual string.

- **sha1**: This function calculates the sha1 hash of a given string. The generated hash is 40 characters in length. Like md5, sha1 is also a one way hashing. If we set the second parameter to be true, then the function will produce 20-character raw output hash string. One thing to remember is sha1, sha256, and md5 are not secure enough to use for password hashing. As they are very fast and efficient, hackers tend to use them for brute force attacking and find the actual input from the generated hash.

- **crypt**: This function generates a one way hashing key for a given string with optional salt string. If you are using PHP 7, then the function will produce an E_NOTICE for not providing any salt during the function call. For hashing, the function uses **UNIX DES** based algorithm or other algorithms available for hashing.

- **password_hash**: This is another useful function that generates hash for passwords. It takes two arguments, one which includes the actual string, and the second is the hashing algorithm. The default hashing algorithm uses bcrypt algorithm, and the alternate option is the blowfish algorithm.

- **password_verify**: We can use this function if we have generated the password using the password_hash function. The first parameter of the function is the entered password, and the second one is the hashed string. The function returns true or false based on the verification part.

- **hash_algos**: If we want to know the list of registered hashing algorithms in the system, we can use this function. This will list all the possible options for hashing algorithm in the current system.

- **hash**: This function takes a mandatory hashing algorithm name along with a string to be hashed to generate a hashed key. There is an optional parameter to get the raw binary output for the hashing. The hash key length will vary based on the chosen algorithm.

PHP has a rich collection of functions and libraries for hashing and cryptography. For further reading, you can consider the PHP.net documentation, along with some other sites mentioned in the next section.

Built-in support through PECL

Since PHP 7.0 release, a raising concern for developers is the performance issue of SPL classes. PHP 7.0 does not bring any improvement to early designed SPL classes, and many developers are now sceptical about using it further. Many developers have written custom libraries and extensions for PHP to improve the data structure efficiency. One of such extensions is PHP DS, a specialized extension for PHP 7 data structures. The extension is written by Joe Watkins and Rudi Theunissen. The official documentation of PHP DS extension can be found in the PHP manual at `http://php.net/manual/en/book.ds.php`.

The library works as an alternative to PHP array, which is a very flexible, dynamic, hybrid data structure. This extension comes up with lots of pre-built data structures such as set, map, sequence, collection, vector, stack, queue, priority queue, and so on. We will explore them in the next few sections.

Installation

The library comes up with different options for installations. The easiest one is to get it from PECL (a repository for PHP Extensions):

```
pecl install ds
```

We can also download the source code and compile the library if we want. In order to do that, we just need to get the code from the GitHub repository and follow the git commands:

```
clone https://github.com/php-ds/extension "php-ds"
cd php-ds

# Build and install the extension
phpize
./configure
make
make install

# Clean up the build files
make clean
phpize --clean
```

If there is any dependency issue, we have to install this package as well:

```
sudo apt-get install git build-essential php7.0-dev
```

For Windows, the DLL is available to download from PECL site. For Mac OS users, Homebrew has support to install this extension:

```
brew install homebrew/php/php71-ds
```

Once the installation is done, we have to add the extension to our primary `php.ini` file:

```
extension=ds.so  #(php_ds.dll for windows)
```

If the extension is properly added, all pre-built classes will be available through `global \DS\ namespace`.

Now, let's get into details for pre-built DS classes from this extension. We will start with the base of all classes, the collection interface.

Interfaces

The collection interface is the base interface for all classes in this DS library. All data structure implementations implement the collection interface by default. The collection interface ensures that all classes are having similar behavior of traversable, countable, and JSON serializable. The collection interface has four abstract methods, and they are `clear`, `copy`, `isEmpty`, and `toArray`. All of the data structure implementations of DS class implement the interface, and we will see these methods at work during our exploration of those data structures.

Another important aspect of the data structure library is to use an object as a key. This can be achieved through the hashable interface of the library. There is another important interface that allows list functionalities to be implemented in data structure classes and also ensures better performance than the SPL equivalent of doubly linked list and fixed array.

Vector

A vector is a linear data structure where values are stored sequentially and also the size grows and shrinks automatically. Vector is one of the most efficient linear data structures as the value's index is mapped directly with the index of the buffer and allows faster access. DS vector class allows us to use the PHP array syntax for operations, but internally, it has less memory consumption than PHP array. It has constant time operations for push, pop, get, and set. Here is an example of vector:

```
$vector = new \Ds\Vector(["a", "b", "c"]);
echo $vector->get(1)."\n";
$vector[1] = "d";
echo $vector->get(1)."\n";
$vector->push('f');
echo "Size of vector: ".$vector->count();
```

As we can see from the preceding code, we can define a vector using the PHP array syntax and also get or set values using array syntax. One difference is that we cannot add a new index using PHP array syntax. For that, we have to use the push method of the vector class. Trying to set or get an index that is not there will cause OutOfRangeException to be thrown during runtime. Here is the output of the preceding code:

```
b
d
Size of vector: 4
```

Map

A map is a sequential collection of key-value pairs. A map is similar to an array, and the key can be a string, integer, and so on, but the key has to be unique. In DS map class, the key can be of any type, including an object. It allows PHP array syntax for operations and also preserves the insertion order. The performance and memory efficiency is also similar to the PHP array. It also automatically frees memory when the size drops to low. If we consider the following performance chart, we can see that map implementation in DS library is much faster than PHP array when we are removing items from a big array:

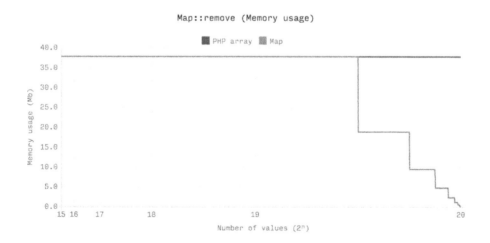

Set

A set is also a sequence, but a set can only contain unique values. A set can store any value, including object, and also support array syntax. It preserves the insertion order and also automatically frees memory when the size drops to low. We can achieve add, remove, and contain operations in constant time. However, this set class does not support push, pop, shift, insert, and unshift functions. The set class has some very useful set operation functions built in, such as diff, intersect, union, and so on. Here is an example of the set operation:

```
$set = new \Ds\Set();
$set->add(1);
$set->add(1);
$set->add("test");
$set->add(3);
echo $set->get(1);
```

In the preceding example code, there will be only one entry of 1 as set cannot have duplicate values. Also, when we are getting the value of 1, this indicates the value at index 1. So, the output will be test for the preceding example. One question might arise here that why not we use `array_unique` here to build a set. The following comparison chart might be the answer we are looking for:

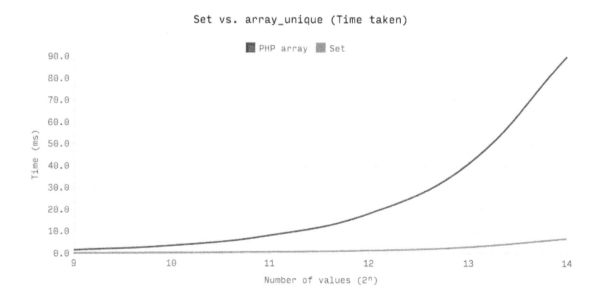

As we can see from the preceding chart, as the array size grows, array unique function will take more time to compute compared to our `set` class in the DS library. Also, the `set` class takes lesser memory compared to PHP array as the size grows:

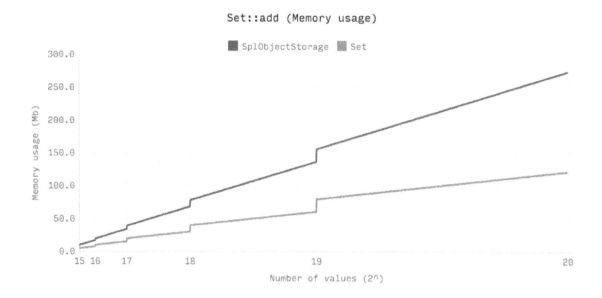

Stack and queue

The DS library also has implementations of stack and queue data structures. DS\Stack uses DS\Vector internally, and DS\Queue uses DS\Deque internally. Both stack and queue implementation have similar performance compared to SPL implementation of stack and queue. The following chart shows this:

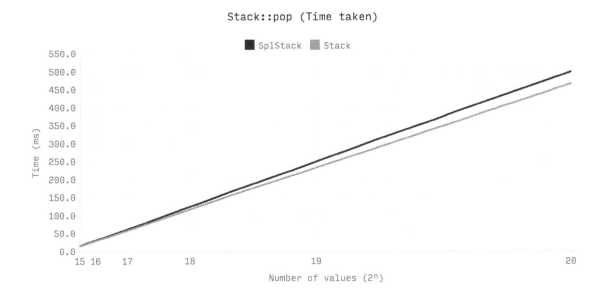

Deque

The deque (pronounced as deck), or the double ended queue, is used for the `DS\Queue` implementation internally. The deque implementation in this package is very efficient in memory usage and also performs get, set, push, pop, shift, and unshift operations in constant time of `O(1)`. However, one of the disadvantages of `DS\Deque` is the insert or remove operation, which has `O(n)` complexity. Here is a performance comparison between `DS\Deque` and SPL doubly linked list:

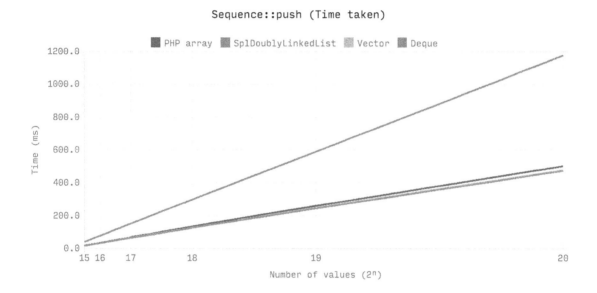

Priority queue

You have already learned that priority queues are important for many algorithms. Having an efficient priority queue is very important for us as well. So far, we have seen that we can implement from our own using heap or use the SPL priority queue for our solutions. However, the DS\PriorityQueue is more than twice as fast as SplPriorityQueue and uses only five percent of its memory. This makes DS\PriorityQueue 20 times more memory efficient compared to SplPriorityQueue. The following chart shows the comparison:

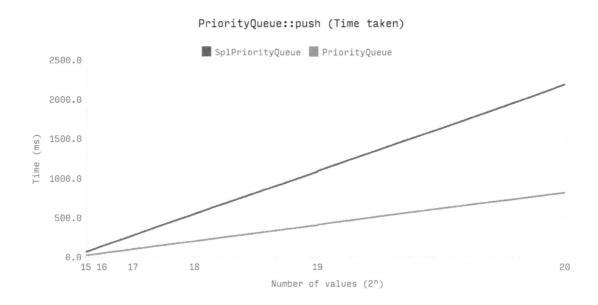

From our discussion in the last few sections, we can conclude that the DS extension is really efficient for data structures and far better compared to SPL for similar implementations. Though the benchmark can vary a little from platform to platform and internal configurations, it shows that the new DS extension is promising and might be very helpful for developers. One thing to remember is that the library does not have built-in heap or tree data structure yet, so we cannot have a built-in hierarchical data structure from this library.

 For more information, you can check the following article as the comparison charts are taken from here: https://medium.com/@rtheunissen/efficient-data-structures-f or-php-7-9dda7af674cd

Summary

PHP has a rich collection of built-in functions, and the list is growing every day. In this chapter, we explored some of the defined functions that can be used in implementing data structures and algorithms. There are many other external libraries available as well. We can select any of the internal or external libraries as per our preferences. Also, there are plenty of online resources to get acquainted with the data structures and algorithm concepts. You also learned about the performance concerns for SPL classes in PHP 7 and got introduced to a new library for PHP 7 data structures. We have to remember that data structures and algorithms are not language agnostic. We can have same data structures and algorithms implemented using different languages or different versions of the same language. In our next chapter, we will explore another area of programming, which is very popular at this moment, the functional programming. So, next, we will focus on functional data structure with PHP.

13
Functional Data Structures with PHP

In recent years, the demand for functional programming language over object-oriented programming has increased. One of the core reasons is that **functional programming** (**FP**) has inherent parallelism. While OOP is used widely, functional programming is quite significantly making a mark in recent times. As a result, languages such as Erlang, Elixir, Clojure, Scala, and Haskell are the most popular functional programming languages for programmers. PHP is not on the list, as PHP is considered an imperative and object-oriented language. Though PHP has lots of support for functional programming, it is mainly used for OOP and imperative programming. The core essence of FP is the lambda calculus, which denotes a formal system in mathematical logic and computer science for expressing computation by way of variable binding and substitution. It is not a framework or a new concept. In fact, functional programming predates all other programming paradigms. It has been there for a long time and will be there in the future as well, as the world is demanding for more concurrent computation and faster processing languages. In this chapter, you will learn about functional programming with PHP and how to implement data structures with functional programming.

Understanding functional programming with PHP

Unlike any object-oriented programming language where everything is represented through an object, functional programming starts thinking everything in terms of functions. OOP and FP are not mutually exclusive. While OOP focuses on code maintainability and reusability by encapsulation and inheritance, functional programming, unlike state-oriented imperative programming, is focused on value-oriented programming, which considers computation as a pure mathematical evaluation and avoids mutability and state modification. When working with OOP, one of the challenges is that the object we have created can bring many extra properties or methods along with it whether or not we are using it in a particular case. Here are the three key characteristics of functional programming:

- Immutability
- Pure functions and referential transparency
- First-class citizen functions
    - Higher order function
    - Function composition (currying)

The concept of immutability tells us that an object will not change after its creation. It will remain the same during its whole life cycle. It has a great advantage as we do not need to revalidate the object whenever we use it. Also, if it requires being mutable, we can create a copy of the object or create a new object with new properties.

So far, in this book, we saw lots of examples of data structures and algorithms using code blocks, loops, and conditions. In general, this is known as imperative programming, where it is expected to define each step of the execution. For example, consider the following code block:

```
$languages = ["php", "python", "java", "c", "erlang"];

foreach ($languages as $ind => $language) {
    $languages[$ind] = ucfirst($language);
}
```

The preceding code actually sets the first character of each name to upper case. Logically, the code is correct and we have presented it here step-by-step, so that we understand what is going on. However, this can be written as a single line using the functional programming approach, as follows:

```
$languages = array_map('ucfirst', $languages);
```

Both of these methods do the same thing, but one is a comparatively smaller code block than the other one. The later one is known as declarative programming. While imperative programming focuses on algorithms and steps, declarative programming focuses on input and output of the function along with recursion (not iteration).

Another important aspect of functional programming is that it is free of any side effects. It is an important feature to have and it ensures that a function will not have any implicit effects anywhere on the input. One of the common examples of functional programming is sorting an array in PHP. Usually, the argument is passed by reference and when we get the sorted array, it actually destroys the initial array. This is an example of side effects in a function.

Before jumping to functional programming with PHP, let's explore some functional programming terms, which we will come across in the following sections.

First class functions

A language with first-class functions allows the following behavior:

- Assign a function to a variable
- Pass them to another function as an argument
- Return a function

PHP supports all of these behaviors and, hence, PHP functions are first-class functions. In our previous example, the `ucfirst` function is an example of a first-class function.

Higher order functions

A higher order function can take one or multiple functions as an argument and also return a function as a result. PHP also has support for higher order functions; `array_map` from our previous example is a higher order function.

Pure functions

A pure function is a function where for an input X, the output will be always Y under any circumstances. The output will never change for the same input for a pure function. So, for pure functions, there are no side effects or dependencies on the runtime environment.

Lambda functions

Lambda functions or anonymous functions are functions without a name. They can be very handy when used as first-class functions (to assign in a variable) or for call back functions where we can define the function in the place of a call back parameter. PHP has support for anonymous functions as well.

Closures

A closure is very much similar to a lambda function, but the basic difference is that a closure has access to its outer scope variables. In PHP, we cannot access outer scope variables directly. In order to do so, PHP has introduced the keyword "use" to pass any outer scope variables to inner functions.

Currying

Currying is a technique of transforming a function that takes multiple arguments to a chain of functions where each function will take exactly one argument. In other words, if a function can be written as *f(x,y,z)*, then the currying version of this will be *f(x)(y)(z)*. let's consider the following example:

```
function sum($a, $b, $c) {
    return $a + $b + $c;
}
```

Here, we have written a simple function with three parameters and when called with numbers, it will return *sum* of the numbers. Now, if we write this function as a curry, it will look like this:

```
function currySum($a) {
    return function($b) use ($a) {
        return function ($c) use ($a, $b) {
            return $a + $b + $c;
        };
    };
}

$sum = currySum(10)(20)(30);

echo $sum;
```

Now if we run the `currySum` as a currying function, we will get the result 60 for the preceding example. This is a very useful feature for functional programming.

Earlier, it was not possible to call a function like *f(a)(b)(c)* in PHP. Since PHP 7.0, Uniform Variable Syntax allows immediate execution of a callable, as we saw in this example. However, to do this in PHP 5.4 and higher versions, we would have to create temporary variables in order to store the lambda functions.

Partial applications

A partial application or partial function application is a technique to reduce the number of arguments of a function or to use partial arguments and create another function to act on the remaining arguments in order to produce the same output as what we would get if it were called with all the arguments at once. If we consider our `sum` function to be partial, where it is expected to take three parameters, but we can call it with two arguments, and later on add the remaining one. Here is the code sample. The `sum` function used in this example is from the previous section:

```php
function partial($funcName, ...$args) {
    return function(...$innerArgs) use ($funcName, $args) {
        $allArgs = array_merge($args, $innerArgs);
        return call_user_func_array($funcName, $allArgs);
    };
}

$sum = partial("sum", 10, 20);
$sum = $sum(30);

echo $sum;
```

Sometimes, we get confused between currying and partial application even though they are completely different in their approaches and principles.

As we can see, there are so many things to consider while dealing with functional programming in PHP. It will be a lengthier process to implement data structures using functional programming in PHP from scratch. In order to solve this problem, we will explore an excellent functional programming library for PHP, called **Tarsana**. It is open source and comes with the MIT license. We will explore this library and also use it as our base for functional data structure implementation in PHP.

Getting started with Tarsana

Tarsana is an open source library written by Amine Ben Hammou and is available on GitHub for download. It is inspired from Ramda JS, a functional programming library for JavaScript. It does not have any dependencies and has more than 100 predefined functions to use for different purposes. Functions in FP are spread over different modules and there are several modules such as functions, list, object, string, math, operators, and common. Tarsana can be downloaded from GitHub (https://github.com/Tarsana/functional) or can be installed via composer.

```
composer require Tarsana/functional
```

Once the library is downloaded, we have to use it by importing the Tarsana\Functional namespace, just like the following code:

```
use Tarsana\Functional as F;
```

One of the interesting features of Tarsana is that we can convert any of our existing functions to a curried function. For example, if we want to use our sum function using Tarsana, then it will look like this:

```
require __DIR__ . '/vendor/autoload.php';

use Tarsana\Functional as F;

$add = F\curry(function($x, $y, $z) {
    return $x + $y + $z;
});

echo $add(1, 2, 4)."\n";
$addFive = $add(5);
$addSix = $addFive(6);
echo $addSix(2);
```

This will produce the output of 7 and 13, respectively. Tarsana also has an option to keep place holders using the __() function. The following example shows the array reduce and array sum of the entries provided in the placeholder:

```
$reduce = F\curry('array_reduce');
$sum = $reduce(F\__(), F\plus());
echo $sum([1, 2, 3, 4, 5], 0);
```

Tarsana also provides a piping functionality, where we can apply a series of functions from left to right. The leftmost function may have any arity; the remaining functions must be unary. The result of piping is not curried. Let's consider the following example:

```
$square = function($x) { return $x * $x; };
$addThenSquare = F\pipe(F\plus(), $square);
echo $addThenSquare(2, 3);
```

As we have already explored some features of Tarsana, we are ready to start our functional data structures using Tarsana. We will also implement those data structures using simple PHP functions so that we have both parts covered, if we do not want to use functional programming. Let's get started with the implementation of stack.

Implementing stack

We have seen the implementation of stacks in `Chapter 4`, *Constructing Stacks and Queues*. For simplicity, we won't discuss the whole stack operation again. We will jump right into the implementation of push, pop, and top operations using functional programming. Tarsana has lots of built-in functions for list operations. We will use their built-in functions to implement our functional operations of the stack. Here is the implementation:

```
require __DIR__ . '/vendor/autoload.php';

use Tarsana\Functional as F;

$stack = [];

$push = F\append(F\__(), F\__());
$top = F\last(F\__());
$pop = F\init(F\__());

$stack = $push(1, $stack);
$stack = $push(2, $stack);
$stack = $push(3, $stack);

echo "Stack is ".F\toString($stack)."\n";

$item = $top($stack);
$stack = $pop($stack);

echo "Pop-ed item: ".$item."\n";
echo "Stack is ".F\toString($stack)."\n";
```

```
$stack = $push(4, $stack);

echo "Stack is ".F\toString($stack)."\n";
```

Here, we use the append function of Tarsana for the push operation, the last function we used here for the top operation, and the `init` function for the pop operation. The output of the following code is as follows:

```
Stack is [1, 2, 3]
Pop-ed item: 3
Stack is [1, 2]
Stack is [1, 2, 4]
```

Implementing a queue

We can implement a queue using Tarsana and the built-in functions for list operations. We will use the array for queue representation as well using this code:

```
require __DIR__ . '/vendor/autoload.php';

use Tarsana\Functional as F;

$queue = [];

$enqueue = F\append(F\__(), F\__());
$head = F\head(F\__());
$dequeue = F\tail(F\__());

$queue = $enqueue(1, $queue);
$queue = $enqueue(2, $queue);
$queue = $enqueue(3, $queue);

echo "Queue is ".F\toString($queue)."\n";

$item = $head($queue);
$queue = $dequeue($queue);

echo "Dequeue-ed item: ".$item."\n";
echo "Queue is ".F\toString($queue)."\n";

$queue = $enqueue(4, $queue);

echo "Queue is ".F\toString($queue)."\n";
```

Here, we use the `append` function to perform enqueue, and the `head` and `tail` functions for the first item in the queue and dequeuer, respectively. Here is the output of the preceding code:

```
Queue is [1, 2, 3]
Dequeue-ed item: 1
Queue is [2, 3]
Queue is [2, 3, 4]
```

Now, we will shift our focus to implementing hierarchical data using simple PHP functions instead of classes and objects. Since functional programming is still a new topic in PHP, implementation of hierarchical data might seem challenging and also time consuming. Instead, we will convert our hierarchical data implementation using basic PHP functions along with some basic functional programming concept such as first-class functions and higher order functions. So, let's implement a binary tree.

Implementing a tree

We will implement a binary tree using a PHP array with a simple recursive function-based traversal. We are just rewriting the functionality using one function instead of a class. Here is the code to do this:

```php
function treeTraverse(array &$tree, int $index = 0,
int $level = 0, &$outputStr = "") : ?bool {

    if(isset($tree[$index])) {
        $outputStr .= str_repeat("-", $level);
        $outputStr .= $tree[$index] . "\n";

        treeTraverse($tree, 2 * $index + 1, $level+1,$outputStr);
        treeTraverse($tree, 2 * ($index + 1), $level+1,$outputStr);

    } else {
        return false;
    }
    return null;
}


        $nodes = [];
        $nodes[] = "Final";
        $nodes[] = "Semi Final 1";
        $nodes[] = "Semi Final 2";
        $nodes[] = "Quarter Final 1";
        $nodes[] = "Quarter Final 2";
```

```
$nodes[] = "Quarter Final 3";
$nodes[] = "Quarter Final 4";

$treeStr = "";
treeTraverse($nodes,0,0,$treeStr);
echo $treeStr;
```

If we look at the preceding code, we have simply modified the traversal function and converted it to a standalone function. It is a pure function as we are not modifying the actual input here, which is the $nodes variable. We will construct a string on each level and use that for the output. We can now convert most of our class-based structures to function-based ones.

Summary

Functional programming is comparatively new for PHP developers as the support for its prerequisites was added as of version 5.4. The emergence of functional programming will require us to understand the paradigm and write pure functions that are free of any side effects when required. PHP has some good support for writing functional programming code and, with that, we can also write functional data structures and algorithm implementations as we have tried to show in this book. In the near future, it might come in handy for optimizing and improving our application's efficiency.

Index

K

Kahn's algorithm
   used, for topological sorting 218, 220
Knuth-Morris-Pratt (KMP) algorithm
   implementing 259, 260
Kruskal's algorithm
   used, for spanning tree 235, 237

L

Last-In, First-Out (LIFO) 12, 77
linear recursion 106
linear searching 183, 184
linked list iterable
   creating 64
linked list
   about 49, 52
   circular linked lists 54
   complexity 63
   doubly linked lists 54
   multi-linked lists 54
   reversing 61
   types 53
   used, for implementing priority queue 93
   used, for implementing queue 90
   used, for implementing stack 83, 84
longest common subsequence (LCS)
   finding 269, 270
Longest Proper Prefix Suffix (LPS) 259

M

maximum recursion depth
   in PHP 120
memoization 255, 256, 257, 258
merge sort algorithm
   about 172
   complexity 176
   implementing 174, 175
methods, Iterator interface
   current 64
   key 64
   next 64
   rewind 64
   valid 64
minimum spanning tree (MST) 231

multidimensional array
   about 33
   used, for representing data structures 35, 36
mutual recursion 108

N

N-ary tree 134
N-level category tree
   building, recursion used 108, 109, 110, 111
nested comment reply system
   building 111, 113, 114, 116
nested recursion 108
Nth position element
   obtaining 62, 63
numeric array 31

O

ordered map 30

P

pattern matching algorithms 258
PHP array functions
   array_diff 288
   array_interest 288
   array_map 287
   array_pop 286
   array_push 286
   array_rand 288
   array_search 286
   array_shift 288
   array_sum 287
   array_unshift 288
   current 286
   end 286
   next 286
   prev 286
   reset 286
   shuffle 288
PHP array
   about 29
   and SplFixedArray, performance comparison 38, 40
   associative array 32
   limitations 48
   multidimensional array 33